MAVERICK!

*The success story behind the world's
most unusual workplace*

RICARDO SEMLER

ARROW

This edition first published in 1999 by Random House Business Books

Permission to use cartoons granted by Miguel Paiva

First published in 1993 by Century
Random House, 20 Vauxhall Bridge Road, London SW1V 2SA

Random House Australia (Pty) Limited
20 Alfred Street, Milsons Point, Sydney,
New South Wales 2061, Australia

Random House New Zealand Limited
18 Poland Road, Glenfield,
Auckland 10, New Zealand

Random House (Pty) Limited
Endulini, 5a Jubilee Road, Parktown 2193, South Africa

The Random House Group Limited Reg. No. 954009

Papers used by Random House are natural, recyclable products made from wood grown in sustainable forests. The manufacturing processes conform to the environmental regulations of the country of origin.

ISBN 0 7126 7886 7

Companies, institutions and other organizations wishing to make bulk purchases of any business books published by Random House should contact their local bookstore or Random House direct:
Special Sales Director
Random House, 20 Vauxhall Bridge Road, London SW1V 2SA

Tel: 020 7840 8470 Fax: 020 7828 6681

www.randomhouse.co.uk
businessbooks@randomhouse.co.uk

Printed and bound in Denmark by
Nørhaven Paperback, Viborg

*For Antonio Curt,
whose soul resides at the head office,
and for Sofia, who has taken my heart
into perennial custody.*

FOREWORD

This is not a business book. It is a book about work, and how it can be changed for the better. It is based on the experience of a company called Semco, which has managed to make money and improve the lives of the people who work for it. Some say Semco is merely a quirky laboratory run by a few impudent and iconoclastic managers. It isn't the real world, they say. It's Brazil. I've heard all the other arguments by now, too – we went too far, we went too fast, we are too big, we are too small, we are too high-tech, we aren't high-tech enough.

But a few people – more excitable or impressionable, perhaps, but also more open-minded – will see in the story of this admittedly peculiar company and its people a new way of running an organization. It is not socialist, as some of our critics contend. It isn't purely capitalist, either. It is a new way. A third way. A more humane, trusting, productive, exhilarating, and in every sense, rewarding way.

ACKNOWLEDGEMENTS

First and foremost to Rick Levine, who devoted more wee hours to this book than he cares to remember. To Suzanne Gluck at ICM, who was naive enough to think we could hook a publisher; to Rick Horgan, Maureen Egen and their colleagues at Warner Books; to Gail Rebuck at Random House UK; and to all other the publishers around the word for sharing our enthusiasm. Not to be forgotten are tough-outside, butter-inside Esther Newberg, Heather Schroder, and the competent team of ladies at Rogers, Coleridge & White in London. And, of course, I am most indebted to the 65 people at Semco who let me interview them for so many hours, and to the hundreds of others at our company who made this story – and so many of our dreams – reality.

Ricardo Semler
São Paulo, 1993

INTRODUCTION

Just the other day, Clovis Bojikian, our Sultan for HR (yes, we still love to mock titles) and I sat around evaluating how close we now were to our dream of 19 years ago. 30 per cent, we agreed. Not very good for two decades of huffing and puffing for democracy in the workplace. The worst part, however, is that we had put that percentage at 50 only three years before . . .

If you ask the serious people, those with blue suits and tie clips, Semco is a roaring success. We are pursued by bankers who enjoy lending money to people who have it, and are stalked to the point of sexual harrassment by stock market underwriters.

By the Grand Scoreboard of Numbers, we're doing fine: since the first edition of *Maverick* in 1993, we have gone from US $35 million in sales to US $160 million, and mushroomed from hundreds of employees to 1,500. Profits and profit-sharing are dandy, salaries are increasing strongly, we have internet companies making money and a half-dozen new joint ventures underway with Global 500 companies. Wunderbar!

But to us this begs, on its knees, the question: so what?

During our meagre years we were deluged with pundits who, personally, behind our backs or in magazine articles, proclaimed our imminent demise. At the Federation of Industries our poor numbers were merrily displayed to other club members as a proof that this democracy nonsense was no way to run a business. Today, a whopping 85 per cent of those Board members have lost or sold their companies.

We could now do a little bit of gloating, but for one issue: we were always adamant that making money and creating a sustainable organization – where people felt enthused to flock to on Monday mornings – had little in common. Sure, I love making money, and I even enjoy a spot of gloating (Jung backs me on this). And yes, making money is a nice by-product of a business that is on the right track. But it is only one of many indicators.

The same way that an IQ test may tell you about people's specific abilities in narrowly defined intelligence but tells you nothing about other vital characteristics, so profits are an indicator, but not much else. How many untold companies have gone to the doghouse surrounded by very handsome numbers? How many businesses make a killing for the owner while slowly killing off all the enthusiasm of the underlings?

Sure, we're happy, and we feel vindicated from the sooth-sayers that told us to beware the ides of March. But rapid growth has brought about a backslide in our hopes of reaching corporate nirvana. Clovis and I are still a bit airy-fairy and touchy-feely, I know, but we ain't givin' up yet.

Our Board meetings have two open seats for the first employees that sign up, and two more for any person in a leadership capacity that cares to show. And we still debate strategy openly, schedule meetings on a volunteer basis, and have leaders interviewed by their future subordinates. But in a time of growth, and in a pattern where we increasingly join with huge corporate partners, Clovis and I are less quirky than we'd like to be.

So the Semco story continues and, should we do badly in five to ten years' time, nothing will alter our faith in freedom and democracy as guarantors of sustainability. *Maverick* is a tale of flying in the face of accrued business wisdom. But it is also a reminder that age-old truths about human nature, respect and integrity can be powerful allies of success. At least that's what the numbers say, if people in striped suits can be trusted.

Recently we inaugurated our new offices, which herald the end of the headquarters and the untimely death of control. The new layout harks of a VIP airport lounge. We resisted the temptation of cutesy billiard tables and beanbags, painted nothing in citric colors and left no place for cribs or dogleashes. How undotcomlike . . .

But we did something else: we told people that they were all welcome to join the new system, which entails a non-territorial concept. Give up your desk and the trappings of personal space, and we will give you freedom. Predictably, only half of our people have taken up the offer so far. Not everyone likes freedom, apparently.

It works like this: instead of one headquarter building, we distribute identical offices across town (four so far). To use a desk, a couch seat or a place at the cappuccino outdoor café (modem-wired) you tap into the website and reserve a place for yourself. At any of the locales across town, presumably the closest to your house, your next meeting, or the theatre you're going to at night. If you need a meeting area, reserve more seats close to you, or a closed meeting room (I find that 70 per cent of the people believe that their meeting falls into the 10 per cent of the situations of confidentiality, so we have lots of closed rooms, also). Because no one knows whether you're at Office A, B, D, or at home, you discover that, hey presto!, you can also stay an extra day at the beach. And no one will know.

As I tell our people constantly: we've all learned how to answer email on Sundays, but none of us has learned to go to the movies on Monday afternoon. Until we learn that, we are email slaves harnessed to the wicked ways of the Profit and Loss Master.

In our new system, the ability to control, once taken away, eliminates not only the headquarters, but all of the insecurity that makes bosses glance, glare and gloat (by looking at their watches and around the office). Now, one issue alone remains: whether people are doing what they negotiated to do, be it the sale of 140 widgets per month, or the Business Plan for a new company. Now, control is passé and a badge of incompetence. Now, you are free.

As we shift into this new gear of growth without bondage, all bets are off as to where Semco will be in seven years time. The last time someone asked, seven years ago, the reply was that of Lewis Caroll: if you don't know where you're going, any road will take you there.

So we have arrived. And feel the corners of our mouth

going from a slight smirk to . . . well, not really . . . a gloat. Now back to the job – 70 per cent awaits.

Ricardo Semler
Senior (con)Sultan
Sitting in the Garden
(During Work Hours)
São Paulo, Brazil
April, 2001

one

NATURAL BUSINESS

Every Wednesday afternoon dozens of men and women file through the front gate on their way to a third-floor meeting room at Semco, the company I lead in São Paulo, Brazil. The guard at the entrance has been expecting them. For years now, executives from some of the biggest and best-known companies in the world, IBM, General Motors, Ford, Kodak, Bayer, Nestlé, Goodyear, Firestone, Pirelli, Alcoa, BASF, Chase Manhattan, Siemens, Dow Chemical, Mercedes-Benz, and Yashica among them, have been making an unlikely pilgrimage to our nondescript industrial complex on the outskirts of the city.

Semco manufactures an impressively varied roster of products, including pumps that can empty an oil tanker in a night, dishwashers capable of scrubbing 4,100 plates an hour, cooling units for air conditioners that keep huge office towers comfortable during the most sweltering heat waves, mixers that blend everything from rocket fuel to bubble gum, and entire biscuit factories, with 6,000 separate components and 16 miles of wiring. But it's not what Semco makes that has executives and management experts the world over waiting months for a chance to tour our plants and offices. It's the way the people of Semco make it.

When I took over Semco from my father 12 years ago, it was a traditional company in every respect, with a pyramidal structure and a rule for every contingency. But today, our factory workers sometimes set their own production quotas and even come in on their own time to meet them, without prodding from management or overtime pay. They help re-design the products they make and formulate the marketing plans. Their bosses, for their part, can run our business units with extraordinary freedom, determining business strategy without interference from the top brass. They even set their own salaries, with no strings. Then again, everyone will know what they are, since all financial information at Semco is openly discussed. Indeed, our workers have unlimited access to our books (and we only keep one set). To show we are serious about this, Semco, with the labour unions that represent our workers, developed a course to teach everyone, even messengers and cleaning people, to read balance sheets and cash-flow statements.

For truly big decisions, such as buying another company, everyone at Semco gets a vote. A few years ago, when we wanted to relocate a factory, we closed down for a day and everyone piled into buses to inspect three possible new sites. Then the workers decided. Their choice hardly thrilled us, since it was next to a company that was frequently on strike. But while no one in management wanted front-row seats to labour-management strife, we moved in anyway.

In the lobby of our headquarters, a standard-issue office building with four floors of steel and glass, there is a reception desk but no receptionist. That's the first clue that we are different. We don't have receptionists. We don't think they are necessary, despite all our visitors. We don't have secretaries either, or personal assistants. We don't believe in cluttering the payroll with ungratifying, dead-end jobs. Everyone at Semco, even top managers, fetches guests, stands over photocopiers, sends faxes, types letters, and dials the phone. We don't have executive dining rooms and parking is strictly first-come, first-served. It's all part of running a 'natural business'. At Semco we have stripped away the unnecessary perks and privileges that feed the ego but hurt the balance sheet and distract everyone from the crucial corporate tasks of making, selling, billing and collecting.

Our offices don't even have the usual number of walls. Instead, a forest of plants separates the desks, computers, and drawing boards in our work areas. The mood is informal:

some people wear suits and ties or dresses, others jeans and sneakers. It doesn't matter. If people want to emulate Thomas Watson and don white button-downs, that's fine. But turtlenecks and T-shirts are okay, too. And I want our people to feel free to put their feet on their desks, just like me. I am pleased to report that more than once a group of Semco executives has been interrupted by people who wanted to use their conference room to hold a birthday party. It warms my heart to see vice presidents eating cake on little plates decorated with Mickey and Minnie Mouse.

We have a sales manager named Rubin Agater who sits there reading the newspaper hour after hour, not even making a pretence of looking busy. I'm sure this mystifies some of our visitors. Most modern managers wouldn't tolerate it. But when a Semco pump on an oil tanker on the other side of the world fails and millions of gallons of oil are about to spill into the sea, Rubin springs into action. He knows everything there is to know about our pumps and how to fix them. That's when he earns his salary. No one cares if he doesn't *look* busy the rest of the time.

My office is on the fourth floor – at least it was the last time I looked, I don't use it as much as other proprietors. Most mornings I work at home. I concentrate better there, despite two sheepdogs that like to bark when I'm on the phone to important customers. I encourage other Semco managers to work at home, too. I also take at least two months off each year to travel, and I like to roam far. There are pictures in my office from two recent expeditions, a balloon safari in Tanzania and a trek through the Khyber Pass in Afghanistan. I never leave a number where I can be reached when I'm away and I don't call in. I want everyone at Semco to be self-sufficient. The company is organized – well, maybe that's not quite the right word for us – not to depend too much on any individual, especially me. I take it as a point of pride that twice on my return from long trips my office had been moved – and each time it got smaller. My role is that of a catalyst. I try to create an environment in which others make decisions. Success means not making them myself.

One of my first acts at Semco was to throw out the rules. All companies have procedural bibles. Some look like the *Encyclopaedia Britannica*. Who needs all those rules? They discourage flexibility and comfort the complacent. At Semco, we stay away from formulas and try to keep our minds open. I knew our rule book was useless when, as a test, I once distributed some additional pages for it. I asked some managers to read the new sections and give me their reaction. Almost everyone said they were just fine. Trouble was, I had stapled the pages together so they couldn't be read without first prying them apart. Funny how no one mentioned that. All that new employees at Semco get today is a 20-page booklet we call *The Survival Manual*. As you will see in Appendix D, it has lots of cartoons but few words. The basic message: Use your common sense.

If you haven't guessed by now, Semco's standard policy is no policy. Many companies have entire departments that generate mountains of paperwork trying to control their employees. Take travel. They have rules that govern how much a person can spend in every possible situation. At Semco, we want our people to spend whatever they think they should, as if they were taking a trip on their own, with their own money. There's no department, no rules, no audits. If we're afraid to let people decide in which section of the plane to sit, or how many stars their hotel should have, we shouldn't be sending them abroad to do business in our name, should we?

We have absolute trust in our employees. In fact, we are partners with them. On the assumption that a capitalist society must be capitalist for all, Semco has a profit-sharing plan – but with a difference. Typically, companies' hand down these plans like God handed Moses the commandments. The owners decide who gets what, when. At Semco, profit-sharing is democratic. We negotiated with our workers over the basic percentage to be distributed – about a quarter of our corporate profits, as it turned out – and they hold assemblies to decide how to split it. It's up to them. Profit-sharing has worked so well that once, during negotiations over a new labour contract, a union leader argued that too big a raise would overextend the company.

Some people have likened the Semco philosophy to socialism, in the old, Eastern European sense. *Nonsenseskaya*. I think we're proving that worker involvement doesn't mean that bosses lose power. What we do strip away is the blind, irrational authoritarianism that diminishes productivity. We're thrilled that our workers are self-governing and self-managing. It means they care about their jobs and about their company, and that's good for all of us.

In restructuring Semco, we've picked the best from many systems. From capitalism we take the ideals of personal freedom, individualism, and competition. From the theory, not the practice, of socialism we have learned to control greed and share information and power. The Japanese have taught us the value of flexibility, although we shrink from their family-like ties to the company and their automatic veneration of elders. We want people to advance because of competence, not longevity or conformity.

When you eliminate rigid thought and hierarchical structure, things usually get messy, which is how our factories look. Instead of machines neatly aligned in long straight rows, the way Henry Ford wanted it, they are set at odd angles and in unexpected places. That's because our workers typically work in clusters or teams, assembling a complete product, not just an isolated component. That gives them more control and responsibility, which makes them happier and our products better. Nearly all our workers have mastered several jobs. They even drive fork-lifts to keep teammates supplied with raw materials and spare parts, which they have been known to purchase themselves from suppliers.

The Metalworkers' Union at first resisted this flexibility. Long ago, organized labour was forced to adopt narrower and narrower job classifications as a defence against giant corporations that pushed ever harder for higher productivity and profits. Eventually the unions realized that they could turn the system against the corporate masters by refusing to allow any deviation from the rules without extra pay. With time, the system became more beneficial to labour then to management – but it really wasn't serving either side.

When the union realized that Semco had no intention of dismantling its power, that the higher profits our factories would generate would mean higher pay for its members, and that we were intent on giving workers a meaningful say in our business, obstructionism eased. We have been allowed to innovate and to let our employees innovate. We are all freer.

Our factory workers, for example, can come in any time between 7 a.m. and 9 a.m. It's their choice, not ours. What if one worker wants to start at 7 and a teammate decides to come in at 9? Surely that would disrupt production? That was our worry, too, so we set up a task force to mediate any problems. It hasn't met yet. Our workers knew that production would suffer if they didn't co-ordinate their schedules, so that's what they did.

At Semco we don't even like to think in terms like worker or boss. We prefer Associate and Co-ordinator. And we encourage everyone to mix with everyone else, regardless of job. In our offices the purchasing and engineering departments have been scrambled so that everyone sits together, near the factory. The idea is that we all can learn from each other. The office decor is anything but plush and sometimes there is grime and oil on the floor. No one cared but me, and now that I have stopped wearing my fancy Italian loafers with the paper-thin soles, I don't care either.

What do the bosses think of all this? I am often asked.

Well, we don't have as many bosses as we used to. As workers began to exercise more control over their jobs and assume more voice in our polices, the need for supervisors diminished. We have also reduced our corporate staff, which provides legal, accounting, and marketing expertise to our manufacturing units, by more than 75 per cent. We no longer have data processing or training departments. Everyone vouches for his own work, so we don't need a quality control department either. After taking a good look at ourselves, we whittled the bureaucracy from twelve layers of management to three and devised a new structure based on concentric circles to replace the traditional, and confining, corporate pyramid.

We've also changed the way our departments do business with each other. If one doesn't want to buy services from another, it's free to go outside the company and buy from someone else. The threat of competition keeps us all on our toes. Recently, we have encouraged employees to start their own companies, leasing them Semco machinery at favourable rates. We buy from our former employees, of course, but they are also free to sell to others, even Semco's competitors. This programme has made us leaner and more agile, and given them ultimate control of their working lives. It makes entrepreneurs out of employees.

This is an extreme case, of course, but we try to maximize the possibilities and minimize supervision for everyone at Semco. Not that we don't have accountability. Before people are hired or promoted to leadership positions, they are interviewed and approved by all who will be working for them. And every six months managers are evaluated by those who work under them. The results are posted for all to see. Does this mean workers can fire their bosses? I guess it does, since anyone who consistently gets bad grades usually leaves Semco, one way or another.

We are not the only company to experiment with participative management. It's become a fad. But so many efforts at workplace democracy are just so much hot air. Not that the intentions are bad, it's just that it's much easier to talk about worker involvement than to implement it. We have been ripping apart Semco and putting it back together for a dozen years, and we're just 30 per cent finished. Still, the rewards have already been substantial.

We've taken a company that was moribund and made it thrive, chiefly by refusing to squander our greatest resource, our people. Semco has grown sixfold despite withering recessions, staggering inflation and chaotic national economic policy. Productivity has increased nearly sevenfold. Profits have risen fivefold. And we have had periods of up to 14 months in which not one worker has left us. We have a backlog of more than 2,000 job applications, hundreds from people who say they would take any job just to be at Semco. As a matter of fact, our last help-wanted newspaper ad generated more than 1,400 responses in the first week. And in a poll of recent college graduates conducted by a leading Brazilian magazine, 25 per cent of the men and 13 per cent of the women said Semco was the company at which they most wanted to work.

Not long ago the wife of one of our workers came to see a member of our human resources staff. She was puzzled about her husband's behaviour. He no longer yelled at the kids, she said, and asked everyone what they wanted to do on the weekends. He wasn't his usual, grumpy, autocratic self.

The woman was worried. What, she wondered, were we doing to her husband?

We realized that as Semco had changed for the better, he had, too.

two

FIT FOR DUTY

The home movie shifts abruptly to a scene of a narrow dirt road on the outskirts of São Paulo. It is the late 1950s. The camera moves in, shaking perilously as home movies will, and three men and a truck come into view. In the truck bed lies a horizontal lathe, a humble tool used for cutting metal. From the reverential expression on the face of the lean, suntanned man on the left, you would think it was fashioned from gold.

It is a glimpse of what it means to start a business. Few moments were as gratifying to my father, that gaunt man in the movie, as when the first machine was delivered to his new plant.

Antonio Curt Semler was born in Vienna in 1912, at the ignoble end of a glorious empire. His father, a successful dentist, wanted Antonio to be a physician. But he had his heart set on engineering, and graduated from Vienna's Polytechnic University instead.

Sensing an imminent decline of opportunities in between-the-wars Austria, he looked for challenges abroad. In 1937, Curt answered an advertisement placed by the DuPont Company and soon accepted a position as production engineer at its chemical and textile plant in Argentina, where he survived the political upheavals of Peronism and eventually became plant manager.

In 1952, Curt visited Brazil and was intrigued by the prospects such a vast, undeveloped country presented. At the time, he was working on a patent for a centrifuge which could separate lubricating oil from vegetables and which, he hoped, would be the mainstay of his own business. At first Rio de Janeiro seemed the right spot. But he changed his mind upon viewing São Paulo from a hill overlooking the city. This was a place, he thought to himself, for an entrepreneur.

It was also the place where this 42-year-old bachelor would meet another Austrian exile, Renee Weinmann, marry and raise a family. My mother's father had moved his family to China and started a profitable business exporting textiles and porcelain from Shanghai. The Weinmanns lived a sheltered life, alongside thousands of Europeans for whom the British and French quarters of Shanghai were islands in an ocean of misery. But as the poverty of the Chinese deepened, their resentment of foreigners grew. My grandfather died just before the Communists took over and my grandmother and her only child left on a freighter, practically expelled by Mao Ze Dong. They landed at the port of Santos, in the south of Brazil, after a month at sea. Soon, my mother was giving English lessons to wealthy citizens of São Paulo, one of whom introduced her to my father.

On the dining room table of their small, two-bedroom apartment in the centre of town, my father plotted a strategy for Semco, a contraction of Semler & Company. He worked constantly, pausing only to allow my mother to reclaim the table so they could dine together. Then he would work late into the night.

Children were a priority, for Curt was already anxious for someone to take over the business. Three pregnancies ended in failure before my sister, Susan, was born. But it was hard for my father to imagine a woman running a rough and tumble business such as Semco. I was born only 11 months later, an unknowing heir to an enterprise scarcely older than I was.

Semco and its owner were obscure, as was the oil-separating machine for which my father had by this time secured a patent. But Brazil was a land of opportunity, ravenous for all sorts of new products. In no time the Semco centrifuge became a market leader, and three Brazilian partners had come aboard with badly needed capital and a knowledge of the country. My father kept working hard, and the 1950s and 1960s responded with more kindness. These were the years of the Brazilian Miracle, when the economy was spurting by

7 per cent annually, a rate unmatched anywhere. Semco, a backyard machine shop only a few years earlier, blossomed into an established manufacturer employing about 110 people and generating revenues of $2 million a year.

The military dictators who ran Brazil, although strictly capitalists, must have been impressed with Stalin: they loved five-year plans. In the late 1960s, they decided the country needed a shipbuilding industry and suddenly there was a five-year National Shipbuilding Plan. My father, sensing opportunity, took on two British pump manufacturers as partners and Semco became a major supplier of marine pumps in Brazil, a line of products for which it is still known.

Passing the company to the next generation is the stated goal of entrepreneurs everywhere. This is mystifying when you think about it. Have you heard of Einstein's son? Why is it that the offspring of industrialists are typically regarded as natural entrepreneurs? Sometimes a son or daughter of an entrepreneur can be an excellent manger, as Thomas Watson Jr of IBM proved in the 1960s and 1970s. But who makes the decision? Invariably, it is the father. And let's be honest: he isn't exactly impartial.

'I want the business to remain in the family's bosom,' the tycoons say. (Remind you of Louis XIV?) So and so 'is the only one I can trust'. But is it better to have the company sink slowly in trustworthy hands than prosper through the efforts of strangers?

And in my case, I hardly inspired much confidence. As a child, I had an attention span that made Jai-Lai seem like a chess match. I thought it was perfectly normal to do maths homework with cartoons dancing across the television screen. My mother still can't understand how they let me graduate with so many D's, or why she and my father were so frequently summoned to meetings with teachers to discuss, among other things, my belief that peanut butter and jelly sandwiches were made to hang from the cafeteria ceiling.

As I grew older, I came to feel downright ashamed of my

unwavering need to occupy stage centre. But some powerful current kept pulling me towards any situation that held the potential for attention and leadership. In high school, I pursued and attained many positions – class president, captain of the track team, photography editor of the year-book. I even ran the lunchtime snack-stand, a concession operated by the junior class to raise money for the class trip the following year. It was here that an aptitude for business first surfaced. I abandoned the policy of freebies honoured by past snack-stand impresarios, lengthened the hours of operation, and encouraged suppliers such as Coke, Pepsi, Kellogg, and Fritolay to compete for our business. I wouldn't say that they fell over each other for the snack-stand account, but our revenues soared. Then I invested the profits in the stock market, and by the following year had earned enough to fly the entire class to a resort. 'At school on business only,' was how my classmates described me in the yearbook.

But this nascent capitalist flair paled beside my desire to master the guitar, in particular a Gibson Les Paul. I was obsessed with rock'n'roll – the Stones, Led Zeppelin, Pink Floyd, Uriah Heep. To me, diversification meant also learning to play the bass and the drums. All this alarmed my father, who anxiously awaited the end of what he hoped was a phase to begin talk of my corporate ascension.

When I was 16 I took a summer job in Semco's purchasing department and found myself studying specs for the half-inch steel plates on marine pumps. My only fun came when a trucker taught me to drive. I was the only kid on my block to get to slide behind the wheel of a Mercedes, even if it was a 10-ton truck, not a 560 SEL convertible.

After the summer I went back to the guitar and my despairing father considered selling out. Soon enough, though, I discovered the depressingly narrow range of my musical abilities. Given my father's desire for a successor and my stint as a snack-stand mogul, business seemed a sensible aspiration.

There was just one problem: in Brazil, all healthy young men must serve in the army for at least a year when they turn 18.

Having waited this long, my father thought it would be the best medicine for me. I would be compelled to get into shape and, if not learn to love the dawn, at least develop a passing acquaintance with it. Whether he was just giving me a hard time or meant it I never discovered. Just in case, I began lobbying my mother. Meal times became sacred, grades improved and my bed was made with miraculous regularity. Weekends were inaugurated by early-morning rising, with the help of two alarm clocks, both positioned on the far side of my room.

Fathers understand this sort of behaviour, and mine kept giving me a 'you-can't-trick-me-son' look. Mothers are another story, God bless them.

'Curt,' mine would say. 'Dickie just can't lose a year of his life in the army.'

I would nod vigorously in the background.

'It'll make him a man,' my father would reply. 'I was in the army myself, you know.'

My mother and I would sit back on the sofa to listen (again) to tales of marches in the snow, cold showers, and the polishing of boots and belt buckles.

Soon I was ordered for a physical at the local recruiting office, so off I went in the middle of the night to sit in line with all the other guys. Any important physical or mental defects were considered then, and I watched several people in the line practise flat feet, nervous breakdowns, and assorted malfunctions. I didn't have the courage for that. The recruiters liked my height, were impressed with my weight and, generally, didn't find me lacking in any of their stringent qualifications, such as having two legs and two arms.

Two weeks later it was time to present my army-approved physique at another military office for a more complete medical examination. Friends had told me horror stories about it. According to tradition, all who were dismissed from service were invited (by a soldier whose physique would have made Sylvester Stallone jealous) to donate blood for the army hospital. An attendant would stick a huge needle in our forearm, hand you a two-litre bottle, and move on to the next victim.

Having passed out on 100 per cent of the occasions on which I have had any contact with blood, I could already picture it: the slow darkening before my eyes, my body lurching forward, the sound of breaking glass, a vision of sandy beaches in the South Pacific. Then a heavy head and many soldiers frowning at me from the ceiling.

Well, if that was the price of freedom . . .

Off I went before dawn, and after the usual five-hour wait found myself in a line with hundreds of naked young men, answering questions about childhood diseases, adulthood diseases, and, especially, venereal diseases. One guy put on an impeccable show of tongue-swallowing and was immediately placed under arrest. Once again I passed. At least I didn't have to give blood, I told myself.

A month later I went for the written examination. By now getting up at 4 a.m. was easy, since I wasn't getting any sleep anyway. The test was long and complicated. I did my best to do my worst and went home in a state of high anxiety. Three days later I learned I had passed again.

I was already outfitted in uniform, cap, and boots, when I was summoned by the officer in charge and, after waiting two and a half hours and then explaining why I thought it was silly to be in an army in a country that has never fought a war and hasn't the slightest chance of breaking that record, was dismissed.

Passing up business school, I entered the São Paulo State Law School, the most prestigious university in the country and one that had educated many Brazilian presidents. I was sure I would prefer its more humanistic approach. But I barely scraped by with below-average grades, in part because I started working again at Semco soon after I enrolled.

three

DR DICKIE

My first experiences in the executive suite distressed me. Everyone was as starched as their shirts.

I tried to fit in, I really did. I even went to a trendy men's store and acquired a complete corporate outfit – navy bluesuit with white pinstripes, white shirt with French cuffs, black shoes. I didn't wear the suit – the suit wore me.

I hadn't been at work long when my father summoned me to his office and told me I shouldn't let anyone call me by my nickname, Dickie. It would diminish respect for me, he said sternly. I should always be known as Dr Ricardo, a title college graduates such as me are automatically accorded in Brazil. Never mind that I had already asked everyone to call me Dickie. The signals to the organization became so confused that to this day I still get memos addressed to Dr Dickie.

Like most self-made men, my father was a traditionalist. He treated his employees paternalistically and considered strikes and labour strife personal affronts. He always remembered that he had founded Semco on a dining room table.

He would wake up every day precisely at 6.30 and follow a schedule as rigid as an I-beam. On Tuesdays, Wednesdays, and Thursdays he would play an early-morning round of golf before going to the plant, lunch at home, then nap for 15 minutes before returning to the office. He would arrive for dinner precisely at 7.45 p.m. On Fridays, he would skip golf and attend the Rotary Club luncheon.

His secretary, Fernande, a short, stocky woman with a serious demeanour, had already been with him 15 years when I arrived, though I never understood why, since they were always complaining about each other. If Fernande arrived six minutes late, my father would not fail to comment. If he corrected a mistake on a letter with a pen instead of a pencil, it would be her turn to fume.

Fernande would often charge out of my father's office banging the door loudly behind her, and I could understand why. An elegant man with an imperial bearing – he had been a member of the Austrian Olympic ski team and still carried himself like an athlete, with his chest pushed forward and his shoulders straight – he demanded respect and not infrequently inspired fear. A stern look was his registered trademark. When I was growing up friends would often leave me at the front door rather than risk an encounter with the old man. At the office, clerks would flip coins to decide who would deliver his papers and possibly become the target of his wrath, for he would often take out his frustration on whoever happened to be closest to him.

When I got my own office next to his, he insisted on installing a sliding door between us. I would be in the middle of a meeting with a customer and – wham – the door would open and in he would march.

My father didn't like my habit of putting my feet up on my desk. He didn't like my habit of working at home. And it annoyed him that I took pains to separate my personal life from the company. If I made a copy of something for my own use, I'd always pay for it. If I needed to send a telex to a hotel where I planned to spend my vacation, I'd pay for that, too. To my father, the business and the family were intertwined and inseparable.

The gap between us was almost 50 years wide, and no matter how hard we tried to blend them, our styles and our ideas would become increasingly incompatible. I knew the transition from father to son wasn't going to be smooth. Slowly, he came to realize it as well.

The tensions between my father and me were compounded by an economy that had shifted into reverse. Despite the general's five-year-plan, Brazil's shipbuilding industry was among the hardest-hit sectors. This was devastating for Semco, for by 1980 90 percent of our business was in marine products such as pumps, components for propellers, and water-oil separators for ship motors. The only profits Semco was generating were from investments of cash reserves, which were diminishing rapidly.

Semco had been run for more than a decade by a group of executives well connected to the maritime industry. As the slump deepened, I became convinced Semco's only chance for survival was to broaden its product line and reduce its dependence on the marine business. It was time, as the Monty Python crew used to say, for something completely different. But whenever I brought up diversification, they would argue that Semco was a highly focused company and that if we lost our specialized skills, we would lose everything. The Old Guard kept telling my father that Semco could hang on, that a new shipbuilding plan was about to start and we would bounce back.

Semco was about to take on $1 million in financing to build a new plant with computer-controlled machinery to assemble marine pump casings and propellers. I was once enthusiastic about such an advanced factory, but as the economy slid I worried about making such a huge investment. If we were going to take on more debt, I thought it should at least be to enter a healthy industry. But I was only 20 and, despite my last name and the inflated title on my business card, Assistant to the Board of Directors, I didn't have much influence. Whenever a critical decision approached, I would usually be sent on a meaningless visit to some out-of-town customer, keeping me away from the office until they figured out what to do.

I was convinced I wanted to be in business – the Les Paul was in the bottom of the closet – but I wasn't sure Semco would be the place at which I would realize my entrepreneurial aspirations. Pushed by me, Semco's auditors at Price Waterhouse had found some companies they thought we might be interested in acquiring. Few seemed synergistic with Semco, but there was one that caught my eye. It couldn't have been a more mundane business – it made ladders, all sorts of ladders. Started by a carpenter, it had quickly become the largest ladder-maker in Brazil, with more employees than Semco. But it had fallen on hard times, so much so that Price Waterhouse refused to be responsible for the numbers in its pre-acquisition audit.

Undeterred, I began to think about leaving Semco and going into the ladder business on my own. I started visiting the ladder-maker nearly every day, getting to know the company and whittling away at the owner's asking price, which started out at more than $1 million, despite the company's problems.

Soon the price started dropping, and I tried to convince my father to lend me the money. 'Let's think about it,' he would say. 'Show me the balance sheet.'

I did, but he wouldn't look at it. He was stalling.

It had nothing to do with ladders, of course. He didn't want me to leave.

I spent most of a year studying the ladder company, and it proved a much better business education than I got in any classroom. I talked to the firm's creditors. I talked to its suppliers. I milked Price Waterhouse for all the strategic thinking I could get.

Then I had a brainstorm. I took out a newspaper ad, in English, announcing that I was looking for a CEO for my prospective enterprise. I said I wanted someone who had managed a Brazilian subsidiary of a multinational company.

I was swamped with responses, perhaps because I hinted that I was willing to give up some equity in the company. I met with about 30 of the most impressive candidates. I would go through the numbers and then ask them to tell me how they would revive the company. By the time I was finished with the interviews I had not only found a CEO – a Bolivian who was president of Black and Decker Brazil – but had also become quite wise.

Ladder sales had continued to slide, and the company's price at last reached a level I could afford: $1. The company's suppliers were willing to extend me additional credit, besides. Though young, I was connected to a well-known company. Perhaps they thought Semco was behind the deal, an assumption I somehow never got around to correcting.

We drew up an exceedingly complicated contract, which was my lawyers' way of warning me that it was a high-risk move. But I reasoned that if I was going to go broke, I would rather it be when I was in my 20s than in my 40s, when I might have additional responsibilities in short pants. Anyway, thanks to all those interviews, I had a plan. I was going to discontinue nearly half the company's products, take all the fresh credit the suppliers would give me and buy enough time to rebuild the business around the items that were still profitable.

On the day we were finally ready to close the deal my father summoned me to his office.

'Let's talk about this some more,' he said.

'It's too late,' I told him. 'I've been at this for a year.'

I knew what was troubling him and tried to ease his anxiety. I told him I would join Semco's board of directors and come to the office whenever he wanted. 'But there's no use me staying here,' I added. 'We're just going to fight. We don't agree on how to run the company, and you've got all these people here you still trust. There was a time when I thought you would give me more power, but I know you're not about to do that.'

That's when my father finally said he wanted to discuss a change in ownership that would give me a majority of Semco's shares and with them the authority to make the changes I believed were needed if the company was going to endure. He also agreed to pay the $30,000 stipulated in the contract if I walked away from the ladder company deal. (That company, incidentally, lingered for a while no doubt because the owner eliminated some products I would have abolished. But in the end the company was liquidated. As for my future CEO, he became the director of DuPont's Brazilian subsidiary.)

'Who's going to run Semco?' I asked my father, just to hear him say it.

I was quiet. He was quiet.

'Better make your mistakes,' he finally said, 'while I'm still alive.'

As it happened, I made all sorts of mistakes right under his nose. That's the trouble with mistakes. You don't recognize them at the time.

And there was one move that wasn't a mistake, although it was terrible risky. Either I could continue to try to convince the entrenched executives that Semco had to change, and endure more of their foot-dragging, or I could make the changes without them. The executives still believed in the shipbuilding plan and were prepared to wait for it, collecting their comfortable salaries all the while. So it would be the second route.

'I'm going on a trip for the next two or three weeks,' my father said towards the end of our difficult conversation. 'Whatever changes you want to make in the organization, do them now.'

I settled into the office my father had used and reviewed the yellow legal pad before me. On it I had scrawled the names of our all top executives. There were about 15 names in all. It was a Friday, and I had set up individual appointments with each of them, starting with Waldemar Maragonni, an imposing man with piercing eyes. He greeted me icily, letting his steel-grey eyes bore through my young skull. I felt like a student handing in a term-paper that was three days late.

'Hello Waldemar,' I stammered.

'Dickie, what can I do for you?' Waldemar said condescendingly.

Come on, Dickie, Say it. Say it.

'Well, you see, Waldemar, I think we've got to make some changes around here.'

No reaction.

'You know that I've been wanting to diversify Semco.'

Still no reaction.

'And,' I went on, 'I feel that we have to make some management changes for this diversification process to work.'

Silence. I decided to summarize the situation thus far.

Surely he would agree with me in the end, and we could part cordially, if not as chums. So off I went into medieval history, tracing Semco's beginnings and Waldemar's contributions in his decade and a half at the company. After a while it occurred to me that I was making a good case for a promotion, not a dismissal. Abruptly changing tack, I rushed up into the past few years, concentrating on Semco's gloomy outlook and the need for new products.

'I couldn't agree more,' Waldemar finally said.

Ah, progress. But no, he's not supposed to agree with me.

'We have started to study diversification,' Waldemar went on. 'I myself will be in Germany and England next month to talk to a few companies.'

'But Waldemar, you've said that many times, and nothing has happened so far.'

'Now it will be different.'

No arguing with that. An hour and a half had gone by. I had only three hours left in the afternoon, and a long list of managers to fire.

'Waldemar, let's make a long story short. I want to conduct this diversification myself, and can't see that happening with a dual command.'

There, I've done it.

'No problem,' Waldemar replied, to my chagrin. 'We'll make a great team.'

I felt the stirring of panic, followed by tension and then frustration. Were all the meetings going to be like this? What if the afternoon ended before I got through the list? The survivors would surely organize over the weekend.

'Waldemar, let me be as straightforward as possible. I need to do this on my own.'

Silence descended like a thick wool blanket on a hot summer day. There we sat, air conditioner whirring in the background, looking at each other.

'Are you saying I'm fired?', Waldemar said after a while.

I cleared my throat and composed myself. 'Yes, Waldemar, I am. It's the only way.'

More silence. Then the inevitable question.

'Does you father know about this?'

'Well, yes. Sort of. Yes. He does. *Yes.*'

'I see,' Waldemar said. At last I saw a physical reaction: he became pale, then ghostly white. I wondered how I looked. Probably worse.

Waldemar got up. 'Well, I'll be in my office Monday morning. Next week we can discuss the transition.'

'Ah, Waldemar, one minute please,' I quickly interjected, getting up also. 'You see, I have in mind a fast transition.'

'And what would that be? Six months?'

'Uh, no, no,' I stammered.

'Three months, then?' Waldemar said moving towards the door.

'Well, no, less . . . I . . . I . . . I . . .'

'You don't mean you want me out in less than a month?' His eyes narrowed as they stared into mine.

'Well, actually, yes.'

'When do you intend that I leave the company?'

Courage.

'Waldemar, I'd like you to take your things home today. Should I need something on Monday, I'll call you there.'

Waldemar went through the doorway, glanced back, then turned and shut the door, firmly. I collapsed on the sofa.

The rest of the meetings were over in a hurry. By 6 p.m. I had fired 60 per cent of Semco's top management. I'd never hired anybody, much less laid waste to so many people in a single, Godfather-like purge. But they had ignored my suggestions to diversify. Semco did not have time for slow, herbal medicine. It needed emergency surgery.

With a mixture of relief and anxiety I made my way to my car and drove through the gates on my way home for the weekend.

I chose a Friday because I had hoped everything would simmer down over the weekend. I had much organizing to do before Monday. I had no managerial experience, but had already lined up someone who had. My new right arm went by the name of Ernesto Gabriele. An excessively thin man in his 40s, Ernesto had enough energy for an entire executive committee (and he would practically be one). Born to an Italian immigrant family in Sorocaba, a small town in the interior of the state of São Paulo, he had held fast during his youth to the dream of studying in America. He didn't speak a word of English or have the money for an airline ticket, much less tuition. But he was determined, and that proved sufficient.

Near his hometown was the Brazilian subsidiary of the Firestone Tire company, and at a school in Sorocaba Ernesto found applications for the University of Akron, where the rubber giant was based. High school diploma in hand, Ernesto filled out a form, requesting a scholarship and promising to learn English. The school had an opening for a foreign student and Ernesto was admitted. He collected donations from the townspeople for his ticket, studied English long enough to confirm his suspicion that he could pick up languages almost overnight, and in July took off for Ohio.

Four years later he had a degree from the University of Akron and a job next door as a Firestone trainee. Rising quickly, he was soon on his way back to Brazil as a junior manager. He kept on rising, too, becoming at the age of 29 Firestone's youngest vice-president.

Ernesto specialized in administration, finance, and restlessness. Highly ethical but short-tempered, he was quick to take offence or create showdowns with colleagues from which he would extricate himself by handing in his resignation. He became vice president of J. I. Case, which makes tractors, then moved to a subsidiary of a German multi-national, where he learned to speak German. His next stint was at a French company, where he learned French. Then he became the assistant to the president of Sharp, the Japanese electronics company, but left after screaming 'bullshit' in Japanese during a business meeting. He went to work in Rio as a vice president of administration for Xerox, but after making 11 trips to the US in one year decided he wanted a less hectic life. Leafing through the newspaper in his Rio apartment one Sunday, an ad, in English, caught his attention. It was for a position as CEO at a ladder company in São Paulo.

Ernesto's résumé intrigued me. How could it not, since he had listed all the companies he had worked for, including ones at which he had spent only a couple of months, along with a complete list of references from each? His openness, coupled with his former employers' willingness to recommend him, impressed me. He had shot up early in his career but had not found what he was looking for. He was obviously brilliant with a passion for organization, but he also had a strong character and inevitably became unhappy wherever he went. That fitted my needs not for the ladder company but for Semco. We were headed for uncharted waters, and I anticipated we would have to change course often. A traditional executive might balk at that, or prove too inflexible.

I met with Ernesto several times before the Great Purge and hired him the Saturday after it. Now I had an alter ego who was as hardheaded and crazy as I was – except he knew how to run a company.

When Monday arrived I began to realize the impact of what I had done. Clients would call and ask for a particular person and we would explain he was no longer with us. They would ask for someone else, and we'd tell them he wasn't there, either. After their fourth or fifth try, you could hear their bewilderment.

Our former executives, I realized, had made themselves the repository of many of our trade secrets, no doubt to ensure their continued employment. They didn't count on anyone as rash as me spoiling it for them, but I didn't count on people as secretive as they were. We had to search through their desk drawers and filing cabinets to discover all the special deals and arrangements they had made with customers.

Naturally, some of these customers tried to talk us into taking the executives back. A German company that licences us to make several kinds of marine pumps even sent two representatives all the way to Brazil to personally plead with me to step aside and let the old managers return. They made it clear they thought we wouldn't survive without them.

I wasn't sure we would, either. But we were going to try.

four

FALSE START

We spent the rest of 1980 gasping for oxygen as we ran from bank to bank, trying to raise cash. We even considered selling the company's buildings. It was no fun having to pre-pay bills from suppliers or sell our products in a market full of rumours about Semco. But soon Ernesto began to work his multi-national magic and our customers realized we weren't going to go bankrupt, at least not right away.

Ernesto installed dozens of new procedures and invented new forms almost daily. Our resident managerial wizard persuaded salespeople to fill out customer-visit reports and keep statistics on orders closed versus quotes offered. Files were rigorously organized all over the company. Employees' bags and cars were searched under a system that randomly selected them for inspection. Everyone was issued a plastic ID card and compelled to wear it. Production schedules were displayed on boards in our new planning and control department. Members of our new time and methods department were dispatched around the plant, searching for ways to speed our workers up.

How inspiring. How capitalistic. Everything Xerox could do, Semco could do, too. Okay, so they actually sold their products and we only had the statistical evidence of why ours were still in the warehouse. A mere detail, we thought, to be rectified any day.

We promoted many Semco old-timers, some of whom are with us still. But we sorely lacked an aggressive leader for our sales department. Truth was, we lacked almost everything in our sales department. Brazil's five-year plans, with their long wind-ups, had made us lax. There seemed to be no need to sell anything; we would take orders, that's all.

Which is why in 1980 we were delivering pumps that we sold in 1975.

So I put an ad in the newspaper for a sales manager. (Sound familiar?) And that's how I met Harro Heyde.

Harro was a strange duck. He was very tall, balding and wore spectacles with lenses like the bottoms of Coke bottles. He didn't own a suit and his clothes seemed pulled at random from the bottom of some dark, dank closet. At our first interview he told me he was an avid cook (*coq au vin* was his speciality) and that he and his wife, a parachute instructor incidentally, lived with two small children in a Bavarian-style cottage, baking bread and raising (what else?) chickens.

Harro had been first in his class at the Institute of Aeronautical Technology, the MIT of Brazil. He spoke English, French, and German, and had held an assortment of jobs, including maintenance director at a huge mining complex in the Amazon and construction manager for the French company Fichet in Algeria. His credentials seemed sufficiently zany for what I had in mind: someone to shake up our sales department.

Harro was willing. Like Ernesto, he had yet to find his niche. Harro started selling on his first day at Semco and never stopped. He would pass a salesperson's desk and ask how a given quote was progressing. The salesperson would tell him the customer was studying it. Harro would suggest a visit. The salesperson would say he would try to arrange one for the next week. Harro would say he didn't mean next week, he meant now. Impossible, the salesman would argue. But Harro would grab him by the arm, and a bunch of magazines from our reception area, and head straight for the prospect's office. Announcing their arrival, they would wait one, two, even three hours – whatever it took until they were seen. Meanwhile, Harro would keep himself entertained by talking to the receptionist about the company, grilling the Semco salesperson about his other accounts, or reading the magazines he had brought with him.

I did what I could to keep him supplied with reading matter. A few days after Harro joined Semco, we signed a licence agreement with a Norwegian company to manufacture a new line of pumps. We knew very little about the technical specifications of these pumps, but in a few days we were scheduled to make a major presentation on the pumps at Petrobras, the state-owned oil company that is among the world's largest. I dropped by Harro's office and asked him if he would look at the material. No problem, he said. Before he could change his mind, I handed him 600 fun-filled pages on hydraulics. *En passant*, I told him I wanted him to speak to the Petrobras engineers. Harro just gave me a leave-it-to-me-kid smile.

He spent dozens of hours studying the stuff, spoke often to the Norwegians, then he made a pitch to Petrobras and came back with a substantial order.

Harro and I hit the road. In two years, we travelled to 16 countries and contacted more than 60 companies to drum up business. We would visit a dozen, sometimes two dozen cities in a month. To protect us from burnout, our rule was one flight per day. We broke it often. On one unforgettably neurotic trip, we gulped down a dinner of marinated salmon in Oslo in an open-air restaurant where the midnight sun reflected off our silverware; took the next flight to New York, where we lunched with executives from the Crane Company; then on to dinner in Cincinnati with representatives from the Day Mixing Company; before spending the night (in the dark, this time) in San Francisco, where we met the next morning with executives from Pacific Pumps, Inc.

I came to appreciate Harro's rowdy jokes and respect his appetite. Once we headed for Linz, Austria, to visit a pump company called Ochsner. Mr Ochsner himself was to receive us, but something went wrong and we didn't get to the hotel until close to midnight, six hours late. Harro immediate made his way to the restaurant, on a quest for his favourite Austrian fare, *knoedel*, a kneaded ball of dough that is a potato substitute. The waiter was apologetic, but we were to leave Austria the next morning and Harro was not an easy man to dissuade. Off he went to the kitchen, not only securing a promise from the chef that his wish would be fulfilled but also that he would be allowed to watch the preparations.

During these trips we hoped we could convince enough companies to let us manufacture their pumps and mixers under licence in Brazil, augmenting our pitiful cash flow and buying us time. But the negotiations were difficult; Brazil's quirky economy and restrictive government regulations were bad enough, and Semco's relative obscurity made our task that much harder. We slipped and slid as we danced along the edge, but someone up there was watching out for us, for we managed to secure seven licence agreements to manufacture soup mixers, oil filters, liquid agitators for mineral tanks, compressors, and other industrial and food-processing equipment. All this reduced marine equipment to 60 per cent of our product line. We were still breathing.

Early in 1981 Alcoa announced plans to build a new aluminium mill in the north of Brazil. It was one of the few large construction projects we could expect in the midst of the recession. Semco bid on the 200 hydraulic pumps for the project, a $3 million job. An order like that meant more hope for our company, which normally had a backlog of 10-months of production work but now was down to a mere two and a half months. We had supplied Alcoa before and thought our chances of getting the job were good. But late one Friday we were told that an Australian competitor, Warman Pumps, had underbid us.

Recovering from the disappointment as much as possible, we turned to our last hope: an order for marine pumps from two local shipyards, Caneco and Emaq, which were building three ships for Petrobras. Both shipyards told us they would rather buy from Semco, as was their custom. Trouble was, one of our competitors had been instructed by its foreign parent to win the job at any cost, and had offered an 18 per cent rebate. They were desperate, too.

Backs to the wall, we offered a 20 per cent discount. There wouldn't be much profit in the job, but the cash would help keep us going until we could figure out what to do next. I remember feeling quite pleased on the flight back from Rio.

At the end of the week, the shipyards told us the competition had offered a 35 per cent discount and thrown in inspections, insurance, and shipping costs, free. Do you know the medical expression 'flatline'? Well, it fitted us. Had there been an electrocardiogram machine in our board room, it wouldn't have registered a heartbeat.

We were on the next flight to Rio, of course, to match the offer. We had no choice. This was surely the last order of the year, and it was only March. Price was secondary – we had to survive until we could pull Semco together. We matched the 35 per cent discount and the shipyards gave us their word that the order was ours. Our heart was pounding again.

A few days later we were sitting at a meeting. I don't remember what we were discussing, but I do recall how jittery we all were. One of us, a superstitious soul, noticed there were 13 people around the table. At that moment I summoned for an urgent telephone call. I picked up the receiver and was told that the Caneco shipyard had been offered an additional 7 per cent discount by our rival and had accepted. Emaq was going along, since Petrobras wanted all six ships to be identical.

All of us were crushed – except Harro. He had that gleam in his eye. At his urging, we had decided to open another front in our battle for survival. We would win the Alcoa job after all.

Alcoa had already reached deals with nearly all the suppliers it needed to build its plant. The only bid it had not yet decided was for the giant mixers that rotate slowly to keep the aluminium from hardening at the bottom of the tanks. We knew little about these machines, except that they were huge, with blades 15 feet long and shafts three storeys high. We asked Alcoa if it would consider a bid from Semco. They told us we might as well forget it, since the winner was to be chosen in just 10 days.

The next afternoon Harro and I took off for King of Prussia, Pennsylvania home of one of the largest mixer manufacturers in the world, the Philadelphia Gear Corporation. We needed its expertise to pull off the job, and it needed Semco, since under out trade laws the machines would have to be manufactured in Brazil. We were ushered into the President's office, where he told us his position on Brazil, sparing no unflattering adjectives or adverbs. Philadelphia Gear once tried to buy a Brazilian company but had been frustrated by the horrendous red tape. From then on, he wanted nothing to do with Brazil or Brazilians.

When I mentioned Alcoa his scowl disappeared. Philadelphia Gear did business with the biggest aluminium manufacturers, but not Alcoa. He immediately saw the chance to establish a relationship with the aluminium giant through a back door in South America. He was smiling now, but turned pale again when we told him the mixers required were bigger than any his company had built. When we told him that we had only a few days to finish the technical work, negotiate the deal, and sign the licence agreement, his scowl returned. Even so, after consulting with his board he decided to go ahead.

Back in Brazil, Harro camped out in the reception area of Alcoa's imposing offices. The procurement manager, Victor Barruzzi, was a tough man, with no interest in cordialities. He was also an early riser, so Harro made it a habit to arrive at his office at around 6 a.m. Barruzzi would pass by and barely nod. Harro would announce himself every hour or so and just sit there, reading Alcoa annual reports and mining magazines. Barruzzi finally gave in and saw him, but only to say that Semco didn't have a chance for the job. Harro somehow managed to set up another meeting with Barruzzi for both of us and, after waiting two hours, we were received. We begged and badgered until Barruzzi gave in and let us bid.

And that's how Alcoa's new Brazilian plant came to boast 26 Semco-Philadelphia mixers, including four that are among the largest in the world.

Now that we were on a winning streak, we decided to attack the Petrobras problem head on. One man, Shigeaki Ueki, the president, was responsible for the oil company's decisions. After countless requests we managed to secure a meeting with him on a Friday afternoon. We told him we believed our competitor was dumping – selling pumps at a loss to worm its way into the Brazilian market. Prove it, he said, and the order was ours. But, he warned, we didn't have much time.

The needle on the electrocardiogram machine jumped. Then we remembered that it was almost quitting time and we still had to get a copy of our competitor's balance sheet from the official registrar. The clerk who received us clearly did not wish to spend the last half-hour of her working week looking through musty files, but somehow my eighteen-days-in-the-desert expression moved her. She found the balance sheet and I scanned it with apprehensive eyes. What if a creative accountant had camouflaged the losses? He might be playing around with inventories, or future earnings. How could I tell? My fingers swept down the columns. Earnings, earnings, where were those damned earnings. Ah, there they were. Nice, fat numbers, in parentheses. As I suspected, a $3 million loss.

In the end, Dr Ueki played Solomon and divided the pump order in half. Semco would have the contract for three of the ships.

If only to show how the world goes round and round but ends up where it started, this same order, which we believed was essential for our survival, was delayed several times. Then the shipyard went broke before it finished paying us.

But that was much later. For the moment, the noose was a little looser.

Nineteen-eighty-one came and went. And 1982. Thanks to the licence agreements Harro and I secured, Semco found itself in the usual position of making money. Lots of money. Well, what for us was lots of money. We even had some cash left over after we paid off our debts. With Ernesto's new corporate controls in place, and our product line greatly enlarged, we were riding a wave of success as Brazil continued to founder.

I couldn't have been more pleased with the new, improved, diversified Semco. Everything seemed so professional. No one could get in or out of our plant without showing an ID card. Even I was stopped by our guards. We had special forms for overtime, phone invoices, copying-machine receipts, everything.

Our pride and joy was our new budget system. The numbers were ready on the fifth working day of every month, all in colour-coded folders. How much coffee was consumed by workers in a subsection of Light Manufacturing III? There it was on chart No. 112, page 67. Ernesto was making us over in the image of Firestone, Xerox, and Sharp.

When I talked to executives at other companies about our system, I liked to tell them about the time the President of Allis Chalmers came down from the US for a visit. He wondered whether we might want to acquire his company's pump operations in Brazil. The deal didn't work out, but we took him on a tour of our factory anyway. He leafed through some of our budget folders and seemed as impressed as a child at his first circus. He didn't expect to find such efficiency – compulsiveness? – at a Latin American company. He told us he was going to order his Brazilian subsidiary, which was many times larger than Semco, to install a similar system right away. Our chests stayed puffed for weeks.

Not too long after that, Allis Chalmers started losing market share and then money. It has now been dissolved and sold piecemeal.

We would come to see a lesson in that. But meanwhile, we were anxious to share our new management skills with the world. It was time for Semco to go out and buy some companies.

five

THE GO-GO YEARS

I began to suspect we weren't being taken seriously when Ray Krinker, senior partner of Price Waterhouse in Brazil, looked across the table at me and smiled. 'A grocery store near my home,' he said. 'That's the best buy in your price range.'

It was 1983. In our typically brash way we had called Krinker, a specialist in mergers and acquisitions, and told him we had $500,000 to spend. We wanted to buy a company. A grocery store wasn't what I had in mind.

I remembered a certain ladder-maker I could have bought for $1 and implored Krinker and his people to press on. They did, and during the next few months I looked at stacks of documents from divisions and subsidiaries that were on the block. We had several requirements: the company had to be No. 1 or No. 2 in its market, have a connection with our own business, and be technologically advanced. It also had to be for sale for the right reasons, which were either because there was no one to succeed the founder, current management was inefficient, or the parent company had lost interest. We weren't in the market for companies that made products of dubious quality or required large infusions of cash, which, of course, we didn't have.

Krinker, an outspoken man with eyes that were alternately twinkling and intense, was invaluable in our quest. He was also ego-levelling. 'A small hole,' he was fond of telling me, 'can sink a big ship.'

I can't say we were a big ship, but we sure as hell were look-ing at many small holes. The companies that were up for sale then – remember, this was still during the recession – weren't very healthy. Most lacked either capital or a market. Some lacked both. Ray helped us avoid them. But that still left plenty of candidates. We would sit for whole afternoons working our way through foot-high piles of annual reports. We would pull one out, read about the product line, look at the numbers, and then decide whether it belonged in the small pile of interesting propositions or the much larger stack of rejects.

No company with half a million dollars has ever felt more powerful. Here were firms with annual sales of $5 million, $10 million, even $20 million, awaiting our verdict. We even got literature from one company with $150 million in sales and another with 4,500 employees.

Of course, we never considered talking to outfits that big. Even so, we had no idea how pretentious we were in thinking we had the expertise to run other companies besides our own. We were a legend in our own minds. Who would dare stop us from fulfilling our destiny as a multinational conglomerate?

I would think back on these times years later, when I read about the whiz kids of Wall Street playing at the same game, buying, selling, and merging companies, oblivious to the rich, complex histories each organization had. These Armani-out-fitted, BMW-driving know-it-alls broke corporations into pieces in the name of short-term profits, and broke the hearts of those whose dreams the corporations embodied. But there was no place for sentiment or tradition or employee motiva-tion in their world. 'Bottom line, what's the bottom line?' they bellowed into their cellular phones. I had become caught up in that way of thinking, foolishly believing I held the power of life and death over the companies whose vital statistics were gathered in the folders on our meeting table. Ray Krinker was right. We should have started slowly. We should have pro-ceeded cautiously. But we were impatient, so we didn't.

We selected 15 companies to visit, negotiated with six, and settled on one: a subsidiary of a Swedish air-conditioning company now known as the Asea Brown Boveri Group. Its Brazilian offshoot, Flakt, sold refrigeration equipment for ships and offshore oil-drilling platforms and ventilation systems for marine engine rooms.

Negotiations proceeded quickly. The deal entailed taking

over the Brazilian marine operation and making it a division
of Semco. The price was about $300,000, which was in our
ballpark. (Okay, it was almost our entire ballpark.) The signing ceremony was to be in Stockholm.

Off I went, stopping to visit other Flakt plants on the way.
Given my state, which was anxious and jet-lagged, I suppose
it wasn't really surprising that the trip was also the occasion of
my first encounter with socialized medicine. For months I
had been waking up with a throat so sore it was impossible for
me to swallow even liquids before midmorning. I also suffered
blinding headaches and gastritis. An extra 50 pounds completed the dismal picture. I hadn't exercised for more than
five years, unless you count huffing my way up the stairs to
my office.

I arrived in Gotebörg the evening before an 8 a.m. meeting.
My host called to say my hotel was a six-minute walk from the
office, so naturally he would meet me in the lobby at six minutes to eight. I had a light dinner in my room and lined up the
pills (two blue, three red and white, and one all-white) my
doctors had prescribed. I took them, painfully because of
my throat, set an alarm, and arranged for a wake-up call at 7,
just in case. Then I went to sleep.

In the midst of a dream I heard the distant ring of a telephone. I answered it in my dream, but it kept on ringing.
Moments later I realized, to my despair that it was six minutes
to eight and the phone beside my bed was ringing. I fumbled
for the receiver.

'Good morning, Mr Semler,' I heard a crisp voice say. 'I'm
in the lobby.'

'Yeah . . . um . . . right,' I stammered. *An excuse. I need an
excuse.* Thinking I was being clever, I explained that I would
be delayed because I was awaiting a most important business
call from Brazil. I went off to splash some cold, Swedish water
on my face, only later realizing that it was 3 a.m. in South
America.

That day I visited an Asea Brown Boveri factory. As we
walked through the plant, I felt progressively faint. Then,
suddenly, everything went black. I had passed out. I was

taken to the medical office and after an hour or so felt well enough to resume my tour. I was feeling fine the next night, when I attended a dinner at the company's headquarters in Stockholm and signed and celebrated our deal.

We took over Flakt's three-floor factory in the suburbs of Rio de Janeiro and half its 60-person payroll immediately. But our understanding of the business turned out to be more limited than we had thought and we proceeded to lose more than $1 million during the next four years before the unit turned a profit.

At the time, though, we thought we were hot. So, naively pleased with ourselves, we continued our hunt for companies to buy.

We sniffed around another outfit in the same field as Flakt, Baltimore Aircoil (BAC), a subsidiary of Merck Sharp and Dohme, the huge pharmaceutical house, but were told we were too late. A deal had almost been completed to sell the company to the largest air-conditioning contractor in Brazil.

We figured the Merck subsidiary was worth $2 million to $3 million. We only had $200,000. But talk is cheap, so we sent a telex to Merck suggesting a meeting. It acquiesced.

Merck told us it had already been offered close to what it wanted and asked if we were planning to bid more. Since we didn't have much cash, we offered Merck an advance payment of sorts – the cash in their own subsidiary's till – and proposed to pay off the rest of the purchase price over five years, under a formula that called for fixed annual payments plus 25 per cent of the unit's profits. A Merck executive, a tall, wiry guy with the cold, hard eyes of a chief financial officer – let out a cynical laugh. But I noticed that another Merck man was looking on thoughtfully. I even thought I saw a slight smile form at the edges of his mouth. As it turned out, some of the Merck people had already concluded they might be better off with the brash young upstarts at Semco.

Extended negotiations followed, ending in a complex contract that was signed at Merck's lawyers' offices in downtown

São Paulo. As we waited for the final copies of the documents, we heard loud noises in the street below. From the window, we saw a huge crowd demonstrating against the government's economic policy. Suddenly, police riot squads arrived and began firing tear gas canisters. Protestors were running all over as the caustic fog spread. One American looked at another. 'What's taking those papers so long?' he said.

The next day we took charge of the BAC plant in the nearby town of Diadema. It was a large, gleaming factory, with flags flying above the entrance. Of the 90 people who worked there, we would retain more than 60.

Since the company was doing well, we left the old management in place, adding only a financial controller. The man we chose for the job, Antonio Carlos Iotti, was a rotund five-footer with thick eyeglasses which, he told me, he even wore in the shower. At his previous job with a large sewing-machine company Iotti had been ordered by a boss to redo an inventory count. He refused. When he received an angry memo from the boss demanding the recount, he sent an even nastier note back. The boss immediately went to see Iotti, intent on a shouting match. He stood at least a foot taller than his insolent employee, but when he lowered his eyes he saw the diminutive Iotti, hands on his hips, glaring up at him, ready for anything. Iotti was the man for us, I thought.

six

KEEPING OUR BALANCE

In two deals we had spent our $500,000 nest egg, nearly doubled our work force, and tripled the number of plants. But with out new financial controls we believed our managers could handle anything. Semco was doing so well I should have known we were heading for a bump in the road.

Make that three bumps. The first had to do with Ernesto.

Years earlier my father had invited two foreign companies to become shareholders in Semco, each with 24.5 per cent of the stock. (He kept the rest, and control.) Semco had the right to manufacture their products, and the two companies had representatives on our board of directors.

My father had a fine relationship with one, but no end of trouble with the other, which accused him – unfairly – of charging family expenses to the business and paying himself lavishly to avoid distributing more profits in dividends.

As Ernesto professionalized the company, he made every effort to be absolutely impartial. That meant giving Semco's minority shareholders – including the troublesome one – as much information as he gave my family. After our second acquisition, Ernesto decided to send out a letter giving his opinion on our overall financial situation. He went into great detail on our investments and production plans. None of the information was particularly sensitive, but he hadn't discussed it with my father, who felt so betrayed he stopped talking to Ernesto.

I sided with my father, though I came to see that my family loyalty betrayed my professional immaturity. I suppose Semco was still very much a family business.

I called Ernesto in and told him my feelings. He replied, in his hot-headed way, that he saw no solution other than his immediate departure. He turned and left for his office, picked up his things, and hurried down the stairs. I stood by the window and watched him walk through the plant gate, realizing that he wasn't even going to take his company car home. I rushed to the parking lot, got into my car, and followed him. When I caught up with Ernesto, I saw he was in tears. I opened the passenger door and he got in. Both of us were silent as I drove him home. It was one of the saddest moments of my life, but it was merely a prelude to the real tragedy, for shortly afterwards Ernesto was killed in a motorcycle accident.

Ernesto's replacement was a short, thin young man named Fernando Lotamorro. Another self-made man, Fernando had started as a travelling salesman and by his late 20s had become a top manager of a large Brazilian company, where he earned a reputation as a first-in, last-out guy. A proponent of meticulous financial controls, he was the ideal person to carry on and expand Ernesto's good work. Or what we then believed was good work.

The second bump involved Harro. He liked the bustle of São Paulo, but he *loved* the country. He would only live in a place where he could raise chickens, which meant his home was an hour and a half commute through world-class traffic to the plant.

As word of his exploits spread, Harro began getting job offers. He didn't seriously consider them until he got a call from a French-Brazilian electrical-equipment company, Merlin-Gerin, which wanted him to run its plant in the rural state of Santa Catarina. He could live and work in a small town where a traffic jam meant beeping the cows out of the way and have room for all the chickens he could ever want and 5,000 roses in his garden.

Harro asked me what I thought. I had to agree the offer was too good to pass up. He stayed at Semco just a few more months before moving south. (Postscript: We kept in touch and 10 years later Harro would rejoin us in a fashion, taking a

25 per cent stake in a new parts and maintenance company we would start together and returning to work at our head-quarters, where the unit is based.)

No one could replace Harro, but sometimes things have a way of balancing out. About the time he left, we welcomed a newcomer who would quickly become a major force behind the astonishing changes that were about to take place at Semco.

I knew our new tough-minded, statistical approach, along with our acquisitions and all the new employees, had created a lot of organizational stress. Ordinarily it would have been silly for a company our size to have a human resources director, but I was convinced we needed one. So I hired a headhunter, went through dozens of résumés, and interviewed the 10 most impressive candidates. All came from much bigger companies; none seemed to fit.

Enter, through a side door, Clovis Bojikian. Born to Armenian immigrants, Clovis was an idealist who started out as a schoolteacher. A proponent of Summerhill-style progressive education programmes, he became a counsellor at a school that served as a training ground for newly graduated teachers from the University of São Paulo and, eventually, its director. His tenure was marked by constant innovation: students were taught to think, not merely to memorize; they were encouraged to question everything, free to set their own schedules, dress as they pleased, and choose their own curriculum.

But Brazil was being ruled by the generals, and they considered Clovis's work subversive. Besides the suspicious lack of discipline, he was teaching kids to be sceptical of history texts that chronicled the exploits of those same military rulers. The generals assembled a special tribunal at the university and Clovis testified for 46 hours. Then he was fired.

The students immediately occupied the school, demanding Clovis's reinstatement. Armed with brooms and in some cases Molotov cocktails, and sustained by cans of food, they spent more than a week on the barricades and the front pages. The generals, embarrassed, finally had the army invade the school. The protestors, rounded up at midnight by machine-gun-toting soldiers, marched out singing the national anthem.

Clovis moved on to the Ford Motor Company in São Paulo, where he worked in personnel and training. After 18 years he had risen to become Ford's human resources manager in Brazil, but in the end such a megacorporation didn't leave enough room for innovation. Clovis moved on to be human resources director at KSB Pumps, which makes hydraulic water pumps and is one of Semco's competitors. Again, he wasn't given much room to stretch.

Here's where the story gets a bit cosmic. One of the members of my father's Old Guard had moved to KSB and took an immediate dislike to Clovis. This former Semco executive hired the headhunting firm that got him his job to find a new position somewhere else for Clovis. And that firm turned out to be the same one I had retained to find Semco a human resources director.

Clovis and I met in my office. Headhunters prefer their candidates to wear blue suits, white shirts, neat ties, and be clean-shaven. Yet here was an excruciatingly thin man in his late 40s wearing an ugly brown suit, a beige shirt, and a white moustache that wound upwards at the edges, à la Buffalo Bill. (At least he had a tie.)

I liked him as soon as I saw him.

Clovis would later reveal that he didn't pay much attention to me at first. After all, he was supposed to have an interview with the president of Semco, and I was the age of his youngest child. Even after I sat down and began a conversation, he figured I was just keeping him company until the real president showed up.

We spoke for nearly three hours, and almost from the start we were completing each other's sentences. We agreed then and there that Clovis would begin as our new human resources director the next Monday. It took about a week for both of us to realize that we hadn't discussed his salary.

The third bump? About a year after Clovis joined us he was offered a job as vice-president of one of Brazil's largest financial companies, where he would run a department with hundreds of employees and earn almost three times as much as he did with us. As with Harro, we talked about the offer. It was tempting, and I told Clovis so. I also said that, should the job disappoint him, we would welcome him back.

I spent almost a year interviewing replacements, without success. Then I stopped looking and simply waited. A short while later Clovis was back at Semco, earning his old salary.

He gets offers all the time these days, which isn't surprising, given what we have accomplished. Thank God he isn't budging.

seven

ANOTHER CONQUEST

By the middle of 1984 we were – your guessed it – ready to buy another company. Don't ask what we were going to buy it with. By this time we had more or less recovered from our first, scary years and our diversification was working. We had no bank loans, still had some cash in the till (enough for working capital, anyway) and were already expanding slightly. It was a solid position, financially.

We heard that Booz Allen & Hamilton, the international consulting firm, had been hired to sell off Hobart Brazil, a subsidiary of the American conglomerate Dart & Kraft that manufactured dishwashers, meat slicers, and other food-processing equipment. With an 80,000 square-foot plant and 150 employees in Brazil, it was way too big for us. We asked for the acquisition documents anyway and were told we should move quickly. Is that all they ever say?

Looking through the material, we came across Dart & Kraft's annual report. To this day, I believe we were the only potential bidders to read it. Mixed in with pictures of the conglomerate's products, including Duracell batteries, Tupperware containers, and umpteen varieties of cheese, were hints that told us Hobart's success came from the marketing synergy of its dishwashers, fryers, scales, slicers, and related products. It was easier to sell the whole line than to try to move the items individually; the company would get more shelf space at distributors, for starters. Other suitors were offering to buy only part of the whole; some wanted the dishwasher line, some the scales business. Only Semco offered to buy everything. Only Semco wanted to maintain the synergy.

The sum of the other bids reached Dart & Kraft's asking price. Our proposal amounted to not much more than half that figure, and because of our lack of cash we would be paying it off over six years. But it turned out that Dart & Kraft was more interested in maintaining the Hobart image, since that name would be on the appliances it would continue to sell elsewhere. Keeping the Brazilian company intact, rather than breaking it up product by product, was appealing.

We found ourselves around a long table at the Brazilian office of Price Waterhouse, completing the deal. We had a list of the issues to resolve, including the price of the specific assets, royalty percentages, and interest rates. We told them the only item we were willing to increase was the time between our payments. (Ha, ha, ha.)

The chief Dart & Kraft executive listened to us attentively. When we finished our presentation, there was silence. Everyone turned to him. He meditated a while, then uttered these words: 'I may be plump and have rosy cheeks, but I'm not dressed in red and it's not Christmas.'

After the laughter subsided, we bargained for seven hours, reducing the payout period and increasing the royalties we would pay. Then we shook hands on a deal.

Hobart Brazil's Ipiranga plant, near São Paulo, had a long but less than glorious legacy, endured by a weary band of employees, some of whom had invested as many as 45 years there. There was much – too much? – history at the plant, which made the changes we would eventually observe all the more surprising.

Built in the 1930s, it was one of those gloomy Gothic factories with high ceilings and tiny windows that would have been at home in Sheffield, England, or Pittsburgh, Pennsylvania. I don't know what company built it, but by 1939 it was owned by the Hobart Brothers, proprietors of a successful restaurant equipment business based in Ohio. In those days the mechanical scales the plant cranked out were the most popular in Brazil, despite 30 local competitors. But over the years so many different managers were sent down from Ohio, and so few had any knowledge of the local market, that success slipped away. Hobart executives have a reputation for keeping to themselves. They weren't interested in wining and dining distributors all over our vast country. And they were tethered to Ohio, dependent on the home office for even minor decisions, slowing their reactions and making them less flexible than they should have been.

The chief beneficiary of these shortcomings was Filizola, Hobart's main competitor, which though founded by Italian immigrants still managed to build strong ties with distributors across Brazil. Filizola expanded steadily and by the 1970s was impinging on Hobart's balance sheet. The folks in Ohio had two options: invest heavily in the Brazilian division, buying new equipment that would eventually reduce costs and prices, or fight it out with whatever fire power was already there and hope for the best. Hobart chose the cheaper strategy and Filizola's market share kept rising.

By the end of the decade a local Hobart executive, Keith Rae, was promoted to general manager. Rae had been with the company more than 20 years, many as a salesperson in Brazil's wildest territories. A man with an unfailing sense of humour and an unflagging honesty, Rae managed to keep the company afloat, but it's a wonder how. He made constant trips to Ohio to report to his supervisors and spent another two months each year drafting and submitting a budget. All this cost him the time he needed to develop new customers and improve the products.

What finally ended Hobart's Brazilian adventure was the electronic scale. By the end of the 1970s it was difficult to sell a mechanical scale in the United States. Still, Hobart's home office thought there would be a market for the more primitive models in the developing world and saw no urgency in retooling the Brazilian plant. Eventually Rae convinced management that the electronic scale was inevitable, even in South America. Hobart Brazil proudly announced its new product was on the way, but then failed to deliver it on time. Meanwhile, Filizola introduced its own electronic scale, establishing technological superiority and cornering the market.

About this time the Hobart family decided to sell out Dart & Kraft. This meant the Brazilian subsidiary could no longer rely on family members who had a long history in South America. Now the operation would be evaluated on cold, impersonal parameters. Dart & Kraft had cash to invest, but would do so only if the products and the market showed promise. That did not seem the case with Hobart Brazil, which had by then slid to fifth place in its field.

Dart & Kraft decided that of the nine offices and plants Hobart Brazil operated all but two should be closed. The plant at Ipiranga was spared, but the classic cycle of fewer sales, diminished investment, and even fewer sales was under way.

Besides scales, the plant produced most of the other Hobart products, including meat grinders and slicers, which sold decently, if unspectacularly, and dishwashers that were still a leader in the hotel, restaurant, and cafeteria market. But after a few years, when the leaner Hobart Brazil proved no more successful than its predecessor, Dart & Kraft hung out a 'For Sale' sign. Keith Rae and his people were both dismayed and relieved. A new owner might not want to keep them; then again, a new owner might make the investment that they so badly needed and dissipate the shroud of failure that now hung over the place.

The Monday after we closed the deal we were all at our new Food Service Equipment plant – Fernando, Clovis, and I. Gloom had given way to anxiety. Everyone wanted to know what the new bosses were like.

Our first move was to reaffirm the philosophy born with our first acquisitions of not changing anything we didn't understand and giving the people already in place a chance before supplanting them with outsiders. It's so easy to blame the managers when a business does badly, but often they haven't had the freedom to manage or the motivation to perform as if the business were theirs.

Keith Rae, by then in his 60s, was promoted to vice president. (To our great sadness, he died about a year after we bought Hobart.) We also had high hopes for João Vendramin, a Hobart engineer who had been trained as an economist. Shy and thoughtful, he would make a superb plant manager, we believed. Another oldtimer, João Martins, had been engineering manager, plant manager, and marketing manager in his 42 years at Hobart Brazil, but the bosses in Ohio thought he was too old to run anything, so they had consigned him to a minor position in training. We raised him back up.

But after a few months in which nothing much happened at the plant, Fernando started to lose his patience. Hobart needed drastic action, he would plead. Soon he was acting like a German Shepherd on a chain, ten yards from a Collie on heat.

'Relax,' I pleaded. 'Give them a bit more time.'

But he would just shove in my direction stacks of handwritten calculations that proved, he said, that the plant was sliding downhill. He kept on insisting that, although he was our director of administration and finance, he still had time to turn Ipiranga around.

Clovis and I discussed it often and, in the end, agreed with Fernando. We were worried about his lack of experience. But Fernando had the aggressive personality that we then believed a successful business required, especially one in a slump.

One sunny afternoon we pointed him in the direction of Ipiranga, let him off the leash, and watched him bound forward, barking all the way.

eight

SYMPTOMS OF TROUBLE

Fernando was convinced that the Hobart plant lacked organization, ambition, and controls, and proceeded to supply the missing elements singlehandedly. He would arrive each day at 7.30 a.m., only to find himself alone in the office until about 9, when people would finally start filtering in, have their coffee, read their newspapers, and only then get to work. And at 5.30 they left for home, leaving Fernando to labour until 9, 10, sometimes even 11 p.m. This didn't please him, and soon everyone knew it.

I wasn't as driven as Fernando, but it was close. He and I would often arrange to meet at 8 p.m. and end up leaving the building together after midnight. The difference between us was that I didn't expect everyone else to stay late. I may have been a bit irritated when, at 6 p.m., I was told that someone I needed to talk to had just left, but I also was surprised when I found a colleague around at 8 p.m. Fernando demanded it.

Iotti, Clovis, and many others at Semco worked long hours, too, and their families were beginning to complain. Iotti lived an hour from the plant and would arrive home almost every night to find his family asleep. Then he would leave the next morning before they awoke. Looking back at that time, it was a wonder no families broke up. I guess it was mostly because we all were convinced the long hours were temporary and that normality would return as soon as we digested our acquisitions and came to terms with Semco's 100 per cent a year growth rate. It took us almost a decade to learn that our stress was internally generated, the result of an immature organization and infantile goals.

Fernando changed everything about the Hobart plant in his

first few months. Sales reps and other employees were fired for lack of motivation or competence, products were over-hauled. Prices were changed. Some production machines were discarded, others acquired. The old Hobart plant was in perpetual motion. But I would soon have cause to wonder whether it was moving in the right direction.

At Ipiranga, and all over the new, improved, giant-sized Semco, we could track with great precision virtually every aspect of our business, from sales quotes to the maintenance records of each of our innumerable welding machines. We could generate all sorts of new reports almost instantly, with dazzling charts and graphs. We were so impressed with our statistical abilities that it took us a while to realize that all those numbers weren't doing us much good. We thought we were more organized, more professional, more disciplined, more efficient. So, we asked ourselves with a shudder, how come we were constantly late on deliveries?

Most of our managers were like Fernando – proponents of classic, authoritarian solutions such as rigid controls and long, gruelling hours. But a few of us were starting to doubt the effectiveness of this approach. I was particularly distressed by the malaise that was all too apparent in our factories, both old and new. Workers just didn't seem to care.

As I thought about it, I realized the tough guys had taken over. And while I initially liked the idea of a disciplined, hard-driven company run by aggressive managers armed with innumerable statistics, I was starting to have second thoughts. Work hard or get fired. That was the ethic of the new Semco. People were being pushed forward. But how much better to have a self-propelled workforce.

During this time I often thought of a business parable I had heard. Three stone cutters were asked about their jobs. The first said he was paid to cut stones. The second replied that he used special techniques to shape stones in an exceptional way, and proceeded to demonstrate his skills. The third stone cutter just smiled and said: 'I build cathedrals.'

As I walked around Semco, I sensed that we had far more stone cutters than craftsmen. What I wanted, of course, was a company filled with cathedral-builders, and there were hardly any of them at all.

If anything, the split between the tough guys and the more sympathetic souls widened over the next few months. But I wasn't worried. I was sure we would find some middle ground and Semco would at last slide into gear and start accelerating.

Then an incident at our annual convention brought me up short. Every year our top 45 corporate officers and their spouses would fly off to a luxurious resort, where we would spend four days recharging and, well, luxuriating. It was the third and last day of one of these junkets. As the managers filed into the conference room after lunch, they saw the cartoon on the stand where the flip-charts were displayed. It pictured an overweight Grim Reaper bearing a scythe and drawing blood from dozens of little people, cowering in corners. There was no doubt about his identity. Was Fernando that overbearing? Was he draining the company's life blood with his autocratic ways?

'Dick, can I see you a moment,' said Renato Bernhoeft, our consultant in organizational behaviour who organized the convention.

'This looks like trouble, Renato,' I said after we adjourned to the privacy of the hall.

'You bet,' Renato said, puffing his pipe. 'But it might be the opportunity you need to get things out in the open.'

'I don't understand. The first two days of the conference went well – no open disagreements, no hostility.'

'Open, that's the key word. You have two cliques here, Dick, and they kept to themselves. There was no mingling between them.' Renato took another puff. 'But let's be frank about it. These guys are locked in battle. The hard against the soft. The rightists against the leftists.' Renato paused and puffed some more, the way pipe smokers do when they want to make a point. 'You've got to start dealing with this conflict. Semco has to have its own culture. A single culture. Right now, it's a mess.'

'So what do I do?'

'Have you ever seen a group therapy session?'

'With a group of 45 angry managers? No way.'

'I don't think you have a choice,' Renato said, and then told me what he had in mind.

What followed can only be described as terrifying. I went back into the conference room, where the managers were sitting in stony silence. Some were smoking in the non-smoking section, a clear sign of hostility. I walked to the front of the room and tried desperately to remember passages from the psychology manuals of Jung and Laing, even as I realized that Reich was going to be of more help here. After all, he was the inventor of physical psychotherapy, and throwing things at each other seemed appropriate.

'Could you all please pick up your chairs and move them forward?'

'Why?' two or three managers shot back at once.

'Just, please, do it,' I said, trying to be firm. 'Put your chairs in a semi-circle right in front.'

I wanted the audience to be closer to me and each other. I noticed, though, that they were moving carefully, placing their chairs near people they sided with.

When the rearranging was done, I told them it was time for a candid discussion of what was bothering us. I talked for a bit about how we all needed to work together, harmoniously, using all the usual phrases. At least Renato was nodding.

'Just a minute,' Fernando bellowed. 'This kind of talk is cheap. Sure, we'd all like to get along. But first there has to be respect.'

'Well, no one will disagree with that,' I ventured in my best please-lie-down-on-the-couch-and-say-whatever-comes-into-your-mind manner.

'What I mean is, someone will have to apologize for that' – he pointed to the cartoon – 'before any conversation starts,' Fernando demanded.

Silence all around.

'Fernando, surely you can see it wouldn't be productive to go in that direction,' I pleaded.

'It's even worse to accept that cartoon as a basis for conversation.'

'Let's just forget the cartoon, Fernando. It's just someone's way of expressing his feelings.'

'Oh, yeah? What if I decided to express my feelings by punching whoever drew it in the mouth?'

Renato stopped nodding.

'You'd never do that, would you, Fernando?' I said, switching to my kindergarten-teacher voice.

'That's what he deserves.'

Just then Oswaldo Guimaraes, our engineering manager, got up. Everyone knew he had drawn the cartoon. He was famous for his cartoons, though they were usually funny, not bitter. But he drew this one because he thought Fernando had been much too heavy-handed, and it was clear that others in the room agreed with him.

Before he could own up to the artwork I waved at him to sit down, saying it didn't matter whose drawing it was. The issue was out in the open and it was time to deal with it.

Four hours later, all had been said, but there was still a deep split between those who believed in law, order, and organization above all and those who felt that people, motivated by a sense of involvement, could overcome any obstacle. It was a case of what, in German, is called *weltanschauung* – how you see the world. The autocrats at Semco were convinced that nothing would get done if they didn't do it themselves or push their subordinates into doing it. They viewed company tasks much as parents see homework – disagreeable, perhaps, but mandatory. The touchy-feely crowd, on the other hand, was confident there was a better way, and that it involved giving up their power. It was Waterloo versus Woodstock, and I didn't see how our Napoleans and our Timothy Learys would ever be reconciled.

As we concluded the convention and prepared to go home I knew I would have to act. The all-together-now feeling of the Gabriele-Heyde years was long gone and the long hours, which then seemed joyful and ecstatic, were now tedious. Semco was divided and confused to the point of paralysis. Even small problems were difficult to resolve; big ones were impossible.

Studying classic business cases, I discovered we were going through the 'Bureaucracy Phase' or 'Adolescent Phase,' depending on which author I consulted. This is a period in which a business that has expanded starts to suffer growing pains. In response, Fernando had tried to cut through the malaise by introducing time-tested techniques of discipline and control. His goal was to instil a sense of organization, to know what was going on or at least have the impression he knew what was going on. The executives who closed ranks behind him didn't mind if our employees came to work scared or anxious, as long as they got things done.

As a result, some of us who felt differently found ourselves trying to manage wave after wave of personnel problems and discontent. How could I stop it?

While my mind wrestled with this conflict, my body convinced me it was time for a change.

I was visiting a pump factory in Baldwinsville, New York, when I suddenly felt ill and again passed out on the shop floor. I was taken to a physician in town and rested in his office for a couple of hours. He was an old-fashioned family doctor, the type who like to talk with their patients. He was quite worried about me and advised me not to continue my trip without stopping for tests. He suggested I might visit the Mayo Clinic in Rochester, Minnesota, or the Lahey Clinic in Boston. I was headed towards Boston anyway, so Lahey it was.

I called ahead and talked to an internist there, who set up some examinations.

'So, what is it you're feeling?' asked the grey-haired doctor when we met three days later.

'I have a constant throat infection that doesn't respond to antibiotics anymore,' I began. 'Because of this, I can't eat solid food before noon, so I have chronic anaemia. I also suffer fainting spells once in a while, as you know. I take medicine for an accelerated heartbeat and for migraine headaches. I have gastritis and drink milk several times a day because of heartburn. Oh yes, and I get rashes on my back whenever I'm tense.'

I watched him scribble all this down.

'Do you play any sports? Jog? Walk?'

'Only up the stairs to my office, and then I have to grab the wall for a few minutes.'

I saw the faint trace of a smile as he scribbled.

'How many hours a day do you work?'

'Ten. Or twelve.'

'Sometimes more?'

'Well, yeah. Sometimes I come in at 7.30 and leave after midnight.'

'That's more than ten or twelve hours.'

'Yes, but that's not every day. Mostly I leave around 9 or 10.'

'Do you work on weekends?'

'A couple of hours on Saturday, and another few on Sunday.' I thought about the exasperated look I got from friends when, heading off to the beach, I'd first fill the trunk with reams of telexes, memoranda, and trade magazines.

'What do you eat?'

'I can't have breakfast, because of my throat, so I just have orange juice. Then a sandwich at my desk for lunch. For dinner, just whatever's in the fridge – I'm so tired by then that I don't have much of an appetite.'

The doctor finished writing and asked me to move into an adjoining room, remove my clothes, and sit on the examination table. A faint smell of ether came through the door, and I felt a little woozy.

'You're becoming pale, Ricardo,' he said as he put the stethoscope on my heart.

The touch of the cold metal did it. I had a sensation of flying in slow motion over a mountain village. All those tiny homes – they looked just like doll houses. 'Breathe deeply, breath deeply,' I heard the doctor say as he slowly came back into focus.

I came to know the corridors of that hospital well during the three days I spent amortizing every machine the doctor had. I also passed out again, when he injected contrast dye into a vein to take X-rays of internal organs too numerous to list. No part of me was left unexplored.

Finally it was time for a reckoning. The kind doctor had a stack of yellow envelopes in front of him containing my test results. After years of telling my woes to physicians who never came up with a diagnosis, I believed I would finally learn what was wrong. I was nervous, but also relieved. I was sure that he would want me to stay at the clinic for a couple of days – maybe a week or two – having all kinds of injections and treatments. I was prepared for that, and would be phoning my parents and the company shortly to let everyone know that I'd be away for a while. I would buy some novels, and relax. If my first vacation in years was going to be spent in a white gown, so be it. I watched as the doctor put the last X-ray in its folder and looked at me.

'You have nothing whatsoever, Ricardo.'

Excuse me, I thought, staring back at him. Had he mixed up my records with someone else's?

'Are you sure?' I managed to utter.

'Quite sure,' he said. 'Your tests are all perfect. But you are suffering from an advanced case of stress. The most advanced case I have ever seen in a person of 25.'

'What happens now?'

'You have two choices. Either you continue your current life, in which case you will be back with us, or else you must change.'

'Change? How?'

'That's not for me to say. All I will say is that absolutely everything about your life has to change. I'll recommend that you take two aspirins, eight times a day. These sixteen pills won't do very much, except remind you regularly that you have a huge problem to solve.'

Then he showed me the way to the cashier.

We simply do not believe our employees have an interest in coming in late, leaving early and doing as little as possible for as much money as their union can wheedle out of us. After all, these same people raise children, join the PTA, elect mayors, governors, senators and presidents. They are adults. At Semco, we treat them as adults. We trust them. We don't make our employees ask permission to go to the bathroom, or have security guards search them as they leave for the day. We get out of their way and let them do their jobs.

nine

COMING ABOUT

I took the 16 aspirins for just one day. Then I started making changes.

Before I could reorganize Semco, I had to reorganize myself. Long hours were the first issue I tackled. They were one of the biggest symptoms of time sickness, a disease that afflicts far too many executives. So I set 7 p.m. as the time I would leave the office, no matter what. After that, I would go to the movies, read books (but not business books) – anything but work. I wouldn't do any work at the weekends, either. And on to each long business trip I would add a week of pleasure travel.

Next, I resolved to delegate furiously, and to summon up the courage to throw unneeded papers away, so they wouldn't clutter my desk or thoughts. I would follow my intuition more, and listen less to experts.

Yes, I would attack my problem directly, and that problem was not simply the management of a business but something even more fundamental: the management of time. So many executives find that the daily quota of 24 hours is too few to get to everything and still have any left over. I thought long and hard about time in the weeks after my visit to the Lahey Clinic. I realized that if I was going to find a cure for time sickness I first had to identify its causes.

Cause 1. The belief that effort and result are directly proportional. 'Order and Progress', the Brazilian flag proclaims. 'Order *or* Progress' is more like it, since they usually aren't found together. In business, effort is too often confused with result. The sales manager who overflows with charm when talking to

customers and, after closing a sale, takes the rest of the day off
to celebrate is regarded as lazy but lucky, not as a talented
sales executive.

When asked the reason for their success, entrepreneurs are
fond of saying, 'A lot of hard work.' Sounds good, doesn't it?
It plays well at home, too, to families who have been ignored
for years. But if great entrepreneurs were to answer the question honestly, most would probably list such factors as a finely
tuned sense of timing, the ability to recognize opportunity,
friends in the right places, an occasional moral lapse, and luck.
May Horatio Alger forgive me, but hard work by itself is not
enough. To say it is possible to establish a successful business
just by arriving early and staying late is like saying that every
mailman can be Howard Hughes. There is a prevailing conviction that sweat is obligatory, and with each new drop an
executive moves a little closer to financial heaven. I had to rid
myself of this notion. It isn't healthy. It isn't even true.

*Cause 2. The gospel that the quantity of work is more important
than the quality of work.*
This is a variation on the same theme. Early in the century
Max Weber recognized that the Protestant ethic of hard work
had permeated the business world. It is even more of a factor
today. Executives feel pressure from their bosses to outwork
colleagues and build their image and career. By this reason-
ing, having a heart attack because of work leads to true glory
and keeling over at the office is even better – a sign, a Calvinist
might say, of being among The Elect.

Someone who manages his time is often suspect. And if he
goes to the theatre, doesn't carry a briefcase home, spends
weekends with his family, and sometimes even picks up the
kids at school for lunch, then he has already descended into an
advanced state of indolence.

The executive who judges his contribution in hours will
find himself muttering things like: 'Well, we all know how
unfair it was that they didn't promote me. Everyone knows
I'm here at eight in the morning and eight in the evening.'

Or: 'My daughter needs to make an appointment to speak to me.'

Cause 3. 'Things are a little uncertain at the office right now. I'll just have to work a little longer until they straighten out.'
Few excuses are as convincing as the 'we're-just-going-through-a- — —. Fill in the blank: change at the top, restructuring, lay offs, expansion. Almost any change can be an excuse for poor time management. To allow such events to shape one's working day is to become a mere cork that bobs up and down on the sea.

Cause 4. Fear of delegation, and its cousin, fear of replaceability.
Here is where we lay bare some nerves. Fear of delegation is the belief that no one is as competent to solve a problem as you are. This kind of thinking (which at times may be justified) usually results from the belief that tasks will inevitably be done poorly if not done by capable hands – yours, of course. But how often is this really masking the fear that others can perform jobs you once thought only you could accomplish?

This in turn leads to the fear of replaceability. This means postponing vacations, or taking them but leaving phone numbers where you can be reached morning, noon and night – and then being disappointed that no one needed you while you were away.

I'll have more thoughts about time sickness and how to cure it later, in Appendix B. For now, let me say that I have recovered so completely that I no longer wear a wristwatch. I gave it up soon after attending a concert by Brazil's most famous pianist, Madalena Tagliaferro. As I listened to her play Sibelius, I realized that she had been born when Brazil was a monarchy, witnessed the invention of the automobile and the aircraft, lived through two World Wars, and was still performing. It struck me that time should be measured in years and decades, not minutes and hours. It is impossible to understand life in all its hugeness and complexity if one is constantly consulting a minute-counter.

But how could I spread such an idea through a company being run as if every millisecond would dent our balance sheet? I couldn't. There was no way around it. Fernando would have to go. I admired his aggressiveness, energy, and dedication, but he needed a harsh, intimidating environment for his magic to work. If it was magic. After my visit to the Lahey Clinic, I was pretty sure it wasn't.

As soon as Fernando parted company, we began to realize that the bookkeeping system he and Ernesto had installed was actually hurting us. For starters, we now had an accounting department full of people who only stopped cranking out numbers to pick up their pay cheques. And we had so damn many numbers, inside so damn many folders, that almost no one was looking at them. But no one would admit it. Everyone just bluffed their way through meetings, pretending to be familiar with every little detail. In retrospect, we realized that it was during this time that we knew least about what was going on at Semco. It was a classic 'forest versus trees' problem.

So we simplified the budget system, slashing the number of 'cost centres' from 400 to 50 and beheading hundreds of accounting classifications and dozens of budget lines. We also reduced the number of documents we circulated, and the signatures necessary to approve them. Our new system was simpler, with limited but relevant data.

As for our actual spending plans, we would eventually develop two budgets: a five-year plan and a six-month report. Yes, I know the argument against five-year plans. Stalin used them, and look how that turned out. But when we look five years forward, we can ask ourselves whether we want to be in a particular market, or whether we should drop a product, or whether we will need a new factory, among other such questions. So a five-year view is essential.

In contrast, we take an operational view of six months, because we found that in a conventional one-year plan people will invariably believe that conditions will improve just enough to compensate for the problems they know they'll have in the first half of the year. Or vice versa.

In either plan we try to think in 'zero-based' terms. Budgets should always be based on rethinking the company; most of the time, though, they're not much more than last year's numbers projected forward, and are about as good as warmed-up coffee at two in the morning.

My constant insistence on seeing only the big numbers is the subject of interminable jokes at the company. The finance people say they only arrive at the big numbers by adding up all the little ones. Therefore, they go on, a budget with only the big numbers actually requires more work than one with every little detail. This is an expensive fallacy, but one that is difficult to eradicate.

One last word on budgets. The receipt of cold numbers, even when they are current and correct, is not enough. In addition to comparing the numbers that arrive every month with the budget, it is essential that they be compared with the expectations of the person who is going to use them. At Semco, we introduced a programme that requires each executive to make an educated guess about the revenues, expenses, and profits for his department at the end of each month. A few days later, the official report is distributed. The comparison gives everyone a sense of how much each manager actually knows about his area.

Simplifying our budget process didn't solve all our problems. But it did help us see them more clearly.

We were still late on deliveries. Authorization forms still spent days bouncing from one person to another; people were afraid to sign their name to anything, for fear they would stand out in the next accounting report. Worst of all, Semco was a company full of fiefdoms: each department defended its turf at all costs. Salespeople thought the people in marketing lived on the moon. The marketers thought the salespeople could see all the way to their navels. The financial types believed the plant managers wanted to fill the stockrooms to the ceiling with inventory. Purchasing thought the people in administration hadn't a clue about how irritated suppliers get when they have to wait for seven signatures before they get their cheque. And production thought the people in sales imagined they were living in Japan, with overnight delivery dates.

My colleagues and I tried various quick fixes for our foundering organization, from suggestion boxes to leadership training to Japanese-style quality circles, in which a range of people from the same business unit, from janitors to executives, sit down together to find solutions to common problems. I tried all the prepackaged ideas I could find, scouring every business book with a title that began with 'How To . . .' or ended with the word 'System' or 'Method'. I read Alfred Sloan's *My Years With General Motors* and Tom Peters's *In Search of Excellence*. I studied popular business writers such as John Naisbitt, Peter Drucker, Alvin Toffler, and Robert Townsend, and academic ones such as Kenichi Ohmae, Marvin Minsky, Itzak Addizes, and Henry Mintzberg. I had two bookcases full of business books, floor to ceiling. I also sought out fellow executives at other companies, grilling them about management styles over lunch. I picked up plenty of ideas and techniques, but I just couldn't make them work in our offices or factories. Our people would be motivated for a while, but then slip back. I began to suspect that Semco's problems went deeper than I had realized.

When I first started working at Semco, I was shocked by the oppression I found. To someone who spent much of his adolescence playing rock'n'roll, the rules and procedures at Semco left me numb. Still, I tried to become the embodiment of a traditional executive – and had, I thought, succeeded. I wore the right suits. I thought the right thoughts. I was so proud when I devised a tardiness programme that docked an employee's wages if he was just a few minutes late. I was a tough guy.

Now, I had a different theory. Semco appeared highly organized and well disciplined, and we still could not get our people to perform as we wanted, or be happy with their jobs. There weren't enough cathedral-builders. If only I could break the structure apart a bit, I thought to myself, I might see what was alienating so many of our people. I couldn't help thinking that Semco could be run differently, without counting everything, without regulating everyone, without keeping track of whether people were late, without all those numbers and all those rules. What if we could strip away all the artificial nonsense, all the managerial mumbo jumbo? What if we could run the business in a simpler way, a more natural way? A natural business, that's what I wanted.

The more I thought about it, the more I was convinced the whole company needed to change. I had no grand plan. There was no blinding revelation. Just a sense that there was a lifelessness, a lack of enthusiasm, a malaise at Semco, and that I had to change it. People weren't gratified by their jobs and often seemed oppressed by them. The traditional attitude about workers was that you couldn't trust them. You needed systems to control them. Yet at Semco the system was dispiriting and demotivating them. So, I thought to myself, why not start by eliminating some of the most visible symbols of corporate oppression.

I had always wondered about the security check our people were forced to submit to on their way out through the plant gate. It bothered me that we treated even veteran workers that way. I asked a top executive about it in my first year at the company.

'Everyone does it,' he patronizingly assured me. 'Theft is so common we need to check everyone, every day. We can't make any exceptions.'

He made me feel so naive for thinking that business could be conducted based on trust that I didn't bother to ask him about the time clocks or the invariably burly watchmen who loomed over them, making sure incoming workers didn't cheat by punching anyone else in.

Nearly every company of any size has its own FBI. Some even have their own J. Edgar Hoovers. Yet these same companies tell their employees they're all part of one big, happy family. How can they rationalize such sanctimonious sentiments when they frisk their workers on the way home? Or deduct vacation time when someone arrives ten minutes late? Or audit the petty cash account of someone who has been with the company for two decades? Or put padlocks on the store-rooms to prevent the entry of 'unauthorized personnel'? What family searches its members for silverware as they leave the dinner table?

Worker are adults, but once they walk through the plant gate companies transform them into children, forcing them to wear identification badges, stand in line for lunch, ask the foreman for permission to go to the bathroom, bring in a doctor's note when they have been ill, and blindly follow instructions without asking any questions.

So I decided to end the searches at Semco. It wasn't hard. I just had a sign posted at the gate that read, 'Please make sure as you leave that you are not inadvertently taking anything that does not belong to you.'

I knew some managers would be appalled. What I didn't anticipate was that shop stewards would complain. Some workers, they said, were worried they would be blamed if a tool disappeared, as it inevitably would. 'Our people want the searches,' the union leaders pleaded. 'They want everyone to know that they're not the ones taking the tools,' In fact, after two hand-held drilling machines disappeared from the Hobart plant, so many workers demanded that searches be resumed we had to hold a plantwide assembly to calm every-one down.

Imagine! Workers wanted to be searched to prove their innocence. We tried to explain that they were forsaking their right to credibility. What happened to innocent until proven guilty? Isolated thefts should not be enough to make them give that up.

I wasn't under the illusion that, by eliminating the searches, we would eliminate thefts. I'll bet that on average two or three per cent of any work force will take advantage of an employer's trust. But is this a valid reason to subject 97 per cent to a daily ritual of humiliation? Yes, there will be theft here and embezzlement there, but that's the case in com-panies with huge auditing and monitoring departments. It's a cost of doing business. I would rather have a few thefts once in a while than condemn everyone to a system based on mistrust.

While I was at it, I took out the big time clock at the plant gate and had small clocks installed throughout the plant and offices. Then we suggested to everyone that punching in for their colleagues would not be appreciated, and let it go at that. Today, the time clocks are there only to help our employers keep track of the hours they work.

Have thefts and time-card cheating increased or decreased? I don't know and I don't care. It's not worth it to me to have a company at which you don't trust the people with whom you work.

Nothing seems more medieval than dress codes. Office personnel are supposed to stroll around in suits and ties or dresses, but who remembers why? It's like this because . . . well, it just is.

The receptions is the calling card of the company – how silly is that? What customer, supplier, or banker would cancel a deal when he sees a casually attired receptionist? What buyer has failed to do business with a company because a salesman wasn't sufficiently fashionable?

Dress codes are all about conformity. People want to feel secure, and dressing like everyone else is one way to accomplish it. If everyone at IBM wears blue suits and white shirts, then even a trainee will feel he is part of the company if he is so attired. But the flip side is that these same people will come to depend on other forms of officially imposed unity, such as a uniform language, uniform behaviour, and maybe even uniform thinking. At its worst, the company turns Orwellian and creativity and freedom are smothered by discipline and the weight of shared expectations. Obviously, few corporations let it go that far, but even relatively informal businesses have unwritten codes of conduct. The more elaborate they are, the worse it is for flexibility and, ultimately, profits.

Of course, some people say they like suits and dresses. Clovis, for example, always comes to work in a suit and tie.

Harro, on the other hand, got a roomful of hoots when he pulled a suit from the depths of his closet and wore it to a meeting with an important customer. If I needed any proof of the ridiculousness of dress codes, I had only to recall how our old friend Ernesto Gabriele bought his old ties from home for the clerks in the accounting department, who didn't have any of their own. It was one more example of how Ernesto tried to creative an atmosphere worthy of a multinational, but with their knots tied wrong and their shirt tails hanging outside their pants, the clerks looked as if they were going to a Halloween party.

Why is it that when they come to work on weekends, people invariably dress in casual clothes? Because they feel more comfortable. Well, why shouldn't they feel more comfortable every day? So we told all our office workers and managers they could dress as they pleased. Period. And most gave up suits and ties and dresses in favour of jeans and, on hot days, shorts. Sure, there are moments when more formal attire is appropriate, such as at board meetings and presentations to important customers. But every responsible adult knows how to dress correctly for these occasions. In fact, one of the few complications of our new policy occurred when one of our air-conditioner repairmen was denied entrance to the Citibank Building in São Paulo because he was dressed too casually. To fix an air conditioner! He went home, changed, and went back to work. End of problem.

We hoped eliminating the dress code would help create a company in which office doors would seldom be closed and it would be common for someone to walk in, sit on a colleague's desk, and eavesdrop on a meeting that had nothing to do with him. Today I am a big believer in MBWA, or Management By Wandering Around. Popularized at Hewlett-Packard, it simply means taking time each week to walk around with, as Bob Dylan said, no destination known. You can see how new projects are going, solve some problem in the factory or the office, or just chat in the hall with someone you haven't seen in a long while.

Sometimes, though, you can't break down the walls until

you actually break down the walls. So one day I called in everyone on the third floor, one by one, and asked them what they would think about giving up their individual offices and sharing one big, beautiful work space divided by plants and flowers. We formed a committee and soon enough the wrecking crews arrived. My goal was for each person to have a desk wherever he wanted, which made it all rather complicated. But with our employees pitching in we managed to finish in a month.

My own work area, incidentally, got much smaller. And I still can't find that sofa I used to have.

Suits and ties were easy compared to workers' uniforms. I remember attending a meeting of top managers at which several major investments were approved in a matter of minutes. Then we came to the matter of replacing our factory workers' sky blue work outfits. We spent more than an hour arguing about the relative merits of various hues – which was more sober, which more inspiring, which showed dirt less – without reaching a conclusion. Everyone had a chance to express an opinion on the uniforms, I thought to myself, except the people whose opinions should count the most: the people who would wear them.

Clovis, as usual, as reading my mind. 'What if we took a survey of the workers to see what colour they prefer?' he asked.

'Are you crazy?' was the response from around the table. 'They're going to want yellow, orange, white – it'll be a nightmare.'

What could be expected of workers? The managers argued. Certainly not an understanding of the influence of colours on motivation and productivity. Who could expect them to be practical?

I couldn't believe what I was hearing. I mean, we were talking about the colour of clothing. In keeping with our new thinking – Clovis's and my new thinking, anyway – we put the survey idea to a vote and the naysayers around the table

reluctantly agreed, thinking no doubt that the workers would
want impractical colours and they would have an opportunity
to tell the boss 'I told you so.'

We polled workers in three of our four factories, offering
them a choice of all the colours of the rainbow and a few usually associated with controlled substances. The result was a tie
between light blue and a blue-grey called petroleum blue. So
we had to take a second survey, accompanied by the sneers of
the sceptical directors. 'By now everything could have been
purchased and delivered,' they didn't have to say.

This time petroleum blue won by a landslide. Even the
critics reluctantly conceded that it was more practical than
our old sky blue, because grease stains wouldn't be visible. We
told ourselves the time we spent distributing and tabulating
the survey twice was worth it.

Emboldened, I took on a really serious problem next. At
Semco, one of our biggest headaches was parking. We didn't
have nearly enough spaces at our São Paulo head-quarters.
After much discussion among mangers, we solved the problem democratically: we abolished reserved spaces for big shots
and apportioned them by department in proportion to their
size. Directors and managers ended up with eight spaces,
administration had ten, clerks and other office workers ten,
machine operators fifteen, and so on. Within each department, all spaces were available on a first-come, first-served
basis. Only after a few executives were forced to leave their
cars outside the gates and saw to their astonishment that
their instructions continued to be carried out by the workers
who had parked inside the gates did they acknowledge that
respect is not a function of the distance from car door to plant
door.

In the next few months, Semco abandoned fancy embossed
business cards in favour of cheaper, standardized ones; asked
executives to share secretaries (about whom much more
later); eliminated private dining rooms; and allowed managers
of the same rank to have different kinds of desks and chairs
and occupy offices of varying sizes. No longer would it be

possible to discern a person's status by the grade and grain of his office furniture or the plushness of his carpet.

Democracy is a lot of work, I kept telling myself and anyone who would listen. It needs to be exercised with conviction and without subterfuge or exception. And it begins with little things, like neckties, time clocks, parking spaces and petroleum blue uniforms.

ten

BY THE PEOPLE

An incident not long after Fernando arrived at Semco should have warned me that he and I were destined for trouble. I had talked him into accompanying me to the headquarters of the Metalworkers' Union of São Paulo for a bargaining session. The trip was unusual because in Brazil companies always make the unions come to them.

There was no mistaking the union office. Dozens of large, stocky workers, dressed in overalls and blue jeans, lined both sides of the corridor. How were we going to get past all those angry-looking men?

Fernando didn't slow down, so neither did I. As we got closer, the workers looked even more menacing. Some moved away from the walls they had been leaning against and stood straight up. A discreet entrance was out of the question. Not only were Fernando and I both more than six feet tall, but we were also dressed in grey flannel suits, with sober striped ties.

The workers started to murmur. 'It's them,' one of them hissed.

We walked forward until we were surrounded.

'It's them, the bosses,' said another.

Threatening looks abounded. Violence did not seem out of the question. Just as I was about to try to explain who we were and what we wanted, the union chief appeared.

'Relax, guys,' he said. 'These two aren't from Taurus.'

Taurus, a weapons manufacturer, had just fired the workers for striking. The union members were expecting a visit by representatives from management and assumed that's who we were – which explained their welcome.

Fernando and I recommended breathing and the workers seemed more amiable. Some even smiled. I smiled back with great enthusiasm. But Fernando walked on, fists still clenched.

The union leaders, not used to being hosts in such circumstances, told us our visit was a great honour. In fact, Walter Schiavon, the union director for our region, explained that most companies did everything they could to demean and intimidate the union leaders, starting with keeping them waiting when they arrived to bargain.

'They make us feel unimportant, as if the managers are so busy they can barely fit us into their schedules,' Walter said. 'We become impatient and irritated, and are less attentive when the negotiations begin.'

'Ah,' said Fernando, looking over at me. 'We must learn to do that, Dickie.'

I squirmed a bit in my chair. Fernando was half-kidding, of course, but it was that other half that bothered me. I had been thinking about softening our hard line towards the union. Fernando clearly wasn't with me.

'That's just the beginning,' Walter went on. 'They make us sit across from the window, so the light shines in our faces. But they are in shadow, so it's hard to see their reactions.'

'And sometimes the chairs we sit on have one leg shorter than the others, so we don't feel secure,' another union man said.

'And our chairs are shorter than theirs, so we have to look up at them,' Walter added.

I looked over at Fernando. He was smiling.

Once everything was handmade and expensive. Then Henry Ford set up his assembly line. Industry began to cater for an emerging middle class, increasing volume, diminishing costs, and providing goods for the multitudes. But if the artisans of the eighteenth and nineteenth centuries could perform highly skilled tasks with little or no supervision, Ford's factory workers, who had virtually no skills, required foremen to watch over them. And who were those foremen but polished versions of the same workers who also needed supervision. And their supervisors needed department heads. And the

department heads needed vice-presidents. So mass production spawned a huge bureaucracy.

The industrialists and their shareholders could hardly have
done better. You won't meet anyone named DuPont living
under a bridge, or need to feel sorry for Henry Ford III, no
matter what Lee Iacocca says. Little by little, though, labour-
ers started wondering about their end of the stick. Factory
workers, especially in the United States and Europe, began to
question the merits of burning themselves out, physically and
mentally, while toiling in unhealthy environments. Unlike
artisans, their decision-making power – their influence over
the conditions they worked in – was negligible. Even in the
largest businesses, it is rare that more than half a dozen people
decide corporate strategy and determine the destinies of
employees. In the face of such a brutal concentration
of power, workers feel infinitesimal.

Tired and deflated by the heat and the smoke and the endless monotony of their jobs and depressed by feelings of
insignificance, workers formed unions that soon enough
began to increase wages and eventually imposed a strait-jacket
of rules that sought to give their members some control over
their lives. The battle was joined and the result was an
increasing inefficiency.

In recent years some companies have sought a way out.
Mostly they are younger firms, less encumbered by traditional thinking. They are devising new formulas to make
peace with their employees and increase their involvement
with the company and its goals. I wanted to move Semco into
their camp. But I knew that we couldn't begin to defuse the
hostility and distrust that had built up over the years without
first improving communication with the shop floor.
Information was always being filtered through the bureaucracy, which was limiting and distorting it. I suspected it was
time for a change when we hired those time and motion specialists to analyse our workers' routines. We thought these
experts would help increase our workers' productivity. Much
later, the workers told how they had quickly learned to slow
down the analysts' timers, which made their study a washout.

What we needed was a new approach. Despite Fernando's scepticism, I went ahead and asked our employees at each of our four business units to form committees comprised of representatives from every part of the operation but management. Machinists, mechanics, office workers, maintenance workers, stockroom personnel, draftsmen – every group would have a delegate on these committees, which would meet regularly with the top managers at each plant.

Only a handful of companies in Brazil had factory committees, and their members were usually the most obstreperous, uncooperative workers on the payroll. Almost all these groups had been shoved down the throat of management unions as a condition for ending a strike. A factory committee at a General Motors plant had instigated a two-week strike in which it barricaded the main gate with trucks, held managers hostage inside an office building, burned partially assembled cars on the assembly line, and made Molotov cocktails to lob at the police.

We prayed our committees would have more polite ways of dealing with us. But we gave them a board mandate anyway, telling them they were to a look after the workers' interests. Members would even have time off, with pay, to dedicate themselves to their new job, which we fully expected would lead to demands for shorter working hours, higher pay, improved working conditions, and maybe even better food in our cafeterias.

We didn't want the unions to think these committees were designed to replace them, so we negotiated their charters with union leaders, and gave them a seat on each committee as well.

What we didn't expect – but should have – was the hostile reaction to our committees from Brazil's business community. The Federation of Industries, representing the nation's industrial aristocracy, was especially peeved. The business magazines attacked us, too, in articles with such headlines as, 'These Guys Run Their Boss's Plant'.

For all the concern, our factory committees were hardly a threat. At first, they hardly existed. Older, veteran workers didn't want to join because they were uncomfortable taking part in what they believed was 'the boss's role.' They had worked under the traditional system for one, two, even three decades, always being told what to do and how and when to do it, and they didn't want to change. Some younger workers weren't interested in the committees, either. Perhaps they were suspicious of our intentions. Or maybe they were scared by the increased responsibilities that go with increased participation. Possibly they just didn't want to pull up to the same table as our top managers.

'I always hated the bosses,' recalled Demerval Mattos, a lathe operator at the marine pumps unit at our Santo Amaro plant. 'The owners of the company were my mortal enemies. I didn't want to sit down and talk to them.'

Even so, Demerval joined a factory committee. So did João Soares, a welder at the dishwasher division at the Hobart plant. At the first, tense meeting, João and his colleagues were tongue-tied. 'For three or four minutes, nobody said anything nobody knew how to start,' Soares would later say. 'Everybody was nervous. Some were so frightened they never did speak, though the meeting went on for hours.'

For his trouble, Soares was elected head of his committee, which hardly increased his enthusiasm. Eventually, though, he and others would find these committees one of the most rewarding experiences of their work lives. 'I saw top management sitting at a table with me and listening to what we had to say and willing to do something about it,' Soares said. 'I saw this was a place where the employees could grow and the company could grow.'

Consider the evolution of Oseas da Silva, another lathe operator at the marine pumps unit. 'I was,' he says, 'a very radical person. But by being on the committee, I learned that with dialogue you can achieve your goals.'

When Semco won a national award for labour relations in 1989, I decided that, since the factory committees were responsible for the honour, a committee member should accept it, even at the risk of breaching government protocol. So Oseas da Silva, former radical, shared a podium with a president.

But that was much later. At first, once they had found their tongues, the committee members concentrated on three issues: money, money, and money. Most were reasonable about it, though. They asked us to survey other companies to find out what their workers were paid, and when Semco lagged behind the industry average the committees gave us time to phase in increases.

Another concern was job security. Committee members didn't feel they could sit across the table from their bosses and speak freely if they could be dismissed for what they said. That seemed reasonable, so we guaranteed that they wouldn't be sacked while they served on a committee and for one year afterwards.

That got things rolling. Soon we were being besieged with suggestions and demands. One committee produced a list of 23 items, including transportation to and from work and first-class medical insurance. (They eventually got the latter, but not the former.) The committees were also curious about the bosses' perks. 'They all had cars,' said Soares, 'they all belonged to clubs, they all had very nice lives.'

Our annual convention provoked their scrutiny, too, especially when I had to cancel a meeting with a factory committee because it conflicted with one of our retreats. 'Glad you brought that up,' a worker representative said. 'Just what is this retreat going to cost?'

We told the truth – the meetings were never less than five figures.

'A hell of a waste,' the worker muttered. He wanted to know why we had to meet in such a pricey hotel, why our spouses had to come, and just what we did there, anyway. Now we have much cheaper conventions, with fewer managers, and much less fun.

Through years of heady growth, painful retrenchment, and unpredictable reorganizations, through acquisitions and initiatives, these committees, which seemed so menacing to so many, assumed uncountable managerial responsibilities and were vital to Semco's success.

They started conservatively, creating subcommittees to modernize locker rooms and bathrooms, buying the materials themselves and sending us the bills. Some committees elected mayors for the factories to care for common spaces such as gardens and reception areas, maintain lighting, even change the furniture. Factory committees organized teams to paint offices and machines and ran 'adopt a tree' programmes that forested our machine shops. At Santo Amaro the committee asked one of Brazil's foremost artists, Tomie Ohtake, to sketch a new design for the plant's interior, and workers plan to execute her vivid, geometric patterns when business permits the added expense for paint.

Eventually the committees broadened their concerns, butting into our business, which was the running of the business. They helped us identify surplus managers, casting suspicious eyes towards people with titles such as strategic planning manager, data processing manager, even marketing manager. They were constantly questioning expenses that executives thought were reasonable, from the gardener who did our landscaping (and made more in a week than janitors made in a month) to the rent on our factory buildings. They took over plant cafeterias, set production goals, and suggested major changes in products.

I remember scheduling a 'Chat at Lunch' session with the committee at Santo Amaro to discuss sales and billing prospects. That morning, without telling me, they sent a delegation to our sales and purchasing departments for a briefing. When the time came for the meeting, they knew more about last-minute developments than I did.

When plants faced hard times, their factory committees would take the initiative and lower wages or increase hours, saving money and protecting jobs. When layoffs were unavoidable, the committees got involved in the sensitive and unfortunate task of deciding who would go. Together we tried to be socially just, taking into consideration such factors as a worker's history with the company, loyalty, ability to find a new job, and family responsibilities. A person with seven children or a spouse in the hospital, for example, would have an edge over someone fresh out of school with no responsibilities. And under a separate procedure the dismissal of any Semco employee who had been with us for more than three years or was over 50 years old had to be specifically approved by a long list of people.

But sometimes the committee members complained that in our effort to be equitable we dragged out the process, talking too much, agonizing too long, and increasing the pain. Perhaps that was an unavoidable price for corporate democracy.

eleven

ONE CHANGE LEADS
TO ANOTHER

Fernando, the last of our Attilas, was the first key manager to be expelled by the new Semco. He was very smart and very capable, but unequivocally autocratic. After he left Hobart we decided we couldn't take the risk of hiring someone new to run the unit, which had already suffered too much culture shock. I was anxious to show that improved performance and a 'touchy-feely' style were not mutually exclusive. This was as good a chance as any.

I redecorated Fernando's office, replacing his bleak oil paintings with modern posters, including one of a neon ladder that seemed to climb one of the walls, and early one Monday morning I moved in. But the new general manager didn't spend much time there. I immediately started wandering around.

My first stop was the sales office. I wanted to talk to Mara Mantovani, our marketing manager. A thin, handsome woman, she had fought constantly with Fernando and was known to make deprecating remarks about the plant's management.

She looked up, surprised, from her desk. 'I was just coming over to see you,' she said.

'Let's just meet here,' I said, sitting down.

She looked around anxiously, as if regretting that she hadn't straightened up before I arrived.

'Let's start with you telling me what bothers you most at Semco.'

'Uh, lots of things,' she said, shifting in her chair.

'Tell me the three or four most important ones.'

'Well, for once, I don't have the autonomy to print brochures, to organize trade fairs, to send out mailings. I needed Fernando's approval for everything. And that took a long time.'

'As of today, Mara, we'll be having a weekly meeting at 9 a.m. each Monday for all those in leadership positions. Just present your proposals and convince the people there. If we can't agree, we'll vote.' I paused for a moment to let the idea sink in. 'So, what other problems do you have?'

'Oh, lots. I sometimes need to tell a sales rep what kind of expense account he has from us, and I can't decide that myself.'

'That's the same sort of problem as the first one, isn't it?'

'Maybe it is. The weekly meeting, right?'

'Right.'

'What about staffing? I need another assistant, and I can't get one.' Mara raised her eyebrows, hoping I would immediately authorise one.

'The weekly meeting,' I sang out. 'The people there will be putting together the budget. What else?'

'I guess everything I can think of will be decided at these meetings, right?'

'You've got it. You'll have to develop your lobbying powers, Mara. And since I have only one vote, I'm going to do a lot of lobbying myself.' I gave her a wide smile as I got up to leave. 'See you in Congress.'

I spent the rest of the morning having the same conversation with the other key managers at our food service equipment unit. Then I headed back to my office, which I declared to be the plant's meeting room, available for everyone. (It soon became common for me to arrive at my desk and find someone sitting in my chair, using the phone or having a meeting. I would just sit on the visitor's side and wait until they were finished.)

The weekly meetings, which started that first day, quickly changed the plant's culture. Instead of waging guerrilla wars with the boss for a raise or a new assistant or the freedom to make a decision, managers now marshalled their arguments for the meetings. The agendas for these sessions were lengthy at first, but over time they shrank as everyone began to make more decisions themselves. People only brought up issues they were genuinely unsure about. And even so, the group would often just throw the problem back in the person's lap. Mara, for instance, was told she should publish brochures in whatever colours she wanted, with whatever layout she wished, and hire however many people her budget allowed to help.

'But what if I put out a mailing and the sales reps don't like it?' she asked.

'It's up to you to decide whether you are going to consult them before you publish,' I told her. 'If you feel confident about it, go ahead. If they don't like it, your rating as Marketing Manager will suffer, and next time you'll be sure to consult them. We're not against mistakes here. If you're not making some mistakes, you probably aren't taking enough risks.'

'But what if they don't like my work?' Mara persisted.

'One of two things. If sales go up, they will learn to trust your judgement.' I paused for emphasis. 'If they go down, they won't.'

'And then?' Mara asked.

'Well, this group puts together the budget, and they'll only include you in it if they think you're a good investment.'

Looking back on it, I can't remember a single decision that I made in that period. Which was just as well, for I am at my best when I am doing the least.

I always smile when I hear executives boast about how par-ticipative they are. 'I want everyone to feel involved,' they will say. 'So I call everybody in, hear what's on their minds, and only then decide.'

What people call participative management is usually just consultative management. There's nothing new to that. Managers have been consulting employees for centuries. How progressive do you have to be, after all, to ask someone else's opinion? And to listen to that opinion – well, that's a start. But it's only when the bosses give up decision-making and let their employees govern themselves that the possibility exists for a business jointly managed by workers and executives. And that is true participative management, not just lip service to it.

Every few weeks the Hobart plant's managers would spend a lunch hour talking to the workers, who would gather in the cafeteria, 200 strong, and talk about anything that was on their minds. No subject was taboo – salaries, profits, new products, hiring and firing policies were all fair game. Through these sessions we started to convince them that everyone at the food service equipment unit should make more decisions and become more involved in the company. Everyone could be a cathedral-builder.

The pot soon began to boil, and before long the old Hobart plant was unrecognizable. Not just physically, of course, but organizationally and, if I may say so, spiritually. Workers who had for years – even decades – reported to the plant and promptly turned their minds off became full-fledged industrial citizens, making decisions not only about their jobs but also about the products they were making and indeed about their company. But at first, the bubbles in the pot were small.

It all seemed to start when a group of women decided to do something about the men's locker rooms, which were always dreadful. If they could be trained to take better care of their area, the women believed, the men might be less careless elsewhere around the plant. One Friday night after all the men had left, the women stole into the locker room and found that it was even worse than they had imagined. Towels, underwear, and toilet paper were strewn about. Dirty clothes spilled out of bins. With felt-tipped pens, the intruders proceeded to tag scattered items with notes: '*I feel out of place here*,' '*I want to go back to my locker*', '*When am I going to get a bath?*'

Corny, right? But when the men arrived on Monday they quickly got the message. From then on the whole plant was much cleaner. Soon, new showers and lockers were installed. Then some of the men redesigned an unused production area, turning it into a games room that was used at lunch and after work. They did all the construction themselves, and invited the managers to a party when it opened.

Soon chaeflera and giboia plants were sprouting between the machines on the shop floor, just as shrubbery had earlier appeared in our offices. Then some of the assembly-line workers decided to paint the factory. Each selected a colour for the column nearest him, while the walls behind each group of five or six workers were painted a collectively chosen shade. One veteran manager consulted a book on the psychology of colours and warned us that some shades the workers favoured would darken the plant, making it depressing and possibly dangerous. Limit the choices, he advised. Better yet, choose the colours for them. It reminded me of the fuss over the uniforms. I told him our philosophy was to leave such decisions to those who would be living with the consequences. When one group of workers picked forest green our resident colourist shuddered. Another group wanted brown. We kept our mouths shut. The plant was closed for an afternoon as workers took up brushes and rollers and turned it into a plant of many colours, including the industrially unlikely shades of pink and magenta. These hues may have looked chaotic, but they were symbols of our desire to let our workers control their destinies.

The office workers watched all this activity with rising jealousy. Why shouldn't they have more say about their walls? No reason at all. So on Friday they all arrived in jeans and overalls and by lunchtime dozens of cans of paint were spread out on the floor. There were boom boxes, too, and singing, while managers and clerks plastered the walls with twice as much paint as our expert said was necessary. No one who entered the offices could tell the paint job was performed by amateurs – and no one who leaned against a wall escaped a reprimand.

The plant may have had the worst food in any institution without bars. So the employees formed a cafeteria committee and took responsibility for selecting a supplier, monitoring quality, and setting prices. Jair Pinto, a clerk in accounting who had been with us for 25 years, was elected its head. Jair was known for his perseverance. He would stalk customers who fell behind on their bills like a Dobermann greeting an unannounced visitor at midnight. Even so, some workers thought he needed a little motivation as far as the food was concerned. One day he arrived at the cafeteria to hear murmurs of discontent rising from the long dining tables. It had something to do with dessert, a substance barely identifiable as pudding. Jair was doubtless wondering what was going on as he started his meal. A worker sitting at his table got up, nonchalantly dumped his pudding into Jair's tray, and walked out without saying a word. Moments later another worker did the same thing. Then another. In ten minutes Jair's tray was a mountain of pudding.

The next day, Jair began to weigh the steaks to make sure they met the 125-gram standard specified in the contract. He was all over the kitchen staff, too. And soon the quality of the food ceased to be a source of complaint.

That didn't end the problems at the cafeteria, though. Semco's policy was to subsidize 70 per cent of the cost of the meals we served. But after consulting with Clovis and some others the factory workers instituted a 'Robin Hood Meal Plan' under which employees paid on a sliding scale based on income. Managers and engineers were asked to pay 95 per cent of the cost of their food, for example, while floor sweepers paid just 5 per cent.

A few supervisors felt unfairly treated and responded by bringing their lunch from home. The rest of the employees decided to do nothing, hoping the supervisors would realize it was cheaper to pay 95 per cent than 100 per cent, which, after four weeks, they did. Today these supervisors defend the 'Robin Hood' plan. They realize what it means to their lower-wage colleagues.

Small changes eventually led to larger ones, as we knew they would. From the shrubbery and paint and dirty lockers and lunch subsidies the workers moved on to concerns central to their jobs and their plant. The factory committee spun off groups that studied the plant's products and how the workers made them, looking for ways to save time and make improvements. These teams weren't created by Semco; they formed spontaneously, as the bracing winds of democracy swept through the food service equipment unit, and often met after hours or during lunch.

One group restructured the dishwasher assembly line, changing it from a sequential assembly process to a batch concept in which dishwashers are assembled in twos and threes by teams of workers who do many different task and spend the time between batches prefabricating the components they will soon need. They also came up with a system in which all the parts for the dishwashers were stocked in open racks in the middle of the factory. Metal tags, green on one side and red on the other, hung on each rack, and the workers would flip the tags when they saw it was time to reorder, ensuring a steady supply. This was a big improvement on the traditional assembly line, in which dehumanized workers have no role in decisions regarding the production process. They just do their minutely choreographed jobs and, if no bolts are available, simply stop working (and love it). In our system, workers were involved in what they were doing and hollered well in advance when the supply of any part was running low. Production wasn't interrupted unless there was a problem at a supplier.

Another team of employees changed the casing on our meat grinder from steel to fibreglass, which made it easier to clean, more modern in appearance, and cheaper to make. Another group dreamed up a new way to pre-weld the base on our scales, saving $27 a unit. And yet another group scrutinized the slicers for cold cuts and other meats. Hobart had been making these slicers for years, based on an old design, and their popularity had plummeted to the point where only a few dozen a month were being sold. The workers realized that a change from cast-steel to stainless steel would make the slicer both more attractive and more hygienic. But stainless steel shows fingerprints, and no one thought customers would want to shine their machines every few hours. A matte finish was the answer, but an industrial engineer on the team calculated that it would take six extra production steps and five additional hours of work. That would make the slicer too expensive.

Annoyed at this stumbling block, the group went off to have lunch together. But one worker had an idea, stayed behind, and gave a slicer a matte finish in just four steps. When his colleagues returned, they were amazed to learn that the new method added less than an hour to the assembly time. A new slicer was born, and sales shot up to several hundred a month.

The strength of these groups was their diversity. They included factory workers, engineers, office clerks, sales reps, and executives. They didn't have a formal head; whoever showed the greatest capacity to lead got the job, calling meetings and moderating discussions. In more than one group, a shop-floor worker guided professionals. Instead of a seniority system, or boxes on an organizational chart that guaranteed power, the groups were held together by a natural system of collegial respect.

There are similarities between this system and the Japanese approach to organizing manufacturing operations, but also important differences. In our groups, younger members didn't automatically submit to their elders. Moreover, once a team decided an issue, it stayed decided. There was no approval needed to make a change. Then again, there were no special rewards for new ideas. It was a spontaneous process; people participated only if they wanted to.

Soon every section of the Hobart plant boasted large scoreboards above the shop floor that tracked the workers' current production against a monthly goal they themselves set. Managers didn't put the scoreboards up; the workers did. They even had a master scoreboard in the cafeteria that showed the whole plant's daily output, product by product.

At first setting goals and monitoring production was uncomfortable for some workers, who were accustomed to arguing that if management's quotas weren't met it was because executives hadn't planned correctly. Now, the workers couldn't mindlessly complain about how the factory was run, since they were helping to run it.

Once again, the slicing team led the way. Its members decided that they were going to make 210 slicers a month. Not 200. Not 220. They calculated the time and effort and the materials involved and concluded that 210 was the right number.

We watched closely that first month, curious to see how they would do. They started strongly, averaging eight slicers a day, right on target. But a shipment of cutting discs from a supplier was late and there was no inventory at the plant. Two members of the group visited the supplier (bypassing their own colleagues in our purchasing department) and discussed the problem with some of the supplier's factory workers (who bypassed *their* colleagues in sales). Two days before the end of the month, the discs appeared. By then, however, they had run out of motors, which came from a plant 300 miles away. Promises for delivery were made daily and broken just as frequently. Team members pestered the supplier and finally their complaints were heard by a sympathetic executive. The motors arrived on the last day of the month.

There were only a few hours left – not nearly enough to install all the motors. But the slicer team made a collective decision: each member clocked out at the end of the day, then returned to the assembly area – on his own time – and worked until 4.50 a.m., when the team had completed 210 slicers. Not one more, not one less.

twelve

THE TROUBLE WITH RULES

For all the board room and locker room debate, most of the changes we had made so far were symbolic. But by late in 1985, the anxiety level had risen perilously among Semco's middle managers. Fernando was gone, but his tough-guy philosophy was alive if endangered.

'You've taken away my power,' supervisors would complain when they bumped into me in halls. 'I can't even tell if my people are arriving on time.' Or: 'How do you expect me to meet this month's sales goal when I don't have control any more?'

They would tell me they were confused. They wanted me to explain Semco's policy. I kept thinking that was what was wrong. There was too much policy at Semco, and not enough thought, judgement and common sense. But I understood why our managers were scared.

If there was a group that was critical to our emerging plan, it was these mid-level supervisors. I never tired of telling them that they, more than me or my colleagues in top management, could be the biggest advocates – or the biggest obstacles – to our efforts to turn Semco into a more democratic and freer company.

Modern corporations are typically shaped like pyramids, with the highest-ranking executives at the top and progressively bigger groups of managers as you work down the hierarchy. Some pyramids are steep, like a bottle of Bordeaux. Others, the more efficient ones, are flatter, like a bottom-heavy bottle of Portuguese rosé. Either way, though, there is always a group of supervisors, department heads, and other professionals in the middle, no longer workers but not yet owners or shareholders. It isn't unusual for these middle managers to be more zealous with authority (tight-fisted with the company's money) than those at the top.

We realized our middle managers needed to be stroked if were going to succeed at what I was beginning to think of as a grand experiment. Like the audience in a Roman amphitheatre, their thumbs-up would ensure that our efforts to increase the participation of Semco's workers thrived. Thumbs-down and the lions would devour us.

Our middle managers had studied at schools that taught traditional organizational discipline and the importance of structure and supervision. They had been reared on competition and trained to accumulate symbols of power, such as parking spaces near the door and embossed business cards. They enjoyed saying things like, 'See that four-door out there, the one with the graphite paint-job? That's my company car.' But democracy cannot be reconciled with expensive and unnecessary icons, especially those that come with radial tyres.

As if the loss of perks and power wasn't bad enough, our supervisors were further troubled by Semco's growth. The acquisitions we had made meant dozens of new managers and hundreds of new workers had to be incorporated into our organization. These people didn't do things our old way, or even our new way.

I decided to hold one large meeting at which our middle managers could air their concerns. It started at 4 p.m. one Friday afternoon. About 40 managers were there. We started by asking them to state the issues they wanted to talk about and before we knew it had a list of 40 items. Many concerned the authority they wanted back – being able to punish workers for tardiness and absenteeism, for example, or to control raises and bonuses for subordinates.

'You have to decide what you want more,' said a production manager at the food service equipment unit. 'If it's billing sales, then you have to let us control our people. They're beginning to think they don't have to obey us, because they can come and go as they like and they know we won't fire them.'

'Your power to fire someone just because he's late too often really determines your month's invoicing?' Clovis asked.

'It sure as hell does,' he shot back. 'The problem with you, Clovis, is that you haven't had to live down there with those guys. Give them a finger and they won't just take your arm, they'll take your whole body!'

Managers around the room were nodding. That's what's wrong with bosses, I thought to myself. So many of them are better prepared to find error and to criticize than to add to the effort. To be the boss is what counts to most bosses. They confuse authority with authoritarianism. They don't trust their subordinates.

'You guys are unable to meet the budget you yourself determined, and now you're using this as an excuse,' said Paulo Pereira, a tall, lanky young man who had come to Semco with Clovis, and worked with him as our personnel manager. Unlike his soft-spoken mentor, he had a reputation for speaking his mind, no matter what.

'Bullshit!' cried a hardline production planning manager. 'All this touchy-feely stuff is bullshit.'

'Yeah,' cried a sales manager. 'It all comes from human resources, which spends the money that we work so hard to make.'

On and on it went, with much gnashing of teeth and muttering under breaths. The managers wanted to know the rules of the game. We kept saying, 'Well, let's discuss it. Let's just come to some agreement among ourselves.' But I could see it was only making them more anxious.

Even though we had done away with the dress code, almost everyone at the meeting wore a suit and tie. (There were no women present.) A conservative bunch, they adhered to a rigid hierarchy, even when complaining. The first to speak were the most senior; then came those just below them, who would unfailingly support their superiors.

I admit I was more than a little to blame for this 'yes man' syndrome. Semco had been known to drive its managers hard and was quick to fire those who did not reach their goals. I myself had dismissed the entire tier of senior managers in one afternoon – no one had forgotten that. So who could blame them for feeling angry, confused, and apprehensive now?

I believed perhaps 20 per cent of the middle managers were actually sympathetic to my efforts to make our factories and offices more democratic. I suspected another 20 per cent laughed heartily at it, considering me a rebel with an inheritance. It was the rest of them who would determine whether I succeeded.

We decided to hold another meeting for the middle managers the next week. And another one the week after. Then it became a weekly affair. The agenda was simply. We would talk only about company policy and philosophy. Operational problems were out. The hardliners, who thought these sessions were useless, quickly dubbed them 'Growing Bees In The Sky'. But I liked the term and used it officially from then on.

As one session led to another, it became clear that we had two choices. We could write a completely new manual incorporating all our new policies and spelling out the emerging philosophy behind them. Or we could do away with the old manual and just not replace it. That way we would force people to make decisions based on common sense.

Guess what we did?

Wrong.

We tried to write new rules. We really did. But at every turn we found ourselves wading into a swamp of minutiae. Take our car fleet, for example. To reduce costs, we set up a central garage to make repairs, track mileage, and send people a memo when it was time to change the tyres or renew the registration. But soon this new department was ensnared in conflict. People's cars would break down and they would call the garage to complain. Or someone urgently in need of his car would arrive at the garage to find there weren't any vehicles available. Department heads received bills for service on their cars, discovered they hadn't budgeted enough, and then spread the word that the auto department was inefficient, or maybe even taking kickbacks from greedy local mechanics who were making the repairs.

From this we quickly concluded that some departments were better not created and some rules were better not written. Common sense would be the best alternative, by far. But we were careful. We didn't want to rattle an already jittery crew. There was no grand announcement of our decision. Over the next three or four months we simply collected all our procedure manuals. (Many months later we did the same with our organizational chart, not that we had consulted it much.) People would ask us from time to time when the new manuals would be ready. Eventually, some began to suspect that an update wasn't going to appear and asked us why. Only then did we say aloud what we had been thinking: that we were trading written rules for common sense.

And that is the system we have today, which is barely a system at all. When you get a company car at Semco, you can do anything you want with it. If you have a friend who is a mechanic, have him take care of it. We want our employees to treat Semco's vehicles as they would the family sedan. We're comfortable having their judgement apply to our car as well as theirs.

But this was all terribly frightening to some of our people, especially at first. We had to do lots of handholding. Clerks in our finance department, for example, weren't comfortable deciding how much Semco should keep as minimum balances in its checking accounts. 'Just think of them as your own accounts,' I would say.

'But Semco has so many accounts,' they would reply. 'What happens if we have an emergency and need cash?'

And I would take a deep breath, and implore them to use their common sense.

Where did all these rules come from, anyway?

They were, I suppose, an unhappy byproduct of corporate expansion. How does an industrial giant act as it grows? First, management concludes that a company cannot depend on individuals. After all, they have personalities and finite life spans. A corporation is supposed to be impersonal and eternal.

Next thing you know, committees and task forces and working groups are spewing out procedures and regulations and stomping out individuality and spontaneity.

In their quest for law, order, stability and predictability, corporations make rules for every conceivable contingency. Policy manuals are created with the idea that, if a company puts everything in writing, it will be more rational and objective. Standardizing methods and conduct will guide new employees and ensure that the entire company has a single, cohesive image. And so it became accepted that large organizations could not function with hundreds or thousands or tens of thousands of rules.

Sounds sensible, right? And it works fine for an army or a prison system. But not, I believe, for a business. And certainly not for a business that wants people to think, innovate, and act as human beings whenever possible. All those rules cause employees to forget that a company needs to be creative and adaptive to survive. Rules slow it down.

Semco had a particularly complicated set of rules on travel expenses. Our auditors often spent hours arguing over whether someone on a business trip should be reimbursed for movie tickets. Well then, what about theatre tickets? What would we do if an employee went to a concert that cost $45? $100? And what about calling home? How often should the company pay? Was a five-minute call reasonable? What if an employee had, say, four children? Are 75 seconds per child sufficient?

See what I mean?

Without rules all answers are suggested by common sense. No, I can't define what common sense is, but I know it when I hear it. Some of our people stay in four-star hotels and others, sometimes with much higher salaries, choose lesser digs. Some people spend $200 a day on meals; others get by on half as much.

A company makes, sells, bills and, God willing, collects. It doesn't need to know if the taxi ride being claimed by a manager was for business. Or if another manager couldn't have stayed in a hotel with three rather than four stars. With few exceptions, rules and regulations only serve to:

1.　*Divert attention from a company's objectives.*
2.　*Provide a false sense of security for executives.*
3.　*Create work for bean counters.*
4.　*Teach men to stone dinosaurs and start fires with sticks.*

The desire for rules and the need for innovation are, I believe, incompatible. (Remember, Order *or* Progress.) Rules freeze companies inside a glacier; innovation lets them ride sleighs over it.

We've found we can replace nearly every rule that those master sergeants called controllers can impose. This does not mean that instructions are not sent out by whoever feels they are needed – but our people are not afraid to ignore procedures that don't seem applicable or wise. There are no absolute truths at Semco, nor are we out to make everyone do things the same way.

There is another, less obvious dividend to the banishing of rule books: people begin to make more decisions on their own, decisions they are usually better qualified to make than their supervisors.

What about the economies of scale? I am often asked. If Semco went out and bought tyres for all the cars in our fleet at once, for instance, wouldn't we get a better price than if employees go out and buy tyres on their own. Probably. Then again, if our auto department scrupulously and blindly followed the manufacturer's overly conservative recommendations on tyre replacement, we would no doubt buy a lot more tyres than we do now by letting our employees decide when they need changing. And I'll bet that's true with many items we used to buy corporately and now purchase individually.

Of course, I don't know for sure, since under our no longer neurotically compulsive budget system we don't keep track of these purchases anymore. But if you want my advice, take a deep breath, pluck up your courage, and feed the policy manual to the shredder, one page at a time. Let companies be ruled by wisdom that varies from factory to factory and worker to worker. To do otherwise only gives those tough guy controllers the comfortable feeling that the company is organized, and provides jobs for dozens of disturbed souls who should be retrained for some useful purpose.

At first it was hard for us. But with a great deal of commiseration and consultation the shock of rulelessnees began to subside, and our middle managers began to remove their armour plates.

I liked to tell them that a turtle may live for hundreds of years because it is well protected by its shell, but it only moves forward when it sticks out its head.

thirteen

WHEN THE BANANAS
ATE THE MONKEYS

They had been there for hours, through the lazy, steamy, Brazilian afternoon. On one side of the long wooden cafeteria table were two union directors and three shop-floor workers. Across from them were three Semco executives. They were all trying to settle a week-long strike that, like most labour disputes, revolved around money. But as befits a company where traditional corporate dogma was being discarded and unpredictability was a way of life, this walkout began when Semco voluntarily launched a programme to give our workers a raise they had neither asked for nor were expecting.

In the three years we had owned the Hobart plant we had proudly watched as workers assumed more of a role in determining how it was run. They set their own production quotas and redesigned the slicers, peelers, and dough mixers they made. Now tension hung over the place like a vulture awaiting the lion's last mouthful. The long silences at the bargaining table indicated that the sides were far apart.

The strike was our eighth in seven years, but all had been brief, so we were hardly experts in them. Clovis was our chief representative at the bargaining table, and his 30 years of managerial experience told him what was on the minds of the men across the table. Workers had practically been bred to distrust anyone who represented money – even someone like Clovis, who had built a career trying to dissipate such feelings. We had come a long way at Ipiranga but in times of stress those early, bitter feelings just seem to reassert themselves. Clovis leaned back, smoothed his moustache, and looked across the table. What would it take, he thought to himself, to create trust if all that had been accomplished here had failed to do it? And how ironic that the walkout was sparked by our efforts to ensure that the wages we paid were fair.

Clovis's chief adversary was the factory committee leader, João Soares. Although aware of his charisma, João had thought of shop-floor representatives as either embittered opponents of capitalism or impassioned leaders. He didn't see himself as either of those. He had suffered through a series of hard-edged factory jobs, but after a few years at Semco had begun to think he had, at last, found a company that would let him have his dignity and even his aspirations. Now, sitting across from Clovis, João wasn't sure.

Given the fits and starts of Brazil's hyper-inflationary economy, we were no longer sure our pay scale was above average, which was where we wanted it to keep our work force stable. So we embarked on a programme to re-evaluate the wages we paid at all levels of Semco. Taking it one business unit at a time, we thought we could adjust the entire company in two years.

Most Brazilian companies determined wages and salaries by referring to orthodox salary models developed in the United States and Europe. At best, these impersonal sets of statistics were applied by pseudo-experts who, if they even visited a company, rarely listened to the employees. The most sophisticated of these plans had nowhere near the complexity needed to gauge our increasingly participative work force or peculiar corporate culture. But we didn't like them for a more basic reason: they were one-sided. We wanted our people to be involved in the process. It was their pay cheque after all.

So we turned to Paulo Pereira, our resident remuneration expert, who, as we might have expected, came to a radical conclusion. The only truly correct pay, he asserted, was an average of what a worker thought he should receive and what a company could afford to pay. That was for business schools, not factories, he realized. But Paulo, an unrepentant idealist, set out to find this point of balance anyway.

In true Semco fashion, his first step was to ask about 30

factory and office employees to visit other manufacturing companies that were about the same size as Semco. They were to interview their counterparts there, comparing skills, responsibilities, and pay cheques. It sounds so utterly sensible to ask workers to do this, but it just isn't done. Indeed, at first we had trouble convincing some corporations to receive our workers. But eventually our people collected comparative information on every job at Semco, from general manager to janitor. And sure enough we had fallen behind, no doubt because we had so little turnover in staff.

The marine equipment plant at Santo Amaro was first to be adjusted, because we believed it lagged the most. After would come the food service equipment division.

At the end of each month there was a barbecue at Ipiranga for all the employees. As it happened, a worker from Santo Amaro had just been transferred to Ipiranga and spent his first afternoon at the barbecue, where he proudly told his new co-workers he had just received a 40 per cent raise. Almost everyone at Santo Amaro got one, he said.

As he made his way around the gathering, indignation rose. When the party ended, small groups of irate workers stayed behind to discuss the outrage. How could workers at Santo Amaro have received a 40 per cent raise and those at Ipiranga get nothing?

How indeed?

The next day, a Saturday, was the end of the month. Dozens of workers were at Ipiranga to meet production quotas. It was an understatement to say their usual enthusiasm was dampened by Santo Amaro's good fortune. Since the workers didn't require supervision, no one from management was on hand to explain the full story of the salary adjustment.

After listening to the grumbling, Soares tacked a note to the main bulletin board. 'We have been tricked,' it said. 'Santo Amaro has received a 40 per cent raise and we didn't. We must go on strike at once, until we are fairly treated.'

When the managers arrived on Monday morning, the strike

was on. It didn't matter that the facts had been garbled – that the average increas at Santo Amaro had been 8 per cent, not 40 per cent, and that any raise above 15 per cent was to be phased in. Nor did it matter that the food service equipment unit was next in line for readjustment.

Soares talked to the regional union director, Geraldo Mello, who was at the plant that morning, and he was even more outraged than João. 'They can't favour their other workers and ignore the Hobart people,' Mello told him. 'We must teach them a lesson.'

When some executives at the plant heard that, they had the classic response: they wanted to make the strikers' lives as miserable as possible. They suggested that we hold on to the pay cheques for the period before the walkout and lock the gates so the workers couldn't sit around the plant, as they all were doing. They even wanted us to suspend health-care benefits. But cooler heads thought we should maintain the Semco way of doing things, no matter how we were provoked, and to my relief they prevailed.

I had come to believe that labour unions were more than a necessary evil. They are one of the few legitimate agents of workplace change. Not all union leaders are sensible, nor is every union's position reasonable. But to pretend a union doesn't exist, or to try to defeat it whenever possible, with whatever means, at whatever cost, is hardly worthy of the term strategy. Executives in the United States who take comfort in the sharp increase of non-union shops are myopic. It's wise to keep all the antennae connected. The ostrich that buries its head in the sand has a bigger problem than limited vision; its rear end is an enormous target.

We all know the usual ways of combating a strike:

1. *Take a stand. Show the flag. Don't back down.*
2. *Guarantee that anyone who wants to work can, even if that means calling in the police.*
3. *Protect company property, with force if necessary.*
4. *Make it hard for the workers by closing the plant and suspending benefits.*

5. *Try to divide and conquer the strikers.*
6. *After it's over, fire the instigators and anyone else you want to get rid of, intimidating others in the process.*

These recommendations are shortsighted and costly. Troublemakers, like weeds, will always sprout up, because management does such a thorough job putting down fertilizer. When we acquire a company or start up a new factory, one of our first moves is to invite the local union leaders over for a visit. Hobart had thanked the heavens it wasn't discovered by organized labour, but we asked the Metalworker's Union, which has earned its reputation for combativeness, to organize the plant and be part of the factory committee.

Recognizing the existence of unions does not automatically mean agreeing with them. We have courteously received union committees just to say no to 18 of their 19 demands. But we recognize the renewing power of unionism, and the importance of not becoming ostriches. He who seeks to keep the union outside the factory gate will soon need pants with a reinforced seat.

During a strike, we follow these rules:

1. *Treat everyone as adults.*
2. *Tell the strikers that no one will be punished when they return to work. Then don't punish anyone.*
3. *Don't keep records of who came to work and who led the walkout.*
4. *Never call the police to try to break up a picket line.*
5. *Maintain all benefits.*
6. *Don't block workers' access to the factory, or the access of union representatives to the workers. But insist that union leaders respect the decision of those who want to work, just as the company respects the decision of those who don't.*
7. *Don't fire anyone during or after the strike, but make everyone see that a walkout is an act of aggression.*

No, I'm not a graduate of the Patrice Lumumba Institute in Moscow, and to prove it let me say that at the time of the

Ipiranga strike Semco only accepted an unconditional return to work. Although we valued dialogue as no other company, we *never* negotiated during a strike.

This was our thinking: almost all companies that follow the first set of rules end up bargaining under pressure and making concessions they later regret. In other words, they start out like Arnold Schwarzenegger and end up as Woody Allen. Under our procedure, there was only one end to a strike – the return to work by everyone, with no pay for hours not worked and no concessions made during the stoppage. Only after the workers came back would we resume negotiations.

So we allowed the striking employees to enter the plant and use the cafeteria for meetings. Breakfast and lunch were served as usual, subsidized by us as usual. Medical care and other benefits continued. But we wouldn't negotiate.

As the strike dragged on, executives would have informal conversations with workers in the cafeteria, trying to win them over. Anyone who ventured into the plant would have thought it had merely run out of raw materials. People were sitting around playing cards and talking. There was no sign of animosity. Some workers wanted to return to their jobs, believing us when we told them we intended to raise their salaries soon. Most didn't.

Then Mello, the regional union director, decided it was time to turn up the heat. Without consulting Soares or the other factory committee members, he went to court and sued us for discrimination. He was convinced a judge would compel Semco to agree to some kind of an increase, giving the workers and the union a victory.

By the time everyone heard about it, the case was on the calendar. Soares felt humiliated. The strike was being handled professionally and even courteously, and going to court was regarded as much too extreme a tactic. Moreover, anything can happen in a courtroom.

'Let's make a deal, Clovis,' said Mello, when the union leader returned to the plant from court.

'The company will comply with any decision reached by

the judge,' was Clovis's clipped reply. His experience, along with intelligence from the shop floor, suggested that many workers were now willing to accept a 5 per cent increase, down from the 40 per cent they had been demanding. There was a risk that the judge would order a larger raise than 5 per cent, but we would take our chances.

So everyone headed for court. After deliberating for three hours, the judge ruled that the strike was illegal. But if the union had lost, we hadn't yet won, since the workers still weren't working.

The next day the mood at the plant was funereal. Several workers sought out João and asked him to talk to management about getting paid for the unworked days. We turned that down, but offered the strikers a chance to work overtime if they came back, so their next pay cheque wouldn't be smaller than usual. They accepted, and the strike was over.

At week's end, Clovis suggested that the managers and strike leaders sit down together to analyse the walkout. This session, which lasted four hours, became known as the meeting at which 'The Bananas Ate The Monkeys'. We said we were sorry for our inflexibility. To prove it, we revoked our policy of not negotiating during strikes. João and his people confessed that the note on the bulletin board had been a mistake because it left the workers no choice but to strike. Had a stranger entered the room, he would have thought that the managers were dressed in overalls and the workers in suits and ties.

The strike taught both sides large lessons. We realized that being participative was not enough. We would have to learn to communicate better, because as much as anything people's perceptions generate strikes. The workers realized that walkouts were hardly an effective method to solve problems, and they have become rare at Semco since then.

A few months after the walkout, incidentally, the new salary schedule was implemented at the food service equipment unit. The average increase was 18 per cent. No wonder the workers were upset.

Almost all businessmen think their employees are involved in the firm and are its greatest asset.

Almost all employees think they are given too little attention and respect, and cannot say what they really think.

How is it possible to reconcile these two positions?

The sad truth is that employees of modern corporations have little reason to feel satisfied, much less fulfilled. Companies do not have the time or the interest to listen to them, and lack the resources or the inclination to train them for advancement. These companies make a series of demands, for which they compensate employees with salaries that are often considered inadequate. Moreover, companies tend to be implacable in dismissing workers when they start to age or go through a temporary drop in performance, and send people into retirement earlier than they want, leaving them with the feeling that they could have contributed much more had someone just asked.

The era of using people as production tools is coming to an end. Participation is infinitely more complex to practise than conventional corporate unilateralism, just as democracy is much more cumbersome than dictatorship. But there will be few companies that can afford to ignore either of them.

fourteen

TOO BIG FOR OUR OWN GOOD

'A great business,' Henry Ford once said, 'is really too big to be human.'

Makes you wonder, doesn't it? Old Henry was proud of Ford factories like River Rouge, with an assembly line that seemed to stretch forever. Today these behemoths are endangered, if not obsolete. Gigantic enterprises are 'downsizing' as fast as they can. They have found that the rational that encouraged their growth, the economies of scale, does not hold forever. Get too big and you quickly discover the diseconomies of scale.

Large, centralized organizations foster alienation like stagnant ponds breed algae. In massive corporations, an employee will know few of his colleagues. Everyone is part of a gigantic, impersonal machine, and it is impossible to feel motivated when you feel you are just another cog. Human nature demands recognition. Without it, people lose their sense of purpose and become dissatisfied, restless, and unproductive. Stalin understood this. Prisoners in his gulags were obliged to dig enormous holes in the snow, then fill them in. It broke their spirits.

As Semco grew, we had begun to suffer some symptoms of giantism, though we didn't recognize them at the time. Our salespeople, for example, insisted on filling out complex forms each time an order was received, stipulating exactly what the customer wanted, rather than just explaining the order and its peculiarities to our engineering, purchasing, and production people. There was nothing inherently wrong with this, except that it generated an enormous amount of paperwork. But the salespeople felt their department would be better protected if they could prove, in writing, that the customer didn't receive exactly what he wanted. Then our engineering department decided it would only hear complaints from shopfloor workers on Tuesdays and Thursdays from 2 p.m. to 4 p.m., rather than simply talking to workers whenever they came around. The teamwork that was flourishing at the food service equipment plant wasn't catching on elsewhere in the company. In fact, cliques were forming among managers, and much of the time Semco seemed to act distressingly like a government agency. We were even keeping visitors waiting at plant gates and reception areas.

We reacted by making the moves the classic organizational studies prescribe.

Semco's structure was what business school professors call a functional system. That meant production managers at our plants reported to the production director at our headquarters; the salespeople answered to the marketing director; the administrative officers to the financial director; and so on. It sounds orderly, but anyone who has worked in a diversified, multiplant company knows that a high percentage of decisions made under this long-distance arrangement are just plain wrong, and take too long as well. It is feudal system, isolating engineering from sales and sales from finance and generating solutions and strategies that serve one department at the expense of another.

No doubt because of this, European companies seem to prefer an organization based on a matrix system. Recognizing that a computer programmer at a distant plant can't possibly be instructed effectively solely from the administrative director's office, the lucky chap is put under dual command, reporting to his local plant manager as well. The matrix system provides a manager with two sources of information, two types of expertise, two perspectives on a particular problem or goal. It allows for a complete picture. But what if the head office wants something done that the plant manager feels isn't necessary? Multiply this conflict by hundreds or thousands of employees and you can see why people in matrix organisations are skilled diplomats, but not necessarily great businessmen. They have learned to survive in an environment that resembles the United Nations by behaving with extreme caution at all times. Of course, you can't try new ideas without taking risks or making mistakes, and people in companies organized under the matrix system generally don't.

Alas, I know all this from experience. So in 1986, after a flirtation with the matrix system, Semco tried yet another organizational plan: autonomous business units. We split the company into separate divisions, with a general manager for each. Theoretically, all the units would be independent. That was bound to breed competition between them, but we believed it would be a healthy competition, unlike interdepartmental warfare.

As a practical matter, however, his autonomous system led us back to a functional organization. That was because the autonomous business units needed some form of internal coordination and they chose what might be called a miniaturized functional system, in which managers inside each business unit reported to the general manager.

And guess what happened next. In no time at all, our managers were studying matrix systems, to alleviate the tension.

Round and round we went, and where we would stop nobody knew.

But wait. It was the dawn of the computer era. Maybe microchip management would save us.

Semco first flirted with computers back in 1980, when Harro and I went to New York and ordered an IBM PC. We had to wait three months for delivery, then learn commands in BASIC to run it. Even so, we had soon concluded that we had no choice but to computerize, and quickly.

Trouble was, we were convinced by our computer specialists that we needed to buy powerful machines that could talk to each other – and hire highly paid, difficult to get, and harder to keep information managers to run them. We even entertained the idea of hiring a systems vice-president to coordinate these information gurus – a prince of processors. As a matter of fact, we ran after a guy named Osiris, desperately trying to pull him away from a French company with all kinds of promises. By the time we had finished negotiating, he had a salary close to mine and someone to sweep the floor in front of him as he walked around. Thank God he didn't accept our offer. We did buy, lease, rent, and steal almost everything the salespeople from IBM, Bull, Fujitsu, and Hewlett-Packard showed us. But hey, we were doing all the trendy things then. We even had a Japanese strategic planning manager.

A master plan hundreds of pages long was drawn up listing the hardware and software we needed. No doubt about it, our information systems department was going to be the brains of the company. We hired analysts, digitation clerks, and programmers. We bought the smartest workstations we could find and hooked them to central data-processing servers that would link all our plants. People who used pencils to update inventory cards as new supplies arrived would now punch codes into computer terminals. Or would they? To make sure, we started brainwashing courses to turn our clerks into 21st-century aparatchiks.

In no time our old systems were no longer operational. Too bad our new, electronic systems weren't operational, either. We waited a month, two months, a year. There were always excuses – the training programme wasn't finished, the hardware had glitches, the software had bugs. It took us too long to realize we were heading down a yellow brick road.

I remember going to see the information system at the Ipiranga plant when I was working there.

'We're close to being on the air,' the resident computer-jockey, Wilmar Fagundes, told me proudly. 'You know, we just got reinforcements last month. We needed four programmers, three systems analysts, and two digitation clerks, but we were short of one of them. To run MRPS.' He must have noticed my blank expression. 'Manufacturing Resources and Planning System.'

I just nodded.

'So now we're hooked up to an IBM 3090, with 12 terminals to be installed,' Wilmar went on. 'Here are the Production Planning Trees.'

I gave him another blank look.

'See, here,' he said, spreading out a pile of enormous white sheets of paper covered with hundreds of tiny boxes. Wilmar was still working on the system, so the design had to be done manually before it could be fed into the machine. 'Every item in production is broken into subsets. Here, this is a simple one: a dishwasher. We have 15 sizes of dishwashers, with 11 variations of each size. Each has approximately 300 components.'

'And that's a simple one?' I said.

'Oh, yes. At the Santo Amaro plant, where we'll be installing the system next, there are products such as the biscuit machinery line. It has 12,000 components, 80 variations of 25 different sizes.

'Anyway, let's take an AM-12 dishwasher. Here it is.' Wilmar pointed. 'This list includes all of its subsets. Like branches of a tree, right? Each branch has its own branches, the components. And the components branch out into twigs.

'Here, this is a dishwasher arm. You know, the hollow metal tube that sprays the hot water on to the dishes. We have that tube in various kinds of metal. See, this branch is the stainless steel tube.' I watched his finger slide along. 'This stainless steel arm has a code. It will tell us if this arm is made here or bought from a supplier or if some of it is made here and some of it is bought from a supplier. This arm is the in the third category, incidentally. So let's look at the production process it goes through, right here on sheet number 257. Um, 256, 258. Where is 257?'

Wilmar muttered under his breath as the orderly stack of white sheets began to fly around the table.

I spent three and a half hours with Wilmar. I saw how the stainless steel arm was ordered by computer, how raw material was set aside – if available – or reordered. How the ordering procedure required three different quotes. How the winning bid was decided by weighing statistical data on delivery, price point-ratios, and payment terms. How inventory items were divided into categories by weight, cost, and the space they took up in a storeroom. How the nuts and washers that held the arm together were made from steel plates that were stocked in the yard and then moved by the computer through seven different areas of the factory and three production procedures – cutting, hole-boring, and welding.

What a difficult way to make money!

I'm sure the people who devised the system envisioned an automated, machine-managed plant where steel plates were gracefully eased through the rear door and elegantly crated dishwashers rolled out the front. Except it never happens that way. I've never been to a plant that doesn't have too many nuts for too few bolts, or shelves of some part for a product it no longer makes. Even in plants that function tolerably well, workers become servants to the Production Dragon, which is fed tons of parts and spits out finished products. This Dragon only smiles when people don't mess with it, or, for God's sake, try a new way of doing things. Sounds like Henry Ford in 1908, doesn't it?

When computers first arrived, they were mostly used for tasks that required the manipulation of huge amounts of information, such as conducting a national census, keeping track of military movements, or untangling huge social service programmes. Now they have evolved to the point where a machine that used to take up a whole room occupies a lap, or even a pocket, and they have insinuated themselves into just about very facet of business. People can't think without a keyboard at their fingers and a monitor in front of their noses. But something curious has happened: computer-generated information, which was the means, has become the end. Instead of helping us organize data, computers are drowning us in it.

The explosion of computer-generated information began at a time when companies were run by executives who weren't part of the computer age, and so could be wrapped around the fingers of computers professionals, who leveraged their special knowledge into a sort of priesthood inventing enchanted words and sacred hymns, throwing hardware and software at people more comfortable with Tupperware, and making most us feel like dimwits. Older executives, especially frightened, thought to themselves: 'I'll hold back this stuff as long as I can, and when that's no longer possible I'll pretend that I understand what they say and buy as much of it as I can.'

The result has been a grossly inappropriate use of these extraordinary machines. Reports are fattened up with charts and graphs and thousands of numbers, most of them unneeded and unheeded. Everything has become excessively complicated and confused, which is exactly the condition computers were supposed to remedy. I can shamelessly say that Semco was swept along on the electronic tide, going from the stone age to the space age in just a few years. But the more I learned about microchip management, the more I came to fear it.

I once visited a small unit of ours three days before the end of the month.

'What do you think this month's billings will be?' I innocently asked the resident computer wonk.

'We already know. We have the number here, in the terminal.'

'How can you? There are still three days left in the month.'

'Oh, no. We stop billing four working days before the end of the month.'

I was shocked. It meant inventory was tied up longer than it had to be, increasing interest costs, and orders would sit for days before leaving the plant, increasing customers frustration. Just picture Federal Express stopping for a few days each month to feed paperwork to its computers.

'Well, we have to fill out the basic invoice, send it to the head office, wait for batch-processing on the central computer . . .'

'Wait,' I interrupted. 'Why can't you just issue the invoices on your own terminal?'

'Because then they wouldn't be automatically recorded in the accounts receivable program, which cross-references all the invoices.'

'I see,' I said, although I didn't. 'Go on.'

'The lot is batch-processed after all invoices from all our units are gathered – we run them in numerical order, for tax purposes – and then our invoices are returned to us. And then we can ship the products.'

'How did you do all this in the past?'

'Oh, that was very primitive. We would wait until the last minute, then type out the invoice. Sometimes we would be here in the middle of the night, getting invoicing out of the way, to make the month's sales larger.'

'How many invoices did you issue then?'

'About 150.'

'And now?'

'About 120.'

Two days later the unit was off the computer and back on the primitive, manual system. And soon invoicing rose 15 per cent, as employees got back to making last-minute shipments in all-our efforts to move finished products out the door. And within a month all the other computer terminals at our business units had been returned to headquarters, and our mainframe there was disconnected. We no longer have all those programmers or keypunch operators; we have dismantled our information systems department and thrown out our systems master plan. We gave all our techies an opportunity to make a living elsewhere and sighed as we sat back and relaxed. In typical Semco fashion, whoever decides he needs a computer goes out and buys one. Whatever anyone feels is necessary is all right with us. The catch is, they have to learn to operate it themselves. Our worries about making one computer compatible with another are over. It's every microprocessor for itself and to hell with the economies of scale.

This much seemed clear: either you can adopt sophisticated, complex systems to try to manage the complications, or you can simplify everything.

Finally, we chose the other path.

And we had the perfect guide – João Vendramin, our balding, bespectacled in-house economist and wise man, who we had the extreme good fortune to inherit in the Hobart deal.

Though he had occasional outburst, João was usually reserved and thoughtful. He certainly *looked* relaxed, having abandoned suits and ties. I can still remember the snickering when João would sit at our mahogany conference table, his feet atop the polished surface. Ever careful about expensive furniture, he would always take off his shoes first.

João would lean back in silence. Then he would suddenly break in, quoting Aristotle or Machiavelli or offering up his own offbeat pronouncement. It got to the point where people would defuse the tension during our meetings by saying things like, 'As João would say about our production schedules, you can't fly bicycles in stratus-cumulus clouds.' And he would just smile.

Who better to send around the world than João? Who better to visit companies that were breaking rules, or eliminating them, and setting out on their own? These were the companies we felt could help us solve our organizational problems.

So off João went to Sweden, where he watched assembly-line workers at Volvo who, instead of performing one task, worked in small teams to put an entire car together. (This system fell out of favour years later, but largely because of union and management problems, not because of a lack of teamwork.) In Delaware, he visited W.L. Gore, a company that had discarded conventional organization charts and created what they call a 'lattice organization' with non-hierarchical relationships between jobs. Gore had stripped the titles from managers' business cards and adopted a system in which salaries corresponded to monthly performance and were adjusted by groups of employees who had the option of cutting an individual's pay to zero (which, according to the late Bill Gore, tended to discourage further work from the party involved). As Samsung in Korea and Toyota, Kyocera, Sharp, and TDK in Japan, João saw other ways in which modern production methods and worker involvement were joined, although their systems depended on such cultural traits as submissiveness and veneration of the company.

'There is no way to treat employees as responsible and

honest adults unless you let them know and influence what is
going on around them.' Vendramin told us when he returned
from his world tour. 'And there is no way to let them become
involved in the decisions that affect them if the plant they
work in has too many people.

'Yes, there are schemes and mechanisms to convince
people that they matter, but they don't work for long. At some
point the workers notice that they are never consulted about
the really important decisions. The only way to change is to
make each business unit small enough so that people can
understand what is going on and contribute accordingly.'

According to Vendramin's diagnosis, Semco was already
afflicted with an acute case of bigness, brought on by our
acquisitions and our success. The cure was logical, if
unfashionable in an age of conglomeration. Factories that had
become too large for their own good should be broken into
units small enough to ensure that the people who worked in
them would feel human again. In a small factory, it is possible
to know everyone by their first name, to debate plans and
strategies, to feel involved, *to belong*.

Vendramin's proposal was that Semco should replicate
itself like an amoeba. So we prepared to divide.

fifteen

DIVIDE AND PROSPER

'It's airy-fairy,' sniffed Henrique Pinto, the dark-haired, moustached general manager of our Santo Amaro plant and one of a dozen or so managers gathered in a third-floor conference room.

'Airy-fairy?' I asked.

'The advantages you're listing on the board can't be measured, but the disadvantages are concrete. And costly. I call that airy-fairy.'

'He's right,' said Clovis. 'The cost of duplicating security guards, receptionists, secretaries, and all the rest is easy to add up. Motivation and the feeling of belonging can't be quantified.' He paused. 'But that doesn't mean that the monetary value attached to the easily measurable items is greater.'

'Then how will we know if we are making the right decision?' Henrique wondered.

'We won't,' I said. 'It's really a leap of faith.'

'We've taken leaps of faith in the past, and fallen,' Henrique broke in. 'Like investing in Flakt. It's been three years since we bought it, and it will take us five more, at least, to see a profit.'

'You're right, Henrique,' said Vendramin, who was sitting with his shoeless feet on the conference table (as usual), staring out of the window (as usual). 'But we made the same decision about the biscuit machinery line. We spent hundreds of thousands of dollars before seeing a return. But then we recovered everything in a single year.'

'So, what now?' Henrique persisted. 'Do we go ahead and divide all the plants, no matter what the cost? What is it you call it, João?'

'The amoeba approach,' Vendramin said with a smile.

We had been discussing the amoeba approach for weeks, with no discernible progress. The engineers and other technically-oriented souls, like Pinto, were sceptical about the gains that might results even if by making our plants smaller our workers somehow became more productive. But our problems – the meetings that ran too long, the power struggles between groups of managers, the impossibility of making everyone in a plant feel like they were a part of something, the alienation I still saw all around Semco, the lack of cathedral-builders – weren't going to go away by themselves. They were, I believed, rooted in bigness, the cure for which, if expensive, was simple. We would divide ourselves like an amoeba – and, we hoped, prosper.

In some cases, it would mean moving workers to a new factory. Other plants would just be split down the middle, like the motel room Clark Gable and Claudette Colbert shared in *It Happened One Night*. In any event, the new units, like those from which they sprang, would be fully autonomous. Managers would be free to manage as they wished, Semco-style. Our centralized corporate staff would provide support in such areas as accounting and human resources and, when asked, offer opinions on strategy. But if a unit didn't need the people at head-quarters, that was fine with us. If a plant achieved the performance we all expected, months would go by before it might receive a visit from any of us. They would deserve our benign neglect.

There were huge costs associated with Vendramin's amoeba plan, as the number-crunchers kept reminding us. What was now one factory would have two of everything, from janitorial staff to loading docks and from data processing departments to parking areas. The two plants would also require that we carry more inventory, in two storerooms. And then there were big-ticket items, such as the cost of additional machines and buying or leasing new buildings.

Sometimes it seemed foolish even to me. But we went ahead anyway, basing our decision on two feelings corporate managers are usually afraid to trust: intuition and faith.

*

In 1986 Brazil underwent a drastic economic transformation. A new economic policy froze prices and cut inflation from 25 per cent a month to zero. The finance minister, a gaunt, serious, quixotic man named Dilson Funaro, was intent on taming an inflationary culture in which everyone raised prices in anticipation of coming rises, perpetuating an unending cycle of increases. Funaro was terminally ill with lymphatic cancer and knew it. This was his chance to make history and he was determined to make the most of it, even if it meant fining and closing companies and arresting executives who added so much as a dime to the price of their products.

Never mind that the monthly inflation rate was back to double digits by the end of a year, or that a few suppliers found ways to bypass the rules, either because they imported raw materials whose prices were quoted in unfrozen dollars, or were more creative about assessing special 'freight' charges or other new fees, or, better yet, had a monopoly on the market. But for a while the plan worked, Funaro was a hero, and the demand for products from a euphoric country surged.

Our Ipiranga plant manufactured two distinct lines: mechanical products and electronic products. The former included dishwashers, mechanical scales, meat-grinders, dough mixers, and cold-cut slicers; the latter consisted of electronic scales and printers that retailers used with them. The electronic products were a problem. We purchased many of the components from importers, so our costs continued to rise. But since the price for our scales was a matter of record, it would have been easy for any customer to lodge a complaint if we increased our prices. Our hands were tied.

Before the economic plan, we had been selling up to 300 scales a month, for revenues of $3 million a year. After it, sales shot up to 500, 700, then 1,200 scales a month, but since our price was fixed but that of our suppliers wasn't, we were losing money with every sale. And that wasn't all. The plant was unable to keep up with the demand; orders piled up, our inventory became unbalanced, and hundreds of scales would sit in the production area, waiting for a single microchip that just wouldn't arrive, no matter how we implored suppliers.

And on top of that, 10 per cent of our scales were being returned to the plant for quality problems. Customers would plug them in at stores hundreds or thousands of miles away and watch them sputter and die.

What all this meant was that we were rapidly losing control of the business. That made the Ipiranga plant an ideal candidate for the amoeba treatment. We decided to segregate the electronics side of the business, moving it to a new plant at Jabaquara, ten miles away. To run the new unit, which we called DBData, we chose a person named José João Fiasco. (I know. But what could we do? That was his name.)

Fiasco was a heavy, well-dressed man with a high IQ and impeccable manners. He had been born to an upper middle class family and had both an engineering degree and an MBA. He had been a successful sales administration manager at Santo Amaro, but had no management experience or any direct contact with workers. He was, however, a true believer in Semco's policy of trusting its employees.

His top lieutenant was Rogerio Ottolia. I had met Rogerio two years earlier, when he managed a plant Clovis and I were considering buying. Rogerio impressed us with his enthusiasm and unflappability in the face of our persistent questions about engineering, finance, and sales. The deal didn't work out, but we hired Rogerio first chance we got. An electronic engineer by trade, Rogerio had a loping walk and bright, dark eyes. He would prove to be a never-ending source of innovation.

Off they went, packing up the machinery and inventory and setting out with 30 other employees to their new, 15,000-square-foot shop. Once they settled in, the mostly young work force, some of them electronics experts, created an entirely new culture. The Kids, as they soon were known, culled through the inventory and discovered, among other items, three years' worth of expensive integrated circuits for a scale that was no longer in production, several hundred displays that didn't fit the housing of the scale they were making, and hundreds of transistors that didn't work on any scale but were somehow never returned to the supplier. The villain was

MRPS, which had been ordering some items at double and triple the proper rate. Not wanting to risk a repetition, The Kids set up a just-in-time inventory system and installed a Brazilianized Kanban, based on the Japanese system in which components and raw materials are colour-coded according to their use in the assembly process and stocked near the machines, so workers can immediately see when they are running low.

Soon sales at the new unit were adjusted to meet its production capacity, and the defective sales were recalled and fixed. In just a few months, DBData became Semco's flagship operation, with productivity twice that of the food service equipment plant, inventories reduced by 40 per cent, and defects down to less than 1 per cent.

What caused this success? The Kids innovated all over the place. Each day started with a short meeting attended by all the plant's employees, who wore white coveralls, Japanese-style. Financial information was regularly posted on the bulletin board, and an open office plan encouraged easy access to everyone by everyone. My favourite innovation was a board at the plant entrance with the name of each employee and next to it a wooden peg. As each person arrived in the morning he would hang one of three metal tags on the peg: a green tag stood for 'Good Mood', a yellow tag for 'Careful', and a red tag for 'Not Today – Please.' Maybe it was cute, but The Kids took it seriously, selecting their tags carefully and paying heed to those of others.

Incidentally, the green tags usually predominated.

The remaining employees at Ipiranga were divided into two units: those who made dishwashers and those who made the slicers and peelers and other food preparation products. The mood improved there, too, especially on the dishwasher side, where assembly workers – going one better than the slicing team – altered the production system, stocking the components on the shop floor and working in teams that moved about the plant as needed, rather than remaining on the same spot. A welder might assemble machines one day, then drive a forklift the next. Similarly, machinists would change from tool to tool, depending on the need.

The sceptics had always argued that we would need many more people and machines when the plants were divided. In fact, each of our three new units had its own plant management, sales staff, and financial department. But when it came to the work force, we were astonished. We had asked each of the three general mangers to choose the people they wanted in their units, much like kids choosing sides for a playground baseball game. Iotti, who was taking over the dishwasher unit, and Wilmar Fagundes, our computer expert who at this point was heading the mechanical products unit, made out their wish lists. We added them up, then included the people working with Fiasco at DBData, and realized that there were still a dozen or so workers who hadn't been spoken for. Each manager planned to use more outside subcontractors and have employees double up on skills and tasks, so they would work more efficiently. (The extra people were mostly retrained for other jobs.)

Quality also rose at the two Ipiranga divisions, as it had at DBData. And all three units eventually began delivering products the next day, which was unheard of in Hobart's history, or in Semco's for that matter.

Rather than creating waste by breaking up our plants, we were eliminating it. My guess is that as Ipiranga grew bigger and more complex, there were more nooks and crannies where marginal or unproductive employees could hide. The paper shufflers multiplied, too.

How big is too big? The British author, Anthony Jay, in his book, *The Corporation Man*, reminds us that we have been hunters for five million years, farmers for nearly 300 generations, and industrialists for a relative blink of an eye. Through virtually all of human existence we have been part of small groups, usually of five to fifteen people. How can a corporation ignore so much experience and expect its employees to adapt to groups of 1,000, much less 10,000?

By all means hire 10,000 workers, if you have the products

and the markets. Just organize them in small business units. A company can be gigantic with 1,000 employees if they are all under the same roof. Similarly, there are small companies with more than 50,000 workers, but you won't find more than a few hundred working together. The truth is, there isn't a programme at Semco that won't work at a company with 5,000 or 10,000 or 100,000 employees, so long as giantism is contained by breaking up the work force into small units.

How small is small enough? For some companies the magic number is 500. For others, the maximum might be a few dozen. Usually, though, people will perform at their potential only when they know almost everyone around them, which is generally when there are no more than 150 people. That is our experience, anyway. Then again, we only had 200 employees before we split up the Ipiranga factory, and interoffice mail would take two days to move from one department to another, a distance of less than 300 yards. Giantism, again.

Yes, some factories are harder to divide than others. You can't just take a piece of an auto assembly line and move it across town. The challenge is to find the correct criteria for division – by product, by market, by machine, whatever. If the equipment is impossible to move, then divide the existing factory in two, but make sure there are different people in each unit responsible for such areas as sales, marketing, production, finance, human resources, and all the rest.

In times of robust economic growth we have found our divided plants make more money than they did when they were larger. And we have also found that smaller plants bounce back from bad times or a crisis much faster than larger ones.

From all this I have come to believe that economy of scale is one of the most overrated concepts in business. It exists, of course, but it is overtaken by the diseconomies of scale much sooner than most people realize.

sixteen

THE INMATES TAKE OVER
THE ASYLUM

The Santo Amaro plant was the next candidate for division. We decided that, with its healthy backlog of orders, the marine products division had outgrown its allotted space and needed to find new quarters.

We began our search in the traditional way, leaving everything to the plant's general manager and keeping our plans secret, to avoid frightening the employees. The manager contacted several real estate agents and they soon found several interesting buildings. The trouble was, they were in places that many of our workers, especially those who depended on public transport, would have a hard time getting to, so we stood to lose a large number of them.

Then we realized that we were conducting the search in a manner contrary to our new principles. We weren't being participative. So we assembled the unit's 120 employees and we gave them all the pertinent facts – the reasons for moving, the budget for the new space, and everything else we could think of. Search committees were formed and by the next Monday the workers had come up with dozens of suggestions for a location.

A few weeks later we closed the plant for a day and everyone piled into buses to visit the three most likely possibilities. Then, at a series of assemblies, the workers picked their next workplace – a vacant factory not far from the Santo Amaro plant, on a street called Nacoes Unidas.

It was an excellent choice in every respect but one: it was next to a factory that was frequently on strike. We moved in

anyway. We never considered overriding our workers'
decision. Our credibility would have gone to hell.

Having found their new plant, our workers didn't stop there.
They designed the layout, in the process pushing us all
another step forward.

Instead of a series of lathes and then a series of welding
operations and so on, all in a long line Henry Ford-style, the
workers formed small groups of different machines. The idea
was to have, at each of these clusters, a team whose member
would fashion a product from beginning to end, giving them
accountability for the product's quality and the enormous
satisfaction that comes with complete a task. What's more,
these workers would know how to operate all the machines in
their cluster, not just one, and do whatever else was needed,
too, even drive forklifts to and from the storeroom. This type
of organization, which had first been adopted by the workers
on the dishwasher line at the Ipiranga plant, was known as a
manufacturing cell.

Frederick Winslow Taylor wouldn't have approved. Before
there was a Henry Ford, there was a Frederick Winslow
Taylor. In fact, there might not have been a Henry Ford without a Frederick Winslow Taylor. He more than anyone was
the Godfather of the modern factory, in which thousands of
nameless, faceless drones carry out unrelentingly repetitious
tasks under ever-vigilant supervision. It was Taylor's belief
that workers were most efficient if their jobs consisted of a
small number of distinct movements, all scientifically choreographed to fit their anatomy. Taylor broke down complicated
manufacturing processes into numerous such tasks, each of
which was to be assigned to a set of workers. This segmenta-
tion and specification of labour, all carefully codified through
rigid job descriptions, was, Taylor maintained, the indisputable key to maximum productivity. And so one worker
would shovel coal out of a bin into a pile, and another would
shovel it out of the pile, carry it a few feet and dump it into
another pile, and still another would shovel it from that
second pile on to a conveyor belt. And all three laboured

under the watchful eyes of a foreman. Multiply this grim little tableau by hundreds or even thousands of workers and you have today's gigantic temples of mass production.

Nor are the stark lessons of Taylorism confined to factories. A few years back, the late, unlamented Eastern Airlines was sold to Texas Air, a company many times smaller. What caused this strange inversion? Taylor and his job descriptions, in my opinion. For years, Eastern dominated many of the best routes on the East Coast. It grew steadily, but as it did Eastern's pilots, flight attendants, and ground service personnel began to insist on detailed job descriptions. With the support of their unions, the airline's employees strictly limited themselves only to what was in these descriptions, refusing to do anything else. The idle time of a baggage handler did nothing to alleviate the temporary lack of a ticket agent or maintenance worker during a crunch. Eastern found itself having to hire more employees, while workers already on the payroll weren't always busy.

By contrast, Texas Air hired non-union workers who were willing to perform all sorts of tasks. On days off, a pilot might sell tickets; during peak hours a flight attendant might handle baggage. Texas Air took off and eventually swallowed Eastern, a much bigger company that had become inefficient and overloaded with employees. (I don't mean to suggest that Texas Air didn't have its own problems, which I believe were chiefly the result of its failure to make workers feel more involved in the company.)

Whenever I find myself in a conventional factory, I am reminded of how little we have advanced since Taylor. He still intimidates students of management. (Maybe it's his imposing name. Perhaps people would feel freer to question his teachings if they remembered that he didn't study at MIT or the Stanford Business School.) I believe Taylor's precise job descriptions limit workers' potential and constrain the possibility of job enrichment, which dampens their motivation. Just think how much better job descriptions would be if they included not only what employees do but what they want to do.

'My dear sir,' Taylor would undoubtedly ask if he could, 'isn't your factory going to become a humongous mess?'

In the terms Taylor is familiar with, probably yes. He would never condone a system in which, depending on what needed to be done, a person could be a lathe operator or a grinder, assemble the final product, maintain the machinery, drive a forklift loaded with supplies, help clean the work area or even paint the walls of his corner of the plant. Taylor would be appalled if workers started to make thingamajigs and screw together whatnots entirely on their own. Or if they discovered that making suggestions, innovating and whistling at work are not forbidden.

In such a system the driving force of productivity is motivation and genuine interest, not predetermined routines and hulking foremen. That's the difference between Taylorism and Semco's manufacturing cells. We don't believe in fragmentation. We want workers to understand that they are part of a whole. And we want them to figure out the best way to do their jobs. They're probably going to find more efficient ways of doing them than Taylor or his followers ever would have.

From our food service equipment and marine products plants the manufacturing cells spread throughout Semco. I assume these layouts are designed by the factory committee in consultation with our engineering staff, but I don't really know for sure. It's been a spontaneous process, different at each plant.

But if these cells made workers happy, they were giving some of our fiscal types heartburn. The cells sawed off the branch on which these sparrows of salary systems were perched, condemning the analyists to one hundred years of solitude. Top managers almost always prefer the tranquillity of traditional methods to the risk of apparent disorganization that will rain down on any company that slowly frees its employees from working conditions based on narrowly defined parameters.

In their squeamishness our managers were no different from some union leaders, who wasted little time reminding us that the workers all had job descriptions that precisely determined their pay. (I guess that made them Taylorists, too.) What would Semco's multi-dimensional workers receive? Would they be paid like welders or forklift drivers or machinists? Naturally, the union wanted us to pay them as if they were in the most lucrative category all the time. So even if someone only spent 30 per cent of his day machining, and the rest of the day driving a forklift, he would be considered a higher-paid machinist.

We disagreed, of course. But keeping a minute-by-minute log of what a worker was doing was out of the question. Instead, we developed a 'basket of jobs' approach: every year workers reflect on their various duties and the approximate time they spend doing each of them. Then it's just a matter of consulting a salary survey and doing the maths. As jobs and activities change, their individual formulae change.

Some managers had another worry about the cells. They thought that if we let our workers take over their factories, they would never let us install any machinery that would eliminate jobs. But our workers knew what labour-saving machines could do for our ability to compete, and we've had many occasions where a factory committee will actually promote a new machine they think we need, even at the cost of some jobs.

What's more, workers in our cells have a way of managing more and more of the manufacturing process. Take quality control. We used to have separate departments at each unit to evaluate our products. But with time our workers took over this role, enabling us to eliminate jobs. Workers also recruit and expel new members of their teams. Today, anyone who applies to be a machinist at Semco will be interviewed by a group of machinists, not an executive, which is the worst thing that can happen to him, because he might be able to talk his way past a manager but not past people who know all about being machinists and may one day be his co-workers. If they say yes, the person has the job. I've not heard a case in which shop-floor workers have opposed someone and a manager has gone ahead and hired him. I can't imagine a Semco manager taking such a risk. Nor do I know of a case in which someone is approved by everybody on the shop floor but rejected by the manager. In our system it isn't possible for one person to overrule everyone else.

Can I definitely say our manufacturing cells have made Semco more profitable? Some of the pluses and minuses have been tricky. True, our manufacturing cells don't respect the so-called economies of scale. Instead of buying, say, 20 machine casings at a time, we tend to buy casings in much smaller quantities, since many items are stocked in the cell, and there's no space for extras. That is more expensive than buying in bulk.

Then again, maintaining large inventories of casings can tie up capital. Our inventory levels have fallen to very low levels with the cells, and each year we do away with more and more stocking space. Indeed, some of our units turn over their complete inventory 17 times a year, as against an industry average of slightly more than three such rotations.

In some cases, it takes cells longer to make a product than it would on a traditional assembly line. But delivery times have still fallen. And there are all those quality control departments we don't need any more.

More importantly, it is clear that workers in our cells have much more interesting jobs than those who mechanically repeat the same, simple set of tasks the whole day. And the cells have made people work much more closely, so our plants are much more finely tuned. This has translated into greater productivity.

Meanwhile, back at Santo Amaro, things were looking up, too. Henrique Pinto and the employees at his mixer unit now had the whole plant to themselves, and were becoming more organized and more productive as time went by.

There was a backlog of orders for biscuit machinery they made that translated into two years of production. We had already spent four years and well over half a million dollars to get into that market, and were now seeing the return on our investment, much to the disappointment of those who considered our entrance into the business a mistake.

The unit needed more office space, better ventilation and a new kitchen. Given the rosy cash-flow projections, it seemed prudent to invest more in the plant. Anyway, the expense would have been far greater had not our workers done much of the work themselves. The ventilation system was designed by Semco-Flakt engineers. The kitchen was supplied mainly by the Hobart unit and installed by a company in partnership with them. And most of the construction and painting was performed by the workers at Santo Amaro. It was just another example of what can happen when you reject Taylorism.

seventeen

SHARING THE WEALTH

All of us were ready to retire. Or better yet, become consultants.

We thought we deserved it. We had unleashed an extraordinary force and were overwhelmed by the results. With prices under control throughout Brazil, 1986 had been a good year for Semco. Without plants divided, autonomous, invigorated, and at labour peace, and our workers more involved in their jobs than ever, 1987 was better.

The food service equipment plant was going great guns, especially the new, worker-designed assembly line for dishwashers. The Kids at DBData, in their white uniforms, were at least as impressive. Santo Amaro had 80 per cent of the market for biscuit-making machinery. And at all our plants, the factory committees, famous for their obstinacy at other companies, had helped us cut expenses drastically.

Because of all this, Semco was making money – $2.2 million in 18 months. I realized it was time to give everyone a stake in the added wealth they were creating. It was time for profit-sharing.

No more than a half-dozen Brazilian companies had profit-sharing at the time, and all of them had merely implemented off-the-shelf plans that unilaterally and arbitrarily doled out the rewards according to top management's dictates (or whims). The companies wanted to motivate their workers, but at the same time retained the power to treat some employees better than others. This is a formula for resentment and division.

We decided we wanted a new kind of profit-sharing plan, one that would not only be fully comprehensible to our workers but also controlled by them. Before we could share the wealth, however, we knew we would have to share something even more valuable: information.

No one can expect the spirit of involvement and partnership to flourish without an abundance of information available even to the most humble employee. I know all the arguments against a policy of full disclosure. Employees will use the numbers to argue for raises in good times, or be frightened by the numbers in bad times. Even worse, trade secrets will be leaked to the competition.

Maybe. But the advantages of openness and truthfulness far outweigh the disadvantages. And a company that doesn't share information when times are good loses the right to request solidarity and concessions when they are not.

The origins of corporate secrecy can be traced to the insecurity of executives who possessed the technical skills to scale the corporate pyramid but weren't mature enough to handle the height. They wanted to be seen as different from those who had not attained their perch. By keeping their salaries secret, they felt they would keep themselves apart from others. And, of course, if they had one secret, it was easy to make others believe they possessed more, and so were even more powerful, since in the modern organization power rests with information.

The problem with secrets is that people usually just assume the worst, whether it's about profits or salaries. We took a poll a few years earlier in which we asked everyone at Semco how much money they thought the company made. This was before we had made many changes, and our employees apparently thought we were unconscionably greedy. How else can we explain the widely held belief that our profits were between 20 and 30 per cent of our revenues? (Most companies would be pleased with a profit of 7 or 8 per cent.) After that, I didn't need to be convinced that we would all be better off if our employees knew the whole truth.

When we told our managers that we wanted to share information about our financial performance with our workers, many were alarmed. They thought the first thing the employees would want to know was how much we were paid.

So we held our first meeting to discuss the monthly operating reports with a few dozen representatives of the factory committees and what was the first question they asked? How much money does a top manager at Semco make?

We answered truthfully: $50,000 to $100,000 a year, including bonuses. The shock was palpable. After all, this was a country where the minimum wage was $1,500 a year. From that day on, our managers have been known by the factory workers as maharajas. (Incidentally, the gap between Semco's lowest- and highest-paid employees has grown much narrower since then.)

The truth may not be pretty, or easily explained, but it is always better out in the open. We don't tack lists of salaries on a bulletin board, but the information is mostly available for the asking. Yes, several executives requested that their salaries be kept confidential, and we obliged because their privacy is important, too. But it didn't matter, since enough salaries were known to give everyone an extremely accurate idea of pay at all levels of the company.

It was soon clear that if our executives were ashamed of their salaries, it might be because they felt they weren't really earning them, for if they merited their pay they could easily prove their worth, whether it was based on specialized knowledge, experience, education, or the mastery of a large department with a big budget and staff. Executives should be proud of what they earn, and their salaries ought to provide everyone with an incentive to rise.

In time our workers came to accept Semco's executive pay and didn't try to get us to lower it, as we were warned would happen. But they weren't shy about letting us know when they thought we had too many highly paid executives floating around.

We soon made all sorts of financial information available besides salaries. Of course, not everyone could understand it. Some workers didn't know the difference between profits and revenue. So with the union's help we began classes to teach them to read balance sheets, cash flow statements, and other documents. I don't know of another company with such a course.

Clovis went to the initial session and couldn't wait to tell me the first question. 'What we want to know,' one worker said, 'is how does the company cook the books?'

It has been rooted in the corporate consciousness that profits belong to those who invest the capital. Of course, this is the rule even at companies at which the founder originally invested very little and which grew largely because of the energy and talents of the employees. Entrepreneurs aren't dumb.

But some companies, looking for new ways to motivate workers, began to share the profits with them. This is hardly a socialist conceit: few ideas are as capitalist as profit-sharing, which rewards with part of a company's earnings the people who help generate this blessed surplus. Nor is it new. What is an annual bonus, after all, but a form of profit-sharing?

Some early profit-sharing plans were structured to return a portion of the proceeds generated by employee suggestions. From there it was but a hop, skip, and jump to plans that shared the total profits. A good idea became a trend, a trend became a fad, and a fad became a movement as companies sought a quick fix for uninterested, unmotivated work forces. But many just shelled out the money, leaving employees in the dark about how the amounts were arrived at. This undercut the plan's effectiveness, and recent studies have found that in a high percentage of cases profit-sharing doesn't work.

In 1986, Semco sponsored a seminar that brought together leaders of half a dozen companies with profit-sharing plans for a debate before an audience of 300 executives, consultants, and labour leaders. The panel's conclusion? There wasn't one, which was more than a hint that profit-sharing is hard to get right.

The truth is that profit-sharing doesn't create employee involvement, it requires it. It works only when it crowns a broad and comprehensive programme of participation. Semco wasn't interested in having a few executives decide who got what. We wanted the beneficiaries to make those decisions.

But which beneficiaries? By now Semco had eight autonomous units in four plants making dozens of products for
three sectors of the economy. Delivery times for our products
ranged from one day for a digital scale to two years for a
turnkey biscuit factory. That's complexity. Would this special
payment to our workers be based on the total profit made by
the whole company, or the profit of each plant, or the profit of
each independent unit, or even the profit attributed to each
team of workers within those units? How would an employee
from a unit that failed to make a profit and didn't get an extra
cheque feel working in the same plant as a person who
received a large additional payment because his unit did well?
Should the distribution formula be weighted to consider
salary, length of service, or performance? Don't payments
that are proportional to a worker's earnings reinforce the gap
between the lowest- and the highest-paid employees? Indeed,
doesn't the distribution of profits represent an immense
amount of money for the company but, once it's divided
among a thousand workers, become only a modest sum for
each? Is it worth it?

There were decisions to make, and the fear, especially on
my part, that an improperly implemented profit-sharing
plan could undo gains we had already achieved. As was our
policy, we ignored rules and precedents and worked from
reality, holding shop-floor discussion and meetings with
factory committees and union leaders over the next year and
a half.

How much of our profits would we return to those who
helped make them? That was the starting point. We weren't
about to pick a number out of the air, or let our workers do
that, either. So we negotiated. We began with Semco's total
profits, the revenues minus expenses. Then we agreed that 40
per cent would be deducted for taxes, 25 per cent for dividends to shareholders, and another 12 per cent for reinvest-
ment – the minimum the company needed to continue to
prosper. That left 23 per cent.

Then the workers went to work thrashing out the distribution issue by themselves. An accounting clerk named Claudio,

who represented the factory committee at Santo Amaro, then one of our most profitable plants, summed up the major sticking point at one of the first meetings: 'Why should we share our profit with plants that aren't making money?' he said. 'It isn't fair.'

There was a lot of discussion on what was fair. Finally, the employees decided that the Semco Profit-Sharing Programme (or SemcoPar) would work like this: each quarter, the profit made by each autonomous unit is calculated and 23 per cent of that sum is delivered to the employees of that unit. (Of course, given the Brazilian economy we don't always have profits to share and we won't give consolation prizes.) What happens to the money after that is up to them. They can vote to divvy it up by head count or they can consider years of service with the company, salary, or other criteria. They can decide that, rather than distribute the money, they will use it for some other purpose, such as for loans so workers can buy houses. But whatever they decide, it only applies for that quarterly payment. Three months later they have to decide all over again.

That's the theory, anyway. In reality, every Semco unit has always decided to split the money up evenly. That means everyone gets the same amount. Not the same percentage, the same amount. Someone making $10,000 a year receives the same profit-sharing cheque as someone making $100,000 a year.

This is not how profit-sharing conventionally works. Many companies simply take a percentage and then apply it to an employee's salary, which makes profit-sharing more valuable for those at the top. Our employees have skewed the system the other way, which is fine with us. Now profit-sharing helps balance our salary structure and enables us to recognize and reward those without fancy degrees who nevertheless contribute ten hours of their best effort every day.

As principal shareholder – and patron – of SemcoPar, I have to admit I initially thought 23 per cent was awfully high. At other companies it runs between 8 and 12 per cent. But I kept telling myself I stood to make at least as much money in partnership with a motivated workforce as I would as the sole beneficiary of the fruits of less inspired workers.

What would you rather have, the tail of an elephant or an entire ant?

eighteen

MILES OF FILES

We were in yet another meeting, hacking our way through an agenda of small, bureaucratic items like so many weeds in an overgrown garden, when we came to the purchase of $50,000 worth of filing cabinets. Several departments had been waiting for months for the cabinets and in desperation had decided to pool their requests. I guess they thought we would be more impressed by their plight.

The discussion had turned to possible suppliers and prices when someone at the table said, 'What the hell are people putting in their files, anyway?'

We went around the room and everyone seemed to have his own explanation for The Great File Crunch. 'Well, of course, they wouldn't be filing anything that doesn't need to be filed,' was the majority view. I wasn't sure.

We didn't buy a single new filing cabinet that day. Instead, we decided to stop the company for half a day and hold The First Biannual Semco File Inspection and Clean-Out. That was the only way we would know for sure what all those cabinets contained.

Our instructions were simple: we told everyone to look inside every file folder and purge every non-essential piece of paper. They were to ask themselves a question attributed to Alfred Sloan of General Motors: 'What is the worst thing that can happen if I throw this out?'

On the appointed day our office workers arrived in jeans and overalls, ready to dig into our musty, dusty archives. I kept exhorting everyone not to be frightened about what might happen if they pitched one document too many. If it was really important, surely a customer or a supplier or someone would have a copy.

I knew how they felt. I felt that way myself. I was one of Semco's biggest file hogs, with four large cabinets and a request for two more. And that was on top of the two and half cabinets each of my three secretaries had.

After our clean-up, I trimmed down to a single cabinet, and that was pretty much how it went throughout the company. People would laugh when they saw six-year-old telexes, ancient catalogues, business cards with the names of people they didn't remember and companies they had never heard of. They also came across plenty of documents they desperately needed only a few months before, but just couldn't find. The clean-up went so well that when everyone had finished Semco auctioned off dozens of unwanted filing cabinets.

That made us think more about our compulsion to collect. We realized that we were filing lots of documents we had no conceivable reason to keep, making more work for ourselves than a natural business required. Just how much of our clerical work, we asked ourselves, was similarly unnecessary?

As our thinking evolved, we began to focus on our so-called support staff. I kept thinking of a story I had heard about an assistant cashier who had applied for work at Semco. At her interview, she was asked to describe her current job. 'I stamp the pink copies and hand them to another girl,' she said. When our interviewer pressed her, he discovered that the woman didn't know anything about her employer, except that it paid her to stamp the pink copies and hand them to another girl.

Which is why Chaplin's *Modern Times* is one of my favourite movies. The issue is with us still. Can people truly be inspired by purely repetitive clerical work performed without any sense of context? How much of it is really necessary? What if we could eliminate all those dead-end jobs and keep only positions with the potential for making people feel gratified? Could we run our company without secretaries, receptionists, and personal assistants? I suppose I don't have to tell you my answer to those questions.

Of course, I didn't think for a moment that our executives would take my word for it. So I staged a demonstration: I sent a ten-page article from *The Harvard Business Review* to Clovis, whose office was next to mine. A simple thing, you think. Not quite. First, I gave the article to Irene Tubertini, one of my secretaries, and asked her to have it copied, then to bring it back to me so I could write a short comment on it, then to send it on to Clovis. But because the article was long, it first had to go to our central mailroom to be copied by a clerk who handled long documents. The mail is only picked up twice a day – between nine and ten in the morning and four and five in the afternoon. Since my test began at 11 a.m., the article sat in Irene's outbasket for most of the first day. By the time it got to the mailroom, the clerk had left for the day, so it wasn't copied until the next morning. By then it missed the morning pickup and sat in the mailroom for most of that day. The article took 22 working hours to travel the ten feet from my office to Clovis's.

My idea was to phase out clerical positions, redistributing their necessary functions among everyone else. As a first step we suggested that secretaries would be more efficiently used if they didn't have to wait on their bosses, serving them coffee, paying their personal bills, making their telephone calls. (There was a significant side benefit to eliminating this last task: we would end those neurotic little telephone wars in which the caller seeks to prove how important he is by refusing to come to the line until the callee is already hanging on.)

I remember meeting with a group of about 30 secretaries. I told them we wanted to eliminate their jobs in a year or two and asked them to start thinking about what they would like to be doing at Semco in five years. Then we tried to push them in the appropriate direction, matching them with openings and sometimes creating new jobs for them.

Gradually, a few receptionists and secretaries made the switch to marketing, sales, and even engineering. An office boy became one of our best draftsmen. Irene Tubertini helped start the Semco Foundation, working with another former secretary in the human resources department to research possible projects. (We eventually settled on helping intelligent but impoverished Brazilian children attain proper schooling.)

In the end, perhaps 40 per cent of our clerical workers moved on to other, more challenging jobs at Semco. But some liked being secretaries and receptionists and found similar positions elsewhere. A few told us they didn't want a more demanding job because it would take too much time away from their families. For them we created a job-sharing programme in which two people split a single position and, we all hoped, would have the best of both worlds.

If the reaction among secretaries and receptionists to my plan was mixed, there was unanimity among our executives about it. They didn't like the prospect of doing their own copying, dialling their own phone, and going downstairs to greet their visitors at the front desk. Some thought we were merely trying to cut expenses and argued that we were being pound-foolish.

'It's going to cost you a hell of a lot more to have a highly paid guy like me filing my own papers,' they would snarl.

One manager came to see me armed with his Hewlett-Packard calculator. 'My secretary tells me she spends 30 per cent of her time filing,' he said, pecking away at the tiny key-pad. 'Let's say I'm 30 per cent more efficient than her.' (Never mind that she knew how to file and he didn't.) 'It still will be at least 21 per cent of my time. Over a year that means there's going to be $12,000 in additional costs to the company. And I'm just talking about filing.'

'Let's just try it,' I kept pleading, to all of them. But the most effective way to make the point was to be the canary on the miner's helmet. Again.

Soon after I took control of the company I accumulated my second and third secretaries, and I managed to keep all of them busy, too. But doing what? Filing papers I would never again have the slightest need for, of course. So I went from three to two to one and, eventually, to no secretaries. I did my own filing, which meant I filed fewer papers – instead of 50 to 60 a week, I found myself filing two or three documents a month. You can take more risks with your own papers than anyone else can, I realized.

Freed from most of the constraints of paperwork, I started working more at home, with an answering machine, a personal computer, and, later, a fax. I encouraged others to work at home, too. 'I need to be here,' some would protest. But once they tried it and found out how much more efficient they were without all the distractions, they became Work at Home evangelists, too.

We found that in an office without secretaries it paid to reflect before adding to the paperwork. We still make extra copies if there is a chance someone will feel left out. (By the way, when we distribute a memo, we always list everyone getting it in alphabetical order, to avoid silly guessing games about prestige.) But generally, the fewer copies the better. And we think three times before filing anything. Read it, understand it, act on it, and throw it away – that's our motto now.

This is not as easy as it sounds. I remember when a new manager brought me a beautifully bound report that powerfully argued against the feasibility of building a new, high-pressure compressor for a petrochemical plant. I was impressed with his analysis and, after flipping through the pages and reading his recommendation, looked up to tell him so, while casually throwing the report in the bin under my desk. 'You're right, it's not worth doing,' I said, watching the blood drain from his face until it was more or less the shade of our fanciest bond stationery. He had worked for 15 years for a multi-national corporation and wasn't used to seeing the product of several long days tossed out after a few minutes of consideration.

I asked him why he thought his report should be filed. I had, after all, agreed with him. He looked at me blankly for a few moments, then conceded with a sigh that it had served its purpose and would do nothing more than take up space. From that day on, he answered memos with terse hand-written notes in the margins.

Another time, dozens of ball bearings worth many thousands of dollars were ordered from abroad, but when they arrived we discovered they were much too big. The supplier wouldn't take them back. It was a costly blunder, but it was difficult to know which department was responsible, purchasing, production or engineering. The three department heads began exchanging memos, and inevitably the sniping escalated. After a few weeks of guerrilla warfare I called the three of them to my office. Conspicuously displayed on my desk was the file of the incident, by then dozens of pages of reports and memos, all held together by a huge metal clip. I still have that clip, but not the reports, for I ceremoniously threw them in the bin before any of my guests could speak.

That didn't end the paper wars at Semco, but it certainly discouraged them. Who wants to write a bitter, incriminating memo, after spending hours reading files and conducting interviews, if he knows it is destined for the shredder?

I knew we would never eliminate memos entirely, but I did find a way to make them more readable and effective and less time-consuming.

One day, after a prolonged debate at one of the meetings we started holding on the issue of excessive paperwork, I conducted an experiment with a group of top managers. I began by reciting the following list:

School Bus
Mayor
Broken Glass
Children
Strike

Then I asked those at the meeting to divide into small groups and write a news story based on these facts, including a headline. There were no restrictions on style or length.

Thiry minutes later, everyone compared their articles. They were, of course, quite different. You could tell from the headlines:

'*School Children Hurt On Visit to Mayor*'
'*Traffic Jam Holds Up Mayor's Speech*'

'Mayor Throws Child Out of School Bus'
'Mayor Christens School Bus With Champagne Bottle'

The point is, facts can be almost irrelevant. What matters is how they are presented.

Suppose the marketing department is asked to assess whether a new product will make a profit. At a traditional company, it would issue a hundred-page report that would include market surveys, demographic assumptions, economic scenarios, competitor intelligence, manufacturing details, and more, all of which, in this age of What-You-See-Is-What-You-Get software, would be illustrated with graphs and charts.

Trouble is, it could still be read in as many ways as there are readers, as the stories of the mayor and the school bus prove.

If you really want someone to evaluate a project's chances, only give them a single page to do it – and make them write a headline that gets to the point, as in a newspaper. There's no mistaking the conclusion of a memo that begins, 'New Toaster Will Sell 20,000 Units for $2 Million Profit.'

And so Semco's Headline Memo was born. The crucial information is at the top of the page. If you want to know more, read a paragraph or two. But there are no second pages. All of our memos, minutes, letters, reports, even market surveys, are restricted to a single page.

This has not only eliminated unnecessary paperwork, but it has also helped us avoid meetings that were often needed to clarify ambiguous memos. Concision is worth the investment. The longer the message, the greater the chance of misinterpretation.

Of course, one-page memos took some getting used to. People sometimes had to rewrite them five or ten times before managing to synthesize their thoughts.

This wouldn't have surprised Mark Twain, who once apologized for writing a long letter because he didn't have time to write a short one.

nineteen

AFFIRMATIVE ACTIONS

On the day Laura de Barros joined our human resources department there was an assembly of workers, managers, and union leaders in our courtyard at Santo Amaro. In nine years dealing with benefits, training, recruitment, and personnel evaluation elsewhere, Laura had come to believe union officials were seven-headed monsters – and workers who had anything to do with them were to be fired immediately. But then, she had only worked for conventional companies. Now she was working for a boss who invited union leaders to his plant and then sat down and talked with them. I left a good job to make less money at Semco, she must have been thinking. Here am I working for an anarchist, not an entrepreneur.

But it was soon apparent that Laura was a bit of a rebel herself. She became our human resources manager, working with Clovis to foster change and nurture daring initiatives, such as the programme we called The Semco Woman.

I was the one who gave her the idea. One day in 1986, about a year after Laura joined Semco, I put the kind of note on her desk, for which I am famous: 'What about a project for women?' it read. 'Let's talk when I return from vacation.'

Corporations aren't completely to blame for prejudice. It's been inculcated in the family, at school – and probably everywhere else – long before anyone reaches working age. Even so, companies can combat and correct bias. Businesses, like schools and parents, train people. They help individuals advance. That gives them an opportunity to rectify past wrongs.

It usually doesn't take much to evaluate a company's commitment to fairness. Don't bother with records and statistics, a look around the offices is often all that's needed. If nearly everyone is white, or attractive, you can bet a company is biased.

Corporations must clearly and consistently demonstrate fairness, and I believe exceptions can be costly. If there is even a hint that hiring or promotion does not depend on merit, credibility with workers will be threatened. Even if only one in ten workers is hired or promoted unjustly, who do you think people will talk about? Fairness for employees is like quality for customers – it takes years to build up but collapses over a single incident.

Before I got back from my trip, Laura and a colleague, Flor Bassanello, had developed the embryo of a programme, forming groups of women at each of our business units. Getting them to complain was no problem – they wanted more money, of course, as much as men with similar jobs made. They also wanted recognition, at least, that they worked a double shift, taking care of families when they got home from work. (I don't have to tell you about Latin American machismo, do I?)

The groups started meeting during lunch. Discrimination, lack of opportunity, relationships with colleagues, problems at home – all was grist to the mill. Soon there were about 75 participants, from illiterate cleaning women to managers with fancy degrees. The gender agenda more than compensated for their diversity.

There is a Brazilian expression, 'to have space', which means to have earned respect, a place in the organization, the attention of others. Laura hoped that by creating a space for the women of Semco, they would begin to aspire to more than the traditional possibilities. And sure enough, it wasn't long before the women issued their first demand: they wanted Semco to modernize the locker rooms and office bathrooms, including the installation of bidets. This item, which was included in the minutes of their meetings that, in typical Semco fashion, were posted on bulletin boards all around the company, provoked howls of derision from some men. I wish I could say it was totally benign. But the women kept meeting, and their numbers kept growing. They were serious, and before long almost everyone knew it.

The first Semco Woman's Convention occurred in December 1986. One hundred strong, the women boarded a bus and spent a workday at a hotel near São Paulo.

Clovis and I opened the session. We told the women that to remedy discrimination it is sometimes necessary to engage in it. Thus, they could count on Semco for support, at least for a while. And the company would continue to grant them a reasonable amount of time to meet. But if they were going to gain power, we said, they would have to take the initiative and go on from there. Then we left.

Laura later told me that at first the women were reserved and ill-at-ease. That was understandable. Few had been to a convention before, some had never been to a hotel, and several had argued with husbands, financés, parents, and bosses over their attendance. (This was in Brazil, after all.)

Laura led the women through a series of dance-like-exercises. The lights were dim, the music soft and rhythmic. The women swayed back and forth, not speaking, engrossed in introspection. I know this sounds awfully touchy-feely. But in time the atmosphere overpowered even the most reserved of the conferees and the women were laughing, crying, and hugging each other.

Then they improvised a play in which they took parts based on traditional men's and women's roles at work. The idea was to show how submissive most women are, and how overbearing most men are, especially the bosses, who were played by women with greasepaint moustaches and pillow pot bellies.

That's all Laura would tell me about the convention. But the women apparently succeeded in convincing each other that there was more to be done, for from then on their movement caught on. Maybe even caught fire. It was standing room only at their lunchtime meetings, in spite of male supervisors who would sometimes find some 'urgent' task for a woman subordinate just as a session was about to start.

By this time the bathrooms had been redone, after lengthy negotiations over the startling cost of all that new plumbing. Their next issue was more significant. Under Brazilian law mothers were entitled to extra money for day care only until their children were six months old. Then they were on their own. Few companies in Brazil provided more, but that did not discourage our women, who came up with a programme and sold it to us. Semco now pays all day care costs in a child's first year, a little less in the second year, still less in the third, and so on until the sixth year, when children are in school full time.

All of us are pleased with the plan, and so are people at the many companies that have copied it.

Soon enough the Second Women's Convention rolled around, a two-day meeting that I'm sure was that much harder for some husbands and bosses to accept. More than 100 women took part, including one participant who was about to go into labour.

It opened with an exercise called 'the Wailing Wall', in which the women scrawled graffiti on a ballroom wall specially coated for the occasion. The object was to let everything out. Heaven knows what they wrote: I wasn't told. There was also dancing and singing, like the year before, but the mood at the convention was more businesslike this time. Semco had begun eliminating clerical jobs that added little extra value, so the women spent part of the session planning training programmes to help them make the transition. After their return they began to evaluate all managerial positions that became open to see if any of them were qualified to fill them. They weren't asking for an edge, just trying to make sure they would be considered.

Some women did rise. One became a projects engineer, working on heavy machinery such as ship pumps and large mixing systems. Another, also an engineer, sold cooling towers. And several women pried their way into the maritime industry, a traditionally male domain, selling spare parts at dockside.

But to my surprise attendance at the lunchtime meetings tapered off. And at about the same time the Brazilian economy hit an air pocket and we had to make a round of layoffs that hit women, many of whom were the last people we had hired, especially hard. I was beginning to think the project had failed.

Laura disagreed. She believed the movement's objectives had largely been accomplished and that there wasn't much more an organized effort could accomplish. Now it was up to each women to take the initiative and advance.

Don't worry, Laura would say. When a problem requiring collective action arises, the women will, too.

About a year or so later a struggle developed between two rival unions. One had called a general strike across the country that, if successful, would have been a major blow not just to the companies involved but also to the other. So it decided it would strike first, and sent organizers from plant to plant to stir up support.

Semco was a favourite target. Because it was always in the news, a walkout at one of our plants would mean a great deal of publicity. The second union sent us one of its best (worst?) men: Horacio Pinipa, a radical more feared than admired by our workers. Horacio didn't like Semco, either; he felt left out of negotiations conducted by our factory committees. If he wanted to get even, this was as good a chance as he was likely to get.

To this day many Semco employees still cannot explain why they let Horacio talk them into going on strike. (These were a different group of workers from those at the Hobart plant.) Standing on a truck equipped with a powerful public address system, Pinipa went on and on, calling me names and trying to pit the factory workers against the office employees, who were resisting the walkout. At one point an engineer named Alberto grew so disgusted he stalked over to the truck and demanded the microphone. Pinipa almost hit him, then continued hurling insults – until he hurled one too many. 'This bunch of women at Semco, they don't do anything useful,' he sneered. 'They're just there to go to bed with the managers.'

About 40 women formed into a furious caucus in a first-floor conference room in no time at all. Then they surrounded

Pinipa. Pointing fingers at him, they screamed at him to take it back.

Pinipa said he wasn't going to take back a damn thing.

Lia Guerra, an excitable Chilean, tried to take a swing at him. She was held back by some other women, but she kept yelling at Pinipa to come down off the truck and fight.

That was when our telephone operator, Iracema, nearly lost control, went to her car, and took out the gun she kept in her glove compartment. (She had to drive home each night through the worst neighbourhoods in town, and the gun made her feel safer.) Flor managed to talk her into putting it back, though she wasn't planning to use it.

Pinipa, by this time cowering inside the truck cab, let us know he was ready to end the strike, and we guaranteed him safe passage to the third floor so he could sign the peace treaty. When he was finished, Laura said she had a message for him.

'Horacio, some of your members wish to meet with you now.'

'Why?' the shaken union man said.

'I think they want to exchange a few ideas with you.'

'Tell them I can't. I have a lot to do when I leave her.'

With that, this brave, radical union leader bolted down the stairs and past the women gathered at the door.

Laura was right. This movement was only waiting.

twenty

TRADING PLACES

We spent years trying to hire Marcio Batoni. We first interviewed him in 1983, when, while a young production engineer at Vigorelli, the sewing machine company, he ingeniously developed a new milling machine using many components the company already had in stock.

To our disappointment, Marcio took another job as production director at a German company named Cyklop, which makes packaging machinery.

We looked him up again early the next year. He came to see us just as he was about to leave on a month-long trip to Germany during which time he would be trained at Cyklop's expense. Given that, he decided it was unethical to resign upon his return.

But we are nothing if not persistent, so the following August we tried again to bring Batoni into the fold (though Clovis and I decided that this time it would be 'three strikes and we're out').

After many discussions, Marcio finally decided to join us. But he couldn't leave Cyklop in a fix, so he gave four months' notice. We winced, but on reflection decided we would have liked to be treated that way if he were leaving us.

When he finally arrived, we immediately designated him plant manager of Santo Amaro. A little while later he took charge of Semco's materials handling and purchasing as well. Then he became our engineering manager. By 1988, Batoni was general manager of our refrigeration systems unit where, despite a horrible economy, he managed to keep sales and profits rising. (When we bought the unit from the Americans it was doing $1.2 million in sales a year: Batoni upped it to close to $4 million, with a 10 per cent profit margin after taxes.)

Far be it from us to leave well alone. Marcio had gained experience with our marine products while running the Santo Amaro plant, so he seemed a good bet for the Nacoes Unidas plant, where those same products were now being manufactured.

This kind of movement, which may strike some as hectic and disorienting, has become a way of life at Semco. Indeed, helter-skelter career paths such as Marcio's have been institutionalized under a job-rotation programme in which 20 to 25 per cent of our managers make a shift in any given year. I'll bet fewer than a third of our people have not yet rotated at least once.

Man is by nature restless. When left too long in one place he will inevitably grow bored, unmotivated, and unproductive. The cure, I believed, was to encourage managers to exchange jobs with one another. Someone in accounting, for instance, would arrange to swap jobs with someone in sales. They would start planning a year or so in advance, to give each time to learn the other's duties and make the transition smooth. But as with other programmes at Semco, we wanted our employees to take the initiative. We didn't want them to leave it to us to decide who went where.

We felt that a minimum of two years and a maximum of five years in a job were ample. Anyone who wanted to stay put longer could, provided he could continually create new challenges for himself. Otherwise, it was find a partner and dance.

We have witnessed several successful corporate transplants that shocked traditionalists. One of our best-managed units, the dishwasher division, which requires critical decisions in marketing and production all the time, is run by an accountant who was for many years our Controller. Our electronic hardware and software products unit, which makes scales, is led by a mechanical engineer. Our current controller was, until recently, a sales manager. Or take Batoni, who has so far led three different business units at Semco.

We don't like our people to be imprisoned by their degrees or résumés. Nor do we let a lack of formal education limit anyone's potential. We've had a financial director and a technical director who had nothing more than high school diplomas. Another technical director had virtually no schooling at all, but that didn't stop him from leading a team of engineers from Brazil's most sophisticated universities. If a scale assembler wants to be a systems analyst, we'll try to make it happen. If a secretary wants to be a sales engineer, we will help finance her studies.

There are so many benefits from job rotation, both for employees and employer, that it's a wonder so few companies encourage it. It obliges people to learn new skills, which makes life interesting for them and makes them more valuable. It discourages empire-building, because people can't very well sustain an empire if they pack up and move every few years. It gives people a much broader view of a company: a financial controller who constantly nags a salesperson about payment terms will regret it when he switches jobs and discovers how difficult it is to deal with a real, live customer.

Rotation forces a company to prepare more than one person for a job, which is an excellent organizational discipline and generates additional opportunities for those who might otherwise be trapped in the middle of the pyramid. It encourages the spread of diverse personalities, outlooks, backgrounds, and techniques, injecting new blood and fresh vision throughout the company. It also depersonalizes the organization; customers and suppliers have relationships with the company, not Mr Frankenstein. Similarly, it reduces the usual traumas when someone leaves a department or even the company, especially if he had tendencies towards irreplaceability – the conscious effort, through the inability to delegate and other related shortcomings, to ensure that he is in absolute control. Nobody wants to pass on a disorganized department, nor look like a dictator or someone who can't select subordinates well.

Of course, rotation must be exercised with care, so specialists aren't lost where they are needed. But this isn't as big a problem as it once was at Semco, since rotation has forced us to develop more than one expert in many fields.

What if someone with a unique talent decides he needs a

change at the wrong time? Well, if he really wants a change, he'll move somewhere else no matter what we do, and then he'll no longer be with us at all. We'd rather have him around to consult, even if he's in a different department. But we've never had a case in which someone with a valuable set of skills wanted to move to another position but did not also take on the responsibility of finding a suitable replacement, even if it took a few years of training to bring him up to speed. They'll say, 'Look, I have a guy who's been with me for three years and in another two, he'll be ready to replace me.'

And we'd all wait.

Life is pretty dizzying at Semco, rotation or no rotation. I'm sure our managers feel less secure than they would, say, in a comparable position at the subsidiary of a large multinational. Park yourself in a job at a huge corporation and play by rules that are well known to everyone and you'll sleep soundly. Semco managers are likely to be confronted with challenging situations all the time. There's no risk of boredom here.

At times maybe Semco is too interesting. Our employees are always complaining that we make too many changes, too quickly. We were always creating new programmes – and I was always disappointed when my ideas couldn't be implemented that same week. But then, I have always been too impetuous. I remember when, as a high school sprinter, I ran in an important statewide race. I had trained hard, felt confident, and drew the inside lane. When the starter's gun sounded, I was off at fill tilt, the undisputed leader. As I rounded the last curve my head raced on to the finish line, but my legs turned to rubber and refused to follow commands. Next thing I knew, I was sprawled on the track, panting for breath and watching my rivals cross the line. I realized then that taking first place is no big deal, the hard part is making it to the line in one piece.

The pressure is also greater at Semco because we truly believe in the market. We don't protect anybody from the vicissitudes of the business cycle or the crazy Brazilian economy. This is not for everybody – certainly not for bureaucrats who spend careers digging themselves in like soldiers in the trenches.

Because of this pressure, we are great believers in professional recycling, a.k.a. sabbaticals. We call it our Hepatitis Leave. When people tell us they don't have time to think, we ask them to consider what would happen if they suddenly contracted hepatitis and were forced to spend three months recuperating in bed. Then we tell them to go ahead and do it.

Professionals – for the time being this programme is limited to mid-level jobs or higher – can take a few weeks or even a few months every year or two away from their usual duties. They can spend the time reading books or articles, learning new skills, or redesigning their job. Or they can just think. In fact, that's the point of the Hepatitis Leave. It's not designed as a cure for overwork. It's meant to create a hiatus in a career during which our people can stop and rethink their working lives and their objectives. It's a point at which they can plan ahead, sort out priorities, and come back in better shape to tackle their goals. Just so long as they remember when their recuperation period is up.

But sometimes our flexibility backfires. We once spent more than a decade preparing an executive to be a production manager. Then we learned from our 'What-Do-You-Want-To-Be-In-Ten-Years' form that he was more interested in marketing, so we paid for graduate schooling in that field at the country's foremost business school and then transferred him. That's how he became head of the marine products plant.

twenty-one

MINDING OUR OWN BUSINESS

I had a premonition about the letter when I saw the return address. I was certain there weren't any homes in that section of town.

Sure enough, the message inside was spelled out in letters cut from magazines, like a ransom note. It laid out details of a purported kickback scheme between two Semco executives and a supplier of steel plates and had been written, the anonymous author said, to repay a debt owed to my father.

The letter arrived at my home just after we had placed orders worth more than $500,000 with the supplier it named. Since we had not done business with the company, and no other bidders had been consulted, I suppose we would have been within our rights to call in the executives and question them. But we had embarked on a new era of trust at Semco and it seemed consistent with that spirit to discount accusations that were not accompanied by solid evidence or even the accuser's name.

Instead of investigating the executives, Clovis and I decided to investigate the complainant. If the allegations were false, then we certainly didn't want such a person working for us. If they were true, we would take the appropriate action, but we also wanted to know why such an underhand method of exposure was necessary.

The return address was handwritten, and Clovis hired a forensic graphologist to study the scrawl. As part of his investigation, he went through our files. A week later we had his report, which made us glad we had handled the case with discretion. Our handwriting expert was sure the author was the same employee who had written a similar letter, this time signing his name, a year earlier. We had ignored it because the accuser had a history of making unfounded charges against supervisors. It was no secret that he felt he had been unfairly passed over for promotions.

So the two executives were exonerated and the accuser was dismissed. Only then did everyone come to know about the case.

But before you get the idea that we take impropriety lightly, let me tell you about another case. A few months after we took over the Hobart factory, a worker noticed that three parts and service department employees often worked late for no apparent reason. One night he stayed behind, crawled into a small closet, and waited. Watching through a tiny hole in the door, he saw the trio sneaking out parts to their cars. The thieves were caught, fired, and arrested. They had been stealing from us for about a month. I hate to think how long it would have gone on without the help of that worker.

These two cases, I believe, illustrate crime and punishment Semco-style. We will always press charges when we believe someone has committed a criminal offence. Always. But short of actual criminality – or in cases when there is reasonable doubt – we are extremely reluctant to get involved. We don't make written admonishments, suspend people, dock pay or anything of the sort. We don't want to become boarding school deans. We'll talk about what bothers us, but generally won't do anything official. But if we feel someone is truly unfit for employment in our environment, we'll tell him so. If he doesn't change, eventually we'll fire him. But we don't slap wrists.

Like so much of our thinking, our views on discipline are shaped by the conviction that our employees are adults, and should always be treated as such. As Semco changed, we came to stress two points about individual conduct: one, each employee is responsible for his own actions; and, two, what people do in their own time is their own business. We care only about an employee's work, not his private life, so long as it doesn't interfere with his performance on the job.

Once, at one of those barbecues our plants throw when they meet their end-of-the-month goals, a few workers started smoking marijuana. They would have been dismissed instantly at many companies, but not at Semco. We called a meeting with the factory committee and said that smoking marijuana on company property was simply not allowed. We knew the people involved, but didn't mention their names. The object wasn't to punish them, just make sure it wouldn't happen again.

If we don't feel imperilled by our employees' vices, we don't feel responsible for them either. If a worker is an alcoholic, it's not Semco's role to try to get him on the wagon: that's the job of Alcoholics Anonymous. If he chain smokes, it's not our corporate obligation to clear his lungs. If he's addicted to cocaine and wants medical or psychiatric treatment, we're willing to help him get it, but he has to take the first step.

This may seem unfeeling or even out of fashion in an era when many corporations believe – no, proclaim, that it is their duty to assist employees struggling with drugs, booze or personal problems. They mean well, I'm sure. But we don't want to turn our managers into Father Figures, even if it makes them feel warm and cuddly inside. We don't want to be a big, happy family. We want to be a business. No one should ever fall for that we're-a-family line. Ask someone who retires and three days later can't get through the gate. Even a worker who gets sick is forgotten if he doesn't return to the plant soon. A few friends from the company may visit him at first, and the cheques continue to arrive each month, but people in that awful situation soon realize that no company is a family.

The owner of a company in our field is known as one of the most generous bosses in the land. When a worker's son had a serious medical problem that could only be treated outside the country, the owner paid all the expenses, which equalled many years of the father's salary, a sum he could never repay. And he didn't have to, because it was a gift, not a loan. But if, as he walked around his plant, this wonderful, caring, generous owner saw someone doing something he didn't like, he would fire them on the spot (with severance, of course). That's the flip side of paternalism. Employees give these owners a lease on their soul for their working lives, and that can be an expensive proposition.

We won't make that deal at Semco. But that doesn't mean our people can't help their colleagues. We're not against compassion, we just want it to be spontaneous, voluntary, and heartfelt. For instance, when one of our floor sweepers, at a relatively advanced age of 50, learned that his pregnant wife was expecting twins, Lia, who worked in our human resources department, went through the factory and the offices and collected donations of money and children's clothing. No one put her up to it; she did it on her own. And nearly everyone at the company contributed, which made us all feel prouder than we would have had our treasurer just sent a cheque.

Occasionally, Semco will lend employees money, but only for unpredictable emergencies, such as when a worker's house is flooded or a spouse gets sick. As long as we feel an individual can repay us, we will go to almost any extent to get him the cash he needs – one, two or even three years' pay. We will then deduct perhaps 20 or 30 per cent of his pay cheque until we are even. But if a worker has an opportunity to buy the house he lives in, or a car his brother-in-law is unloading, we won't lend him a cent. We don't want to buy into his financial life or participate in his dreams. We might offer a course on budgeting, or help him calculate how big a mortgage he can afford, but that's it. The love and caring we offer comes from our people, not our policies.

And you won't find a running track, swimming pool, or gym at Semco. Many companies build them to help their employees cope with stress. At Semco, we try not to cause stress in the first place.

Does this mean that companies should abolish all benefits and transform the resources they consume into additional pay? Of course not. The amount returned wouldn't enable their employees to buy the same benefits. (Here's one place where there are economies of scale.) So we compromise by having employees manage benefits such as health-care insurance. The company contributes the money, but the employees make the decisions on how it is spent.

It isn't easy living up to our laissez-faire ideals. I remember when Celso Violin, an employee in the human resources department, asked an office maintenance worker, Jose Fernandes, to feed some confidential documents – payroll records, including those of a few executives who were still not disclosing their salary – into our shredder, which is so noisy it's kept way down the hall. Jose started feeding the papers into the machine, but had to leave for a few minutes to pick up some rubbish. A few moments later a colleague rushed into Celso's office: 'You better go out there and see what's happening,' he said, trying to catch his breath.

Celso ran into the hall and saw a security guard leaning over the shredder, reading the papers. This guy was trouble: he took advantage of his immunity as a factory committee member to cause us all sorts of problems. He was the sort of worker who gave the committees a bad name.

'What are you doing?' Celso shouted, knowing the answer but not knowing what else to say.

'Reading,' the guard casually replied.

'You can't do that,' said Celso. 'They're confidential.'

The guard said a few nasty things and walked away. Later, he was called to Paulo Pereira's office and asked why he had been spying. He kept saying he didn't mean any harm. Paulo knew what he was up to – he was trying to prove that some managers were making much more than their stated salaries. And Paulo made sure the guard knew that he knew. Then he asked him what he thought Semco should do about it. This surprised him – but the guard had a surprise for Paulo. He said that, since he meant no harm by looking at the papers, he thought he shouldn't be punished at all.

I'll bet most companies would have fired the guard instantly. When employees break important rules, corporations usually try to make examples of them, as a deterrent. But

Semco is a participative company, and we don't ask a question if we're not prepared for the answer. We followed the guard's recommendation and did nothing – except to tell him we didn't think what he did was right.

At Semco we rarely fire anyone for cause, but when we do, we don't put a notice up on the bulletin board announcing, 'Mr Pilfer has decided to resign, regrettably, for reasons of health.' If an employee has breached our confidence, we say so. If he has left for a better job, we say that, too, wish him well, and sometimes express the hope that he will one day return.

We always try to speak the truth. On those rare occasions when the truth, for some special reason, cannot be told, we say nothing. We believe it is essential that all company communications, especially those intended for the workers or the public, be absolutely honest. We even apply this policy to journalists. All the television networks and major newspapers and magazines in Brazil can talk to whoever they want at Semco, no matter what they have reported in the past, and do. And our people are free to speak their minds, without fear.

We take another step to ensure that communication at Semco flows. Two or three times a year we distribute a questionnaire called, 'What Does The Company Think?' It gives workers another chance to tell us whether they are satisfied with their salaries, have any reason to leave the company, would ever support a strike, have confidence in management, and so on. The results are published for all to see, and enable us to monitor our credibility as well as their concerns.

We even encourage civil disobedience in the company, though we do so subtly. If a request for some item gets bogged down in purchasing, for example, employees know that in a jam they can just buy it themselves and send us the bill. Workers have held protests in our cafeterias because they thought we should subsidize 100 per cent of their meals, not just 70 per cent. Some have refused to wear a uniform. Our reaction is to do nothing, except to explain why things are as they are. If co-existence is impossible, they'll either eventually leave on their own or be slowly and subtly expelled from the system. But we have people who agree with very little of what we think and are still here, unapologetic and unfettered. So what if they don't wear their uniform, as long as they do their job.

A touch of civil disobedience is necessary to alert the organization that all is not right. Rather than fear our Thoreaus and Bakunins, we do our best to let them speak their minds even though they often become thorns in our side.

One of the sharper thorns was a welder at our refrigeration systems factory, where we make cooling towers. In Brazil, people who work in conditions deemed to be dangerous are paid extra – 20, 30 or 40 per cent more, depending on the risk. Our welder and some co-workers asked the factory committee to demand a hazard premium for the hot welding they were doing. But how hot is too hot? We told the workers we would ask a group of Semco engineers to inspect their working conditions, then adjust their pay accordingly.

This seemed to please everyone but the rebel, who said he didn't believe company engineers would be fair. We ignored his objections, and the engineers reported that there were indeed hazardous conditions that warranted a 30 per cent increase. We immediately complied, making the payments retrospective to cover the weeks since the welders first spoke up. But the rebel, naturally, thought he and his colleagues deserved the full 40 per cent premium.

A few weeks later one of these same welders – the man with the most seniority – reached Brazil's mandatory retirement age for full-time employees. He had been with the company many years and because of that had a high salary. But he was a good employee and we decided to rehire him as a consultant, which enabled us to circumvent legally the retirement rules. And, of course, we paid him at the same rate as before.

Then we heard from our rebel. As the next most senior welder, he was hoping to inherit the salary of the senior man. We explained that this was an exceptional case, but he wasn't satisfied. He went to the union, which said he would have to fight it himself. And so he did, in court. And while he was at it, he sued us over the hazard pay, too.

This didn't thrill us, but if a worker wants to sue us, that's his right.

A month or so later we all trooped into court. The judge began by asking if the plaintiff had received the correct severance pay when he left Semco.

'I don't have it,' the rebel welder said.

The judge turned to Paulo Pereira, who was representing the company, waved a finger in his face, and said harshly, 'Why the hell doesn't he have it yet?'

'Because he's still an employee,' Paulo replied evenly.

'Still an employee?' said the judge, incredulous. 'Anybody who sues a company is fired or leaves.'

No, Paulo said, the welder had disagreed with us and decided to go to court, but he was still an employee.

The judge, to everyone's surprise, stopped the proceedings and congratulated Semco for its respect for the rights of its employees.

Then the case resumed and dragged on for six months. In the end Semco won both lawsuits. And the welder? He's still with us, and just as sharp as ever.

twenty-two

HIRING AND FIRING THE BOSS

Anatoly Timoshenko was going into the arena, and the lions were hungry. Gathered in a meeting room at Santo Amaro was as antagonistic a group as he was likely to face in peacetime. If he was lucky they would be his future subordinates.

Timoshenko, a tall, soft-spoken man with a grizzly beard, had talked with all the top executives at Semco, and we had wished him luck. But we had been clear as a Baccarat goblet that we weren't going to move a finger for him. It was up to him.

We had hired Timoshenko several years earlier, after he answered an advertisement. We were looking for a manager conversant with the legal complexities of purchasing agreements and experienced in delivering large orders and managing people. We also wanted someone with a working knowledge of planning, assembling, quality control, cost control, finance, and marketing.

Why such an extensive and diverse set of qualifications? The project we had in mind entailed the construction of entire biscuit factories – each consisting of between $3 and $4 million worth of dough mixers, dough cutters, ovens, conveyors, electronic controls, the works. The thousands of components would be manufactured at our Santo Amaro plant, then assembled anywhere in the world. Our customers, Nabisco, Sunshine Biscuits, and the like, would simply press a button and, *voila*, Ritz crackers and Oreos.

There was no one at Semco who we thought could handle the job. Our ad attracted three candidates, of whom Timoshenko seemed by far the best. He had experience with

Citibank in finance and with several other companies in production. He was enthusiastic, too, until we told him that getting hired at Semco would be unlike anything he had ever endured.

In these days of the new world order, almost everyone believes people have a right to vote for those who lead them, at least in the public sector. But democracy has yet to penetrate the work place. Dictators and despots are alive and well in offices and factories all over the world.

Most companies and employees accept his as immutable. But we didn't believe Semco had to perpetuate a system in which a person is hired who impresses his future boss but does not have the respect of his subordinates. Nor did we understand why we should keep a supervisor who wasn't well regarded by those who were supposed to follow him. So we developed a programme to ensure that bosses were ratified by the people who work under them.

Like many innovations at Semco, I don't exactly know how it started. Initially, we just wanted to know why some people hadn't become the successes we thought they would be when we promoted them, and naturally asked those who worked for them. That led us to draw up a form subordinates now use to evaluate their managers twice a year. It has about three dozen multiple choice questions designed to measure technical ability, competence, leadership and other aspects of being a boss. Here are some examples:

> *The subject reacts to criticism:*
> *a. Poorly, ignoring it*
> *b. Poorly, rejecting it*
> *c. Reasonably well*
> *d. Well, accepting it*

> *When the subject's department achieves a high level of productivity, he/she usually:*
> *a. Takes credit for other people's success*

b. *Gives credit to those who did the work*
c. *Gives credit to the team as a whole*

The subject conveys to his team feelings of:
   a. *Fear and insecurity*
   b. *Indifference*
   c. *Security and tranquillity*

The subject:
   a. *Constantly reminds everyone he is the boss*
   b. *Occasionally reminds everyone he is the boss*
   c. *Rarely makes a point of being the boss*

The questionnaire is filled out anonymously, so no one is afraid to be honest. We weight the questions and answers according to their importance and calculate a grade, which is posted, so everyone knows where everyone stands. Seventy per cent is passing, but most managers get between 80 and 85 per cent. Managers who score below 70 are not automatically dismissed, but a low grade usually creates intense pressure on an individual to change. What we want to see is improvement from one year to the next. Supervisors meet with their subordinates to discuss their grades, so the process of change starts very quickly.

This employee review builds on one of Semco's great strengths, our transparency. At our company people can always say what's on their minds, even to their bosses – even when it's about their bosses. It is instilled in our corporate culture that everyone should be willing to listen, and admit it when they are wrong.

We developed the questionnaire to find out why some managers were failing. But we also had cases in which managers we admired – and repeatedly promoted – got such low marks that it made us wonder how we could be so wrong. We once had a man who ran a large department extremely well, or so we thought. On his first evaluation he got a 40. After looking into it, we concluded that his subordinates were right: he was a great salesman but a terrible leader, and his people were succeeding in spite of him. Solution: we made him the head of a one-person sales staff, and he has shone. With a new leader, his former department did even better.

But such cases are rare. Far more often the evaluation process helps people change. I speak from experience. My first evaluation was conducted by two vice-presidents and my secretary at the time, Irene Tubertini. 'I've prepared a list of all the bad things I want to complain about,' Irene warned before telling me that I often didn't let her know what my priorities were and then got upset when she didn't correctly guess them. Her complaints prodded me to develop a system using labels of different colours to denote the importance of a task – red for extremely urgent, yellow for pressing, green for items that can wait a bit. (I stole the idea from the 'mood' tags at the electronic scale plant.)

Our next step was obvious, if radical. A manager imposed from on high starts with the count against him. Why not let the people elect their boss? In a plant where everyone has a financial stake in success, the idea of asking subordinates to choose future bosses seems an utterly sensible way to stop accidents before they are promoted. It's a wonder it isn't done more often.

So we extended our evaluation system to cover proposed promotions to high-level positions, using another questionnaire to be filled in by middle managers and shop-floor supervisors. But since these subordinates hadn't yet worked for the candidate, we added a step: a group interview – or interviews, since candidates are often asked to return for four or five meetings. I'm sure this tries their patience, but it also gives them an opportunity to learn our business and our culture. And that gives them and us a chance to find out whether we are truly made for each other before we step up to the altar.

It was Marcio Batoni who explained our strange hiring ritual to Timoshenko. Batoni was somewhat in charge of the job opening. I say somewhat because this is Semco, the company at which nothing is straightforward, and no individual can decide whether there is a job opening. An executive can start the process of creating a new job by trying to convince his colleagues that their business unit needs someone new. If there is a consensus in favour of adding a job, then the person or people most interested in the idea puts together a profile of the ideal candidate, listing all major qualities and requirements – experiences, leadership ability, languages spoken – with weights attached to each. As a matter of corporate culture, factors such as academic background and personal appearance are ignored. Semco abounds with people who lack degrees or Italian suits but are first-class employees nonetheless.

The profile and a general job description are posted on all bulletin boards, giving our employees first chance to apply. I know what you're thinking: don't many companies do this? Yes, but here is why we are different: under a programme we call 'The Family Silverware' an employee who meets 70 per cent of the requirements for a job will be chosen instead of an outsider. In other words, our people get a 30 per cent discount on a new job merely for being here. As believers in the power of cultural adaptation, we are willing to bet that someone who meets 70 per cent of the requirements will quickly develop into a 100 percenter on the job.

Only if no qualified internal candidates come forward are outsiders considered. But not all outsiders are treated on equal terms. We make it a point to give ex-Semco employees – orphans, Laura de Barros calls them – an edge. Only a few have tried their luck at other companies or struck out on their own, but many of them have come back, and we have welcomed them.

We also give preference to friends and acquaintances of our employees, because no responsible person at Semco would risk his own reputation by recommending someone who can't meet our standards. But family members are out; only distant relatives are permitted to work for the company, and then only in different plants.

Only after all this fails to produce a candidate do we resort to newspaper ads or headhunters. We prefer three applicants for an opening, but will settle for two.

'We manufacture the ovens, conveyors, and dough mixers, ship them to the site, and install them,' Batoni told Timoshenko at their first meeting. 'All customers have to do is put in the dough and the sweeteners and press the button. What we need is someone who can make sure every one of the thousands of components, every one of the hundreds of individual deliveries, each of the dozens of critical engineering decisions, will be made correctly. And on time.

'The manager of this unit will constantly be in the line of fire.' He looked squarely at Timoshenko. 'Do you feel up to that?'

Timoshenko thought it over for a moment and said he did. But he had one question about our strange procedure: didn't we run the risk of hiring people who were likeable rather than tough? Batoni assured him this wasn't the case. In the admittedly short time Semco had allowed employees to play a critical role in hiring their bosses, they have repeatedly recognized that their self-interest is the same as the company's. A congenial boss might make their lives easier in the short run, but they know that only the success of their department will ensure that they continue to receive profit-sharing payments, or even ordinary pay cheques.

To reassure Timoshenko, Batoni told him of how three months earlier we had replaced our treasurer. A notice of the opening was posted, but no internal candidates applied. Clovis had a friend he thought would be ideal, a 50-year-old treasurer at a company about the same size as ours. His name was Mario Fontes. But several people who worked in our finance department recommended Gil Ostolin, a 30-year-old former Semco accountant who now ran a car dealership with his brother. As an 'orphan', Ostolin got an automatic edge. On top of that, he had been well liked by many of those who were about to interview him.

Several top Semco executives met with both men and strongly preferred Mario. But given Gil's popularity they didn't think Mario had a chance. There was even some talk of abandoning our participatory hiring process just this once – it was *that* crucial a job – but we knew our whole effort to democratize Semco would be compromised.

Both candidates were invited in to meet their potential subordinates on the same day. The jury, a dozen or so people who worked in finance, agreed that if neither scored higher than 80 they would keep looking.

Gil arrived first. Clovis watched as he embraced the men and kissed the women. What an entrance, Clovis thought to himself as he went back to his office to await the result.

Each interview took two hours. After the two candidates left, the questionnaires were filled in and scored.

In the end, affection and familiarity lost out. Mario won, although just barely.

After all this, Timoshenko's interview must have seemed a huge anti-climax. Scoring 84, he started work almost immediately – but probably started losing points right away. It was a challenging project, and the constant pressure to meet the tight deadlines turned Timoshenko into a first-class nudge.

Semco's first biscuit plant was delivered on time, on budget, and exceeded the specifications required. And that was only the start. The division rolled out more biscuit plants, each carrying a healthy profit margin of 12 to 15 per cent after taxes.

Soon we decided to spin off the unit into a separate division that would give it the freedom to chart its own course and ensure that it stayed small enough to be efficient. Naturally, we wanted Timoshenko to run it. But that meant we would need to promote him to general manager, and under our process he would first have to be interviewed and approved by his future subordinates – including many people he had so effectively irritated. What an opportunity to get even.

And it got worse. We told Timoshenko that if he wasn't approved we would try to find another place for him, assuming we had one. If not, he would have to go, since we don't believe in stockpiling talent. People get unhappy waiting on shelves. Anyway, companies and talents are dynamic and needs and interests change. It's like keeping butter outside the refrigerator. It usually melts by the time you are ready to use it.

Because of our policy of giving preference to orphans who want to return to Semco, we think it is healthier for people to oxygenate themselves in the job market than to be put into some internal hibernation.

As Timoshenko entered the room for his interview, the chatter from the several dozen people who had assembled there ceased. Three different camps sat in different sections of the room. By the windows were the engineers, including Almir Vieira and Carlos Okamoto, the leaders of the opposition. They felt Timoshenko had not only been too tough, but had 'micro-managed', which was anathema at Semco. The second group, the division's administrative staff, sat at the far end of the room, at the end of the long mahogany table. Many had had run-ins with Timoshenko and were against him. The last group, the factory supervisors, were sitting against the wall opposite the window. They had counted on Timoshenko to solve their bureaucratic problems and seen him turn promises into reality on the shop floor. They were solidly in his camp.

Timoshenko opened the meeting by calmly pointing out that antagonisms had been built into his former job. Yes, he had pushed too hard. Yes, he had made mistakes. But he would change. It was important to remember, he said more than once, that they all had succeeded.

There were a few nods, but most of the people just sat there in stony silence. After a while, Almir asked to speak. His talents as an electrical engineer were well known. So were his candour and temper. True to his reputation, he angrily accused Timoshenko of mishandling his assignment and placing his own ambitions first.

A few factory supervisors tried to defend Timoshenko, but the engineers and the administrative people kept up their attack. As the afternoon wore on, it was clear Almir and some other engineers might quit if Timoshenko was promoted. A few resignations and the technological backbone of the unit would be lost. Orders for biscuit machinery were already stacked up.

This time, Timoshenko repeated, he would be more flexible. People wouldn't have fixed positions. He wouldn't determine who would run each sub-department. The unit would run by itself for a while, and with time the natural leaders would emerge, Semco-like. He kept saying that he wouldn't be a dictator.

Then he left the room. If the engineers prevailed, we would lose Timoshenko. If Timoshenko won, we might lose some engineers. Despite the value of these technocrats, we decided we would abide by the outcome. Democracy would prevail and, we trusted, Semco would, too.

Well, they couldn't reach a decision that day so a second meeting was scheduled. Meanwhile, Timoshenko did a little last-minute lobbying, going from work area to work area trying to earn a few more points. Some of the administrative staff seemed pliable. Most of the engineers wouldn't even talk to him.

Judgment Day arrived and the three factions took their accustomed places in the room. After an hour of discussion, each employee took a questionnaire and began to fill it in. Timoshenko gazed out of the window, watching the others decide his fate.

Soon enough, the results were read aloud, by group. First came the engineers. Interestingly, their low grades on the questions involving interpersonal relations were partially offset by better marks on questions concerning Timoshenko's technical competence. Next came the factory workers. All their grades were exceptionally high, prompting muttering from the engineers. The marks from the administrative people were in between.

When the results were calculated Timoshenko had a 74 – four more points then he needed. After more debate about the factory workers' grades the group decided to eliminate the highest and the lowest marks on each question and recalculate the average. This time his score came to 70.6. There was more griping, but everyone decided to respect the outcome.

In the end, no one resigned. And Timoshenko eventually made a surprising selection for the job of chief engineer, the person who would be his right arm – the utterly flabbergasted Almir. Soon he and Timoshenko were working on a budget for a unit that would become one of our great successes.

twenty three

MORE THAN A JOB

The changes we had made at Semco, especially the flexibility of job rotation and unpredictability of employees evaluating their bosses, resulted in people taking some strange twists and turns. Life at Semco was becoming more challenging all the time, as Simpliciano Domingos de la Sierra and Alipio Camargo, among many others, could attest.

Simpliciano Domingos de la Sierra was a young man when he came to work at Semco, but he had already endured a lifetime of knocks.

He left his home in a São Paulo slum at the age of 15 and worked for some of the heavyweights of Brazilian industry, large multinational corporations where conditions were often deplorable and management always authoritarian. He soon became convinced that what was good for the bosses was bad for the workers, period.

When we hired Simpliciano as a sheetmetal worker Semco was still in the firm grasp of my father's Old Guard. His new co-workers took one look at his fair skin, and saw the ease with which he blushed, and christened him Camarão – shrimp, in Portuguese. But I can't think of a nickname that was less apt.

'I didn't give Semco an easy time,' Simpliciano recalled. 'I arrived at the end of 1974, and by 1975 I had already organized a strike for higher salaries and a cafeteria – we brought our food from home then, and we didn't have much to eat.'

Camarão won what was merely the first round. He was the kind of person who slept with an eye open. Even after I took over and Semco started to change into a company that was more trusting and tolerant of its employees, Camarão was deeply suspicious. He questioned everything and fought with our human resources people, particularly Paulo Pereira.

Sometimes, though, Camarão would stop talking just for a moment and give Paulo a chance. And once in a while, they would even manage to exchange ideas, for underneath the hostility Camarão had a lively mind. Gradually, very gradually, he began to soften. Like João Soares, Oseas da Silva, and other Semco workers, Camarão moved from mistrust to the next stage, in which he listened to and thought about, and even tried, a few of our ideas. It's understandable, isn't it, that workers who come of age in an autocratic, authoritarian, paternalistic environment become reflections of it. It took time for Camarão to adjust to the innovative, democratic, participative atmosphere at Semco.

I knew Camarão had turned a corner when Paulo told me how, during a meeting, a union leader compared Semco unfavourably to Termomecanica, one of the giants of Brazil's copper industry. 'Everything is wonderful there,' the union guy said. 'There is a first-class cafeteria where everyone eats whatever they want, and can go back for seconds. Medical care is also first-class. And the salaries are among the highest in the region.'

Before Paulo could intervene, Camarão jumped to our defence. 'Look, my friend,' he told the union man, 'I worked for Termomecanica and I wouldn't go back there. Everything you said is true, but a worker there is only a worker. I'd rather earn less money here and be respected. Only at Semco are workers treated like responsible people. Everywhere else they're nothing – frisked like robbers. I even worked for a company where we weren't allowed to speak. I got plans for a part from the engineering department that were wrong, but I kept quiet and made the part anyway. If I opened my mouth, it would have been worse. I would have lost my job. People believe workers weren't made to think, only to work.'

Soon, Camarão had joined a factory committee and, although we didn't encourage it, began to oppose any arbitrary actions of his union. Sometimes he even told us *we* were going too far and being too permissive. 'Semco starts from the principle that employees deserve to be trusted,' he said. 'But not all workers do, you know. We had a coffee break that began at nine and ended ten minutes later. Then Semco bought some thermos bottles and said we could have coffee any time. But some workers went for coffee and then stayed outside talking, when they should have been working. They abused Semco's trust. The same thing happened when a telephone was installed in the plant. I told them it should be a coin telephone, so everybody would be careful using it. But Semco said the people in the office could use a phone for free, so the workers in the factories should be able to as well. But at lunch people would talk for a long time, especially the younger, single employees, who talked with their girlfriends.'

Having demonstrated an ability to see both sides of factory life, Camarão became a supervisor, leading more than two dozen employees. The promotion was a source of immense pride, since his co-workers had pushed him for the job.

But here is where the story takes an unexpected turn. Although Camarão was a natural leader, he may have been a bit, well, heavy-handed. 'The workers couldn't see that if I was measuring how long it took them to do something, it was because we had a delivery schedule to meet,' he said. 'That if I asked for their attention, it was to make sure the product was being made correctly. I was just trying to be professional.'

At about this time there was another of those economic downdraughts and we had to reduce our work force. As was our habit, we looked carefully at the middle of our organization, searching for supervisory levels we could eliminate. No one is insulated from such scrutiny, and although we were delighted with Camarão's ascension, we felt his position was not absolutely essential, given the slump. So he went back to work at the bench, or at least tried to. Alas, the relationship between Camarão and many of his once and current colleagues on the shop floor was poisoned. They resented him, and the tension and hostility was so great Camarão actually asked us to fire him.

Fortunately, we had a better idea: he would open a small company of his own and become a Semco supplier, furnishing us with sheetmetal parts such as casings for pumps and mixers and special shafts for biscuit machinery. Camarão left Semco with a book full of orders and two challenges: to learn to be not only a successful entrepreneur but also a good boss.

We all knew it would be hard to be one without the other.

Alipio Camargo had a nickname too: 'Dr Disagreement'. He was administrative manager of Hobart when Semco took it over, and we quickly learned he was the kind of person who would count to ten when he got angry – and explode by two.

Hobart was an extremely tough company. People couldn't cough without permission. So it wasn't surprising that Alipio was a demanding boss.

Under our control the plant both loosened up and became more profitable, but Alipio had trouble adjusting to us and to success. We shifted him to sales manager, but his tough-guy approach didn't improve. I remember having a meeting with him to discuss whether we should increase prices by 30 per cent. Alipio thought it was necessary, but not all at once, as we were contemplating. Before long he was screaming at me to take the job of sales manager and do whatever I wanted with it. Then he snatched his briefcase and stormed out. Certain he would be fired, he went home and started his résumé.

By then talking back to bosses was a tradition at Semco. But what bothered us was the way Alipio treated subordinates. He once walked into the office and found that a desk had been removed without his consent. He asked what had happened and a young woman said some workers had taken it elsewhere. 'Who authorized it?' Alipio demanded, his anger rising like an incoming tide.

'I think . . .'

'You're not paid to think,' he snapped. 'You're paid to follow orders.'

It was then that we all knew we had to bring Alipio into the programme. At least the timing was right. We had just developed the evaluation questionnaire, and Alipio became one of the first Semco managers to be rated by his subordinates. His score was about 55 out of 100.

At the follow-up meeting with his people, Alipio was told he was an uncaring autocrat who would have to change. Then came a session with Laura de Barros. His attitude may have been appropriate at Hobart, she said, but now he worked at Semco.

Alipio heard the message and started to improve, which was fortunate because we had in mind making him general manager for administration and finance for the whole company. He had all the technical skills, but we really should have known better, for as soon as the promotion went through he immediately began acting like an autocrat again.

The first floor of our headquarters was a mess: papers were piled on the floor and some of the chairs and tables were broken. When a bank manager arrived for an appointment he had to jump over a pile of debris to get to Alipio's office. So our new general manager gathered everyone together and gave them a week to clean it all up. Anything found on the floor after that, he warned, would be thrown out. And while he was at it, he told them he wanted them all to be more businesslike in their manner. No arguing, he ordered.

Alipio hired an office consulting firm, which proceeded to redesign the layout of his floor. Just as the new furniture was about to arrive, he told his people about the new plan.

'You didn't ask us,' they angrily protested. 'You should have.'

With the entire department up in arms, Alipio was forced to back down and give everyone a few days to recommend changes. In the end they approved Alipio's design, with the exception of just three chairs. But now everyone was happy because they had had a voice in it.

About that time Alipio had his second evaluation. This time his subordinates gave him more than 80. Laura met with him once again and told him that while we all were pleased with his progress we knew he could do better. She told him he should talk more with his people, exchange ideas – and be more participative.

Alipio began to hold monthly meetings with his staff. They even went out together for beer and dinner. And that spring they all went to a ranch for a weekend retreat.

In the spirit of togetherness, Alipio began to think about redesigning his area again. This time, he wanted to eliminate the offices. 'The floor was full of little rooms,' he said. 'We didn't need them.'

But Alipio had learned enough by then to know that he couldn't eliminate the offices suddenly and unilaterally. So after paving the way with a lot of talk, he started by convincing everyone to let him remove a single wall from each office. When they were used to that, he removed another wall. And then another.

'Everybody accepted it,' he said. 'For the first time, we were a team.'

Alipio had become a Semco manager. The final proof was when he reorganized his department, bringing in computers and streamlining all the administrative procedures. He believed he could pare the number of employees in his unit from 44 down to 11. Many were transferred; some were laid off. He fully expected to be in the latter category.

And, indeed, soon he had made so much progress consolidating our many bank accounts and eliminating so many accounting cost centres (once more) that the department really didn't need a manager.

'If you have another job for me, great,' he told me. 'If not, I'll move on to another company. But I'd like to stay.'

Eventually he went back to the Hobart plant to head our food service equipment unit.

The pyramid, the chief organizational principal of the modern corporation, turns a business into a traffic jam. A company starts out like an eight-lane superhighway – the bottom of the pyramid – drops to six lanes, then four, then two, then becomes a country road and eventually a dirt path, before abruptly coming to a stop. Thousands of drivers start off on the highway, but as it narrows more and more are forced to slow and stop. There are smash-ups and cars are pushed off on to the shoulder. Some drivers give up and take side roads to other destinations. A few – the most aggressive – keep charging ahead, swerving and accelerating and bending fenders all about them. Remember, objects in the mirror are closer than they appear.

twenty four

ROUNDING THE PYRAMID

Despite our efforts to simplify Semco's structure and prune away managerial excesses, our executive ranks were still bloated. Some of us in leadership positions were all too aware of the company's bureaucratic girth. So were the factory committee members, who constantly complained that there were too many bosses, and that they talked too much and were too slow to act.

Everyone knew what needed to be done. Several years earlier in 1986, our food service equipment plant provided a vivid case study in what is now known as downsizing. Six positions were eliminated: the managers of marketing, finance, production, sales administration, data processing, and technical assistance. (Four left the company and two went to work for other Semco units.) Together they comprised the entire second tier of the plant's hierarchy, nestling right under the general manager's nose.

The purge probably wouldn't have occurred as an evolutionary step, even at this our most daring plant. As it turned out, though, I was doing my stint at the plant, so the nose in question was mine. My predecessor, in a classic effort to turn the plant around, had brought in more managers. But the workers began complaining that the new bosses were getting in the way, dragging down performance, and costing us money.

I agreed that we could run the plant without the people in the second tier, and so did the people in the third tier. Still, I wasn't about to tell anyone how we were going to replace the six department heads. That was – and is – basic to my style. No one can get me to decide a thing; my goal is to get people to decide things for themselves.

'Who'll do the marketing?' someone asked me after the marketing manager, Mara Mantovani, had cleaned out her office and gone to work for her father's small manufacturing company.

'Let's not worry about it,' I said. 'It'll get done somehow.'

And it did. Mara had four marketing people under her in the third tier and they just divvied up her job, task by task, all by themselves. There was no formality to it. No memos. No meetings. No approvals. Among the marketing manager's responsibilities was to see to it that we were represented at trade fairs. When the next event approached, one of her four deputies took care of it. When the account executive from our advertising agency paid us a visit, another of the four dealt with him. Still another took care of the new brochures. In our new arrangement, the marketing department was no longer headed by an individual. It had become a team.

Oh yes, the moral of the story: far from missing the second tier, the food service equipment unit increased sales and profits. Less was more.

Even so, our other plants were reluctant to follow Ipiranga's lead. The resistance was led, naturally, by mid-level managers who feared for their jobs. Once you put something like this in motion, they undoubtedly thought, who knows where it will stop? Bureaucracies are built by and for people who busy themselves proving they are necessary, especially when they suspect they aren't. All these bosses have to keep themselves occupied, and so they constantly complicate everything.

The heart of the problem is the pyramid, the basic organizing principle of the modern corporation. It gets narrower as it rises, rewarding the few who keep climbing but demoralizing a far greater number who reach a plateau or fall by the wayside. What can be expected from the employees on the lower levels, whose opinion is never sought and to whom explanations are rarely given? They know that the decisions that matter, the decisions that will affect them, are made on high. Is it reasonable to ask, year after year, for a special effort from these people, and then reward them with a few public thank you's and perhaps an extra month's salary, while the lucky few at the top enjoy fancy offices and shiny new cars, not to mention bonuses that can exceed a hundred or even a thousand salaries for an ordinary worker?

Those who make their peace with the pyramid and develop specialized skills – accountants, software writers, engineers of various persuasions – can expect job security. But their fate can be to enter and leave at the same time every day, doing what they have done for years or even decades. Is it reasonable to suppose that they will continue to be motivated?

Those who maintain a smidgen of ambition expected gradual increases in power, responsibility, title, and money. Because of the constraints of the pyramid, organizations are often not ready to promote them fast enough to satisfy them, so many firms take the easy way out and create an extra level or two for their over-achievers. What harm does it do? It's just a few more lines on the organization chart.

But soon there is such a pollution of titles and levels – and a diffusion of responsibility and authority – that much of management's time is spent dealing with the inevitable conflicts, jealousies, and confusion. Six or seven levels are common even at a time when flattening-the-pyramid has become a fad. Bigger corporations have 12 or 14 tiers. Given the typical executive's respect for hierarchies, how is it possible for anyone five rungs from the factory floor to know what's going on there? He can't so he distracts everyone around him with memos, phone calls, and meetings trying to find out.

I wanted our people to have more contact with each other. I wanted less clutter. I wanted fewer levels. I wanted more flexibility. I wanted a new shape for our organization.

In the autumn of 1988 my soon-to-be wife, Sofia, and I rented a house for two weeks on the Caribbean island of Mustique. Our plan was simply to sit on the beach and relax. I brought along a small library – Thomas Mann's *Death in Venice*, Machiavelli's *The Prince*, Ibsen's *A Doll's House*, Taylor Branch's *Parting the Waters*, Alex Haley's *Autobiography of Malcolm X*, and a collection of poems by e.e. cummings. Even so, I spent most of my time thinking about Semco: the progress we had made, the distance we had to go.

I had been trying to get people to react in a new way, to make more decisions, to take control of their working lives, to work faster and think faster. But we were still wedded to an archaic structure. We persisted in cramming our managers into the inflexible pyramid. Up, down, or out. Those were the only options. There was some job rotation going on at Semco, but not nearly enough to compensate for the claustrophobia of the pyramid. It was too hard for people to float around the company, accumulating authority informally. The only way to progress was to move up a rung, even if an employee had no desire to take on additional managerial responsible. The pyramid also limited how much anyone could advance financially by honing their skills in the same job, since it was virtually impossible to pay a person more than his boss. Hell, the pyramid even prevented people from talking directly to their colleagues who were too many rungs above them.

Watching the clear, gentle Caribbean waves, it suddenly seemed so obvious. Why not replace the pyramid with something more fluid?

Like a circle.

A pyramid is rigid and constraining. A circle is filled with possibilities. Why not try to round the pyramid?

We began sketching it out in Mustique. Sofia and I would find sticks and draw in the sand, stepping back to ponder the implications of our handiwork. Back in São Paulo, I continued to refine the idea. After a few months, I was playing with three concentric circles – a tiny one in the centre and two progressively larger ones – and some triangles.

That small, innermost circles would enclose a team of half a dozen people (including me), the equivalent of vice presidents and higher in conventional companies. They would co-ordinate Semco's general policies and strategies and be called Counsellors.

The second circle would enclose the seven to ten leaders of Semco's business units and be called Partners.

The last, immense circle would hold virtually everyone else

at Semco – machine operators, cafeteria workers, janitors, salesmen, security guards, and so on. They would be called Associates.

And the triangles? They would be scattered around that last big circle, each enclosing a single person we would call a Co-ordinator. These people would comprise the first, crucial level of management – the marketing, sales and production supervisors, the engineering and assembly-area foremen, anyone who had a basic leadership role in our old system.

There would be six to twelve triangles for each business unit, and they would float all around the large circle, indicating that the people in them were movable. Although two Co-ordinators would be on the same level of management, they could have vastly different skills, responsibilities, and salaries. What differentiated them would be their competence and leadership abilities.

In my scheme, the smallest circle would serve as a corporate catalyst, stimulating decisions and actions by those in the second circle, the people who actually would run the company. Then would come the Co-ordinators, who would be the leaders of departments or specific activities, guiding teams of five to twenty Associates in their areas.

Movement in our circles would be freer than is possible following the rigid career development paths of the pyramid. Co-ordinators with relatively little ambition could stay in low gear and take in the scenery without worrying about crazy drivers or lengthy tie-ups. They could move from one job to another, assuming there was an opening, or another Co-ordinator willing to trade. They could also decide to go back to being an Associate. And since Associates could earn more than Co-ordinators, no one would have to feel his pay cheque depended on his title. A specialized software engineer who was nevertheless an Associate, for instance, could make much more than a Co-ordinator in the engineering department, who in a classically organized company would have the rank of manager and a bigger salary.

My circles would free people from hierarchical tyranny; they could act as leaders when they wanted and command whatever respect their efforts and competence earned them. They could cease being leaders whenever they wanted, or whenever the organization decided they no longer merited it.

Because Co-ordinators would only be Co-ordinators, and could not embellish their titles with phrases such as 'of Engineering' or 'of Accounting', we would avoid the confusing mumbo-jumbo of appellations and ranks common in modern corporations. And because there would be limits on the number of Co-ordinators, Associates would have to take on more responsibility.

How would decisions be made? On the shop floor, each Associate would make all the decisions he felt confident to make by himself; if he was uncertain about a problem, he would consult his Co-ordinator. Similarly, each Co-ordinator would make all the decisions he felt confident to make. He would bring other issues up at a weekly team meeting presided over by the Partner of his business unit. This session would be held Monday morning, after which the Co-ordinators would brief the Associates they worked with on the results.

Decisions that affected all our business units, such as a company-wide wage increase, or decisions that one business unit did not think it should make alone, such as a large investment in new equipment, would be forwarded to another meeting on Tuesday attended by a representative from each unit (not necessarily the Partner), plus all the Counsellors.

Just three circles, four job categories, and two meetings. That's it.

We had endless discussions about the new structure, and passed out circular organization charts that we asked every manager to hang prominently in his office. But for many, the first reaction to the circles was that they were just another bit of silly symbolism from the people who brought them psychedelically painted factories.

'What am I going to put on my business card?' some wondered. Others balked at the term Partner, fearing someone might think they owned part of the company. 'I don't see what the big deal is about,' still others shrugged. After all, how serious could a few circles be?

In fact, the circles and triangles and trendy new names signified the most radical changes we had yet contemplated at Semco. Where there once were foremen, supervisors, and department heads, we would have only Co-ordinators – and there would be far fewer of them, making for a startling shift in the proportion of indians to chiefs. Implementing the new system meant ripping apart the pyramid, clearing away whole levels of management, eliminating a host of titles, and breaking established chains of command. Moreover, under the new rules one Co-ordinator could not report to another Co-ordinator and one Associate could not report to another Associate. This further flattened the hierarchy and would change the way the entire company would relate to each other.

Even so, the implications of the new system only became apparent at budget time (by which point is was too late to go back). Managers – I mean Partners and Co-ordinators – would say, 'Okay, for this new budget I understand we have to call everyone by new names.' But when they tried to, they realized they were in deep trouble.

'This foreman is now called a Co-ordinator,' they would begin. 'And this supervisor, who is the foreman's boss, is a . . . a . . . I guess he's a Co-ordinator, too.' Pause. 'But what about *his* boss?'

As they were struggling with three suddenly equal people, we would remind them: 'You know, there's only one Co-ordinator for this group.'

'Well, why can't we call all of them Co-ordinators?'

'Because the object of this reorganization is to diminish the bureaucracy.'

'So what happens to those people who can't be bosses any more?'

'That's up to you.'

So they realized we weren't just changing from Title A to Title B. We were reducing the number of bosses as well as the variety of bosses.

It was a big adjustment for those who held supervisory

positions before but now didn't qualify as Co-ordinators. Suddenly, they found themselves floating in our new circle, *sans* title and automatic authority. But their pay cheques weren't affected, and I hoped the new, more relaxed atmosphere in the plant would make the transition easier.

Co-ordinators also had adjustments to make. Consider a spare parts supervisor who made $12,000 a year and an engineering manager who made $85,000 a year. Under the old system, they would have to communicate through many levels of intermediaries. But now both would have the same title and might report directly to the same Partner. Every Monday morning, they could find themselves sitting next to each other at the weekly meeting. Their salaries were irrelevant as far as their participation in decision-making was concerned. Each had the same single vote.

The new system also ensured that a suggestion, request or complaint from an Associate would instantly be heard by someone at the decision-making level, a Co-ordinator, who could take it up directly with a Partner at the next weekly meeting. So shop floor workers who are so easy to ignore in conventional systems could get a response in a matter of days.

That was the theory, anyway. But as we began to implement the new system, we soon ran into the problem of 'ghost layers.' Say we had promoted a machine operator to a foreman's position a few years earlier. This foreman reported to a supervisor who reported to a departmental manager. Along comes Mr Semler and his circles. Of these three managers the Partner decides to keep only one, the supervisor, who becomes a Co-ordinator. But the foreman is a good worker, so he is given the option of going back to his old machine, at his foreman's salary of course, which eases some of his pain. But the problem is that his co-workers still come to him for advice and leadership, maybe because he knows a lot or maybe because old habits die hard.

We couldn't tolerate these 'ghost layers' because we wanted to shorten the path people had to follow to get decisions made or complaints heard. The foreman who became a worker again but was still consulted by his colleagues represented an extra managerial tier we thought we had eliminated.

Slowly, we ferreted out our ghosts and goblins. And we didn't stop there. We kept asking, 'What does this management layer do? What does that layer do?' Like any organization, Semco had divisions for finance, administration, marketing, sales, parts, production, engineering, and the rest. Each of these divisions had its own financial manager and administrative manager and controller and on and on. And below each of these individuals were more managers, in more levels. Each reported to the person one rung up, the classic chain of command. As we put the new system in place, we would cull through these levels. It was like a huge game of musical chairs. There were fewer and fewer seats all the time. Of those supervisors left standing when the music stopped, some went back to their old jobs in the factory, some left Semco voluntarily, and some, inevitably, were dismissed. Their tasks were redistributed, but not formally, because we no longer had specific job descriptions, only those four titles. We just said, 'This person isn't here any more . . .' and let the people involved figure out what to do about it, as people had at the food service equipment unit.

I don't know exactly how many leaders we lost, perhaps 30, maybe more. They ranged from foremen all the way to an executive vice-president, Arno Witte.

'This is just semantics,' Arno had said when he first heard me expound on the circles. 'It's not really going to change anything.'

Two years later he agreed with me that Semco had been so transformed that his own job was superfluous – he was an unnecessary level and he was honest and courageous enough to accept it. Arno was a terrific executive; it had taken us years to recruit him. Now, he was leaving to become president of Dunlop Ltd.

Sadly, we lost a lot of talent in the transition. But it was a price we were willing to pay. Conventional companies warehouse people until something suitable opens up, but you know how we feel about that. Anyway, now that our workers could understand our balance sheets, there wasn't any way to stockpile someone at $100,000 a year, or even $40,000.

Semco today is characterized by an absence of structure that astonishes outsiders. Whenever we hire a consultant who is unfamiliar with our company, he usually begins by asking for a copy of our organizational chart. When we tell him there is no organizational chart, we can see the sweat bead up on his brows. 'Well then, we'll need to make one,' he will say condescendingly. The next half-hour is spent explaining that we haven't used an organizational chart for 12 years and we don't intend to use one now.

The organizational chart is the birth certificate of a business, nothing more and nothing less. It is only useful for people who are unsure about the origins of a division or a role. Organizational charts have their place in the modern corporation – locked away in a filing cabinet.

Let those who swear by these charts take this test: pick a department and ask all the people in it to classify their supervisors according to their proven competence and actual decision-making powers. Transform the results of this survey into a parallel organizational chart and compare it with the official version. I'll be surprised if they're close. The truth is, power and respect cannot be imposed in connect-the-dot fashion.

I have called our structure new, but it isn't much different from the organization used 500,000 generations ago when man was a hunter. The person who saw the mammoth first became The Spotter. The one who chased the fastest after the mammoth was The Runner. The one who threw the spear most accurately was The Maskman. Whoever managed to impose himself as the leader was The Chief.

Consistent with this philosophy, when a promotion takes place now at Semco we simply issue blank business cards and tell the newly elevated individual: 'Think of a title that signals externally your area of operation and responsibility and have it printed.' If the person likes 'Procurement Manager', fine. If he want something more elegant, he can have cards saying, 'First Pharaoh in Charge of Royal Supplies'. Whatever he wants. But inside the company, there are only four options. (Anyway, almost all choose to print only their names.)

Although doubters and sceptics abounded when I first drew my circles, even the most cynical observers were astonished to find that things were better off once we got rid of the pyramid and all its rungs and roles. Critics who months earlier told us, 'We just can't get by without so-and-so' were now marvelling at how fast and efficiently our plants were operating without so-and-so.

Traffic jams became rare. Semco was moving at the speed limit.

twenty five

NAME YOUR PRICE

'I think everyone should set their own salaries.'

Paulo Pereira, our brilliant, iconoclastic ex-personnel manager, now Co-ordinator, was tossing another grenade.

At another company everyone would have laughed. But at Semco, revolutionary notions were taken seriously, because you never knew when one would be adopted. So when Paulo blurted out his modest proposal at one of our 'Growing Bees in The Sky' sessions, everyone tried to imagine what such a system would be like.

'Say that again, Paulo?' Batoni requested after a few moments.

'We've implemented the Round Pyramid,' Paulo said. 'We've eliminated rules and cut the bureaucracy. We've tried to make our company transparent, to let our people be free. Why can't we trust our employees to decide how much they should be making? Is that really such a big step?'

I glanced across the table at Clovis. He had a here-we-go-again look in his eyes.

Top managers at Semco received both a fixed and a variable salary, the latter being a bonus – from 25 to 50 per cent of additional pay a year, on average, in good years – based on performance. But no one was satisfied with the way these bonuses were allotted.

Many companies have bonus systems – nothing new there. Most are based on profits. If the budget forecasts a $1 million profit, for example, a manager might earn a certain percentage of extra pay when that goal is reached and more if it is exceeded. Bonuses can also be based on sales volume or invoicing levels. But such conventional formulae can be unfair and counter-productive. Say a year is progressing nicely and a company is closing in on 110 per cent of the pro-jected profit. Then a major client goes belly-up and an accounting adjustment has to be made, bringing profits down to 85 per cent of the forecast. Wouldn't the suddenly bonus-less managers become demotivated? Or say a new tax law brings a mediocre performance up to 120 per cent profit? Aren't the shareholders going to be peeved if bonuses are doled out?

At Semco we tried five or six bonus systems, without suc-cess. Managers would be happy one year, perturbed the next. We tried to tailor formulae for individual plants and cut the period of the payout from annually to semi-annually to quar-terly. Nothing worked. Then we realized that we shouldn't be doing anything to solve this problem. Since democracy was now part of our corporate culture, why not let our managers set their own goals and, when the year was over, decide the extent to which they had met them. From there it would be a relatively simple matter to award themselves the appropriate bonus. And no one would dare complain about the fairness of the system, since the managers would determine their own reward.

Cynics thought a few of them might take advantage and award themselves undeserved or even outlandish sums, but that didn't happen. I like to think it is because everyone at Semco is reasonable and honest. Maybe, but I'm sure our transparency had a lot to do with it – public salaries are a strong disincentive to be conspicuously greedy.

The success of the new bonus system gave Paulo his opening. He had dreamed of implementing self-set salaries almost from the time he arrived at Semco. He got the idea after attending a course on salary surveys and discovering that most systems looked empirically sound but actually were far from it.

Paulo had talked to Clovis and me about self-set salaries straight after that, but we decided Semco wasn't ready. Now, two years later, the few traditionalists left at the company were still hesitant. What about all the elaborate schedules comparing salaries from job to job, company to company, and industry to industry? they reminded us. Should we just throw them out?

Yes, we replied. Surely there was a better way to set salaries, a way that would give our employees a role in a process that is always one-sided.

We were aware that, if we allowed people to set their own salaries, the differences among colleagues would become that much more irritating and disruptive. Conventional salary systems after all, strive for standardization. The system we were contemplating would be individualistic. Executives would be called on to make different calibrations of worth and value. What if someone lacked the experience of a colleague but considered himself more dynamic? If an executive asked for too little and got it, would he be undervalued by those around him?

While Paulo and the Counsellors were stewing about this, I called in Irene Tubertini, the last of my three secretaries. 'How much money do you need to earn to live comfortably,' I asked her, watching her face flush and her brown eyes cloud over with bewilderment. 'How much money do you need so that you will leave for work in the morning with the feeling that you are fairly paid; so that you won't be tempted to look for another job.'

She sat there, not quite believing what she was hearing, wondering what I could possibly be up to. I told her to think about it for a day or two, then give me a number. That would be her salary for the next year. Yes, I was serious, I told her. We intended to ask others the same question, and hold them to their answers.

A few days later Irene told me she wanted to be paid $20,000 a year, which was a shade higher than she had been making. That seemed a little low to me, so I pushed it up by 10 per cent and we had a deal.

Having passed the Tubertini test, we called together those in the highest leadership positions at Semco and their immediate staff and went through the same routine. We chose these people because they were educated, could express their opinions, and were less susceptible to being manipulated by us.

We devised an evaluation form to help them through the process. They listed their age, how long they had worked at Semco, their current role, and how they spent their time – that is, how much of their working day was devoted to making decisions, meeting with customers, working in departments other than their own, and so on. Since we had done away with conventional titles and most other hierarchical distinctions, it was difficult to differentiate between managers without asking them precisely what they did. And we also asked our people how they would represent themselves if they were to leave Semco and look for a similar job elsewhere.

After each manager completed the questionnaire, he gave it to his boss, who also filled it in. That gave us two sets of evaluations for each person.

We didn't want to create a process in which an employee would say, 'I want to earn $1,000 a week,' and his boss would respond, 'You only deserve $750.' This wasn't supposed to be a negotiation. We wanted each manager to focus on his role in the company and his value. So a boss might tell a subordinate, 'You said you consider yourself a veteran, but I think you're still a junior purchasing manager.' We hoped they would keep talking until they came to a meeting of the minds.

Only then did the subject of money come up. Before they told us what they wanted to be paid, we asked them to consider four criteria: what they thought they could make elsewhere; what others with similar responsibilities and skills made at Semco; what friends with similar backgrounds made; and how much money they needed to live. To help them with the first two, we gave them a salary survey from Semco as well as national surveys compiled by such consultants as Price Waterhouse and Coopers & Lybrand. For the second two, they had to look inside themselves.

Then they decided how much they would be paid, just like that.

*

Well, not quite. We had originally planned not to change a salary once a person set it. If it was too high, he would have to live with the fact that the whole company would know he had overpaid himself. If it was too low, he would have to wait another year before raising it. But since this was our first, nerve-fraying trip down this road we felt more comfortable knowing there would be an opportunity for some give and take between a boss and subordinate before a number was finalized.

We needn't have worried. Except for half a dozen people, everyone set salaries that were in line with our expectations. In five of the six exceptions, people set salaries *lower* than we had projected. It wasn't always easy to get them to raise their figure, either.

'I found it difficult to define how much I should get,' said José Violi Filho, who had been recruited to Semco by his friend Iotti.

Violi, who is barely five feet tall and weighs just over 100 pounds, has one of the clearest, quickest minds I have ever come across. He can cut through a business problem or analyse a balance sheet in seconds. He came to us as an assistant accountant, rose to accountant, then chief accountant, plant controller, and corporate controller, with a stint as treasurer somewhere in there. Then he wanted to run a business unit and eventually became the Partner for the food service equipment unit. Then he went back to the financial area as a Counsellor, doubling as a Partner for corporate finance. (See what I mean about careers being hectic.) But back then, he was a country boy, too shy and uncertain to pay himself a proper salary.

His supervisor at the time, Alipio Camargo, rejected the $15,000 a year figure Violi chose. 'You better re-do this,' he said, 'because as it is, we cannot even start to talk.'

Violi raised his figure to $18,000. Alipio disagreed again, saying the right number was $25,000. The case was taken to Clovis, who decided that Alipio was right.

Of those who participated in that first round of salary setting, only one sales manager awarded himself an outlandish sum. He had aspirations of becoming a Partner and just went ahead and set his salary at that level, which was $70,000 per year, about 30 per cent more than he was making, apparently hoping the promotion would follow.

We felt he could become a good sales director, but not right away, and, since we already had a sales director, probably not at Semco. When we told him this, he calmly told us he was under consideration to be managing director at another company. He got the job, too, so perhaps he was right about his salary.

There are three reasons why reasonableness prevailed. First, everyone knew what everyone else was paid. Second, the top people – Clovis, Batoni, Vendramin – are all modest about their pay. (For the record, I am a bit less modest; my salary reached a high of $300,000 in the heady days of 1989, but has been as low as $120,000.) As a matter of corporate philosophy, we try to keep our top salaries within ten times our entry level pay, which is in stark contrast to the rest of the country, where a top manager's salary can be 80 times as much as a worker's.

The third reason our people tended to be modest about salaries has to do with self-preservation. Remember, at Semco our operational budgets cover just over six months, not the usual twelve. Since an unanticipated increase in expenditures has to be offset in a short period, there is little margin for manoeuvring. Our people know salaries account for most of our operating costs, and they think about our six-month budgets when they set them. It's easy to solve a budget problem by eliminating a salary that seems too high, and no one wants to stick out.

After several years of this, the economic impact of self-set salaries has been far less dramatic than we had thought. A 10 per cent increase has turned out to be the exception. Brazilian law doesn't allow for a reduction in salary, even a self-set salary, but when inflation is high real income goes down when salaries are relatively stable. By this measure self-set salaries at Semco have gone way down in some years. Obviously, our people are keeping their salaries in check because of their concern about Semco's welfare. In good times and bad, self-set salaries have encouraged our workers to take that rarest of corporate perspectives, a long-term view. And they have the added virtue of eliminating complaints about pay, which are always among a company's most contentious issues.

About 5 per cent of our work force took part in that first experiment. Now we're up to nearly 25 per cent, including most of our Co-ordinators. I don't see any reason why factory workers can't one day make the same calculations.

Now that our leaders were happy with their salaries – or at least responsible for them – Paulo had another, even more daring proposal. He called it 'risk salary'.

'Each of you now has the correct salary, according to your own estimate of your worth,' he told managers at a meeting of company leaders in 1989. 'I propose to pay you a little less, but in return will give you the possibility of earning more.'

Then he explained his new wrinkle. If Semco did well, an employee who agreed to risk a 25 per cent salary cut – the limit – would receive up to 50 per cent more. Then again, if Semco did poorly, he would suffer the 25 per cent cut.

Employees who didn't have high fixed expenses have taken Paulo up on his offer and risked more; those with non-working spouses and children have risked less. The results, so far, have been rewarding to the players and the company, since with this programme part of our labour costs fluctuates with profits or losses. When business is good, people in the programme make a lot more money. When it isn't, they are helping us cut expenses and lowering their profile in case cost-cutters are called out.

twenty six

THE PUBLIC AWAITS

Based on our new philosophies and policies Semco now boasted one of the highest growth rates in Brazil. Sales, which had been about $4 million a year for decades, had swelled to $35 million, and in just a few years we went from one to six factories and from 100 to 830 employees.

Semco was No. 1 or No. 2 in every one of its markets; we had 85 per cent of Brazil's marine equipment sales, 70 per cent of its hydraulic pump sales, and 65 per cent of its commercial dishwasher sales, and our Hobart scales had gone from 3 per cent to 23 per cent of the market in three years – this despite many competitors, most of them divisions of large, powerful multinationals.

What made it all that much sweeter was that we didn't owe a cent to anybody, since we had no debt. In fact, bank vice-presidents whose secretaries always told us they were in a meeting when we called now were calling our switchboard, trying to make appointments to see us. And never during our expansion did we receive any help from the government.

But success is more than impressive numbers in an annual report. Oseas da Silva, a member of the factory committee at Santo Amaro who had once organized and led strikes against the company, described our transformation in Brazil's largest newspaper: 'It was hard to get used to. You know, like when people are used to living in an authoritarian regime. When they finally let you out of jail, you can't believe it's true. The workers are motivated to work.'

Another Semco employee told a magazine: 'The company became a paradise to work in. Nobody wants to leave.'

It's enough to go to your head. Which I guess it did. So, early in 1988, at the age of 28, I decided it was time to compose

my memoirs. Sofia and I headed for our ranch in the mountains, where there is no phone. For nine days I wrote
furiously, 12, even 14 hours at a clip, working so hard I was
often surprised by the dawn. It all came gushing out, ten years
of experimentation and craziness, frustration and joy. Not
having much faith in electronic gadgets after Semco's experience with computers, I used the word processor with an eraser
on one end.

I drove down the mountains with 750 handwritten pages I
called *Turning the Tables*. I sent copies to Brazil's major publishers and waited. Weeks passed. Finally, one called. I
thought he was my best bet, since he had published both
Iacocca and Morita. We went to lunch and I came back thinking he would make me an offer. He never did.

The other publishers never got back to me, so I called them.
None were interested in my book, although two suggested
that I might print it at my own expense to give to Semco
employees.

That's when I thought of Richard Civita. I didn't know him
personally, but knew his company, Nova Cultural, a large dis-
tributor of magazines and a medium-sized publisher. I called
him and told him my story. He said he was leaving for New
York that night and would read my manuscript on the plane.
Two days later I was told he was willing to pay all of $2,000
for the story of my life and my company. Well, money wasn't
the point, I quickly told myself. I called my lawyer and asked
him to draw up a contract, urging him not to push too hard,
since this was the only publisher in Brazil willing to take a
chance on my story. But he is a tough man, and demanded
that the contract contain a clause calling for the royalty rate to
increase with each 100,000 books I sold. The publisher and I
laughed about that, since we would have been happy if we
moved 5,000 copies.

What did we know? *Turning the Tables* would eventually
sell 400,000 copies and spend nearly 200 weeks on the bestseller list, making it Brazil's biggest-selling non-fiction book
ever. The nation, it seemed, was eager for new ideas. As I like
to say, we were sitting on our surfboard, a tiny speck in the

ocean, when a huge wave of organizational unhappiness broke. We just stood up and rode it into shore.

I was a successful if iconoclastic manager who would soon be a best-selling author, and a minor celebrity. But I had another ambition: I wanted to be an alumnus of Harvard Business School.

I had started thinking about studying at Harvard halfway through high school. It became an obsession years later, when I was taken to Cambridge by friends and was impressed by what I saw. Returning by subway to Boston, I bought an extra token. I put it in my wallet with the intention of using it on the day I was admitted.

The next year I applied to the Business School, against the better judgement of some local counsellors who thought studying in the United States would do nothing for my career in Brazil. They also feared that a rejection, which they evidently believed was more than a remote possibility, would be a blow to my oversized and fragile ego. If I had to go to school in the US, they advised, why not apply to several universities and cut my risk.

Being thick-headed, I applied only to Harvard and anxiously awaited the decision. Finally the letters from Cambridge arrived. Try opening an envelope with your fingers crossed.

I was sure I would be accepted. I was wrong. It took me weeks to recover. I didn't tell anyone, to spare myself the added misery of listening to such comforting remarks as, 'That's not all there is in life, you know.' From time to time, though, I checked my wallet to make sure the token was still there. I don't know why, but I was convinced I would study at Harvard one day, if only that token didn't get lost. I couldn't cheat and put it in a safe place, either. It had to stay in my wallet if it was to work its magic.

Two years later, I applied to Harvard again. This time, I was granted an interview at the school. I scheduled an appointment to coincide with a business trip and off I went to

Boston. I had spent a good deal of thought on my attire, finally settling on the dark wool suit with discreet chalk stripes I chose for my first day at Semco, a starched white shirt, and a sombre tie. After a long internal debate, I decided not to wear a matching handkerchief. But I had devised a boldly different way to drape my overcoat elegantly over my arm. Having made such careful preparations, you can imagine my horror when I checked into the hotel the night before my interview, opened my suitcase, and discovered that my suit was a wrinkled mess. It was 11 p.m. – too late for a pressing. Then I remembered an old trick of my father's: he would hang his suit near the shower and let the steam smooth out the material. Relieved, I sat back on the bed to watch M*A*S*H while my suit relaxed. Then came Johnny Carson. Then came sleep. The hot air in the room woke me with a start and I realized, horrified for the second time, that it was 4 a.m. and the shower was still on. I rushed to the bathroom to find that my suit was damper than Gene Kelly's in *Singing in the Rain*.

But what luck. It was snowing outside, and by morning my spongy look was quite suitable.

My conversation with the Dean's assistant went well – at least I was impressed with my conduct. As I was about to leave, he suggested that I attend a class, which I did. The instructor sarcastically introduced me as 'an elegant gentleman from Brazil', I guess because I was the only one in the room wearing a suit.

I returned to Brazil to once again await Harvard's verdict. After a few weeks the letter arrived. It seemed distressingly slim. I remember holding it up to a light to see if entrance forms were enclosed. I opened the letter. After the 'Dear Applicant' I saw the words 'Regrettably'.

It would be many days before I took the letter out again and read it all the way through. Twice spurned! And the token was still in my wallet.

For the first time I considered abandoning my objective. Then I recalled how I had forgotten my wallet in various places and it had always been returned, token and all. And how I had bought new wallets several times and carefully transferred the token. This had to be a sign. A Sign, I mean.

Many months later, on a day on which I became particularly irritated about losing an order, I decided to send a slightly abusive letter to Harvard telling everyone at that great institution exactly what I thought of its admissions policy. In the last rejection letter, I was told I didn't have enough experience, even though I had been working at Semco for years. So I told them in my letter that by their standards they wouldn't have accepted Steven Jobs when he was starting Apple.

A few months later another letter arrived from Cambridge, and I braced myself for a rebuke. But the letter merely asked me to fill out a few forms and send in my photograph in order to be enrolled for the upcoming semester. What miserable timing! By then so much was happening at Semco that it seemed more educational to stay put.

I finally did become a Harvard alumnus, though. A few years later, after I had led Semco for six years, I decided to attend a programme for corporate executives that consisted of a month of intensive instruction each year for three years. I still had a lot to learn about formal business disciplines and techniques, but I was at least as curious about how the people at Harvard – the professors and the other CEO's – would react to the ideas and programmes we had been implementing at Semco. Would they think we were as strange as I thought they were?

I spent dozens of hours discussing Semco during my three months. It would come up nearly every time a class touched on the theory of managerial organization or labour relations or productivity. I think I can safely say that I amused them with my explanation of our circular organization and self-set salaries.

'Maybe I'll try that when I get back,' they would say, shaking their heads. But somehow I got the feeling that most of them wouldn't.

twenty seven

SWELLED HEADS

Factory committees with real power; offices with open doors, and fewer than the usual number of walls; balance sheets that are posted on bulletin boards; rulebooks tossed into the bin; memos never longer than a page; circles instead of the pyramid; executives that make any sum they say; and a bestselling book chronicling the whole thing. No wonder Semco was beginning to attract attention.

My colleagues and I had made the 'A' list. Invitations flowed in. I was giving 50 or 60 lectures a year by myself. My style was confrontational: my talk to the Association of Railroad Workers was entitled 'The Dying Railroad Industry', I told the Junior Secretaries' Annual Conference 'How to Stop Being a Secretary', and the Convention of Financial Executives was treated to 'Doing Away With the Financial Executive'. When I spoke to the undergraduates at Brazil's main business school, the theme was 'Why Undergraduate Business Schools are Unnecessary'.

Even so, I was also sought out for newspaper and magazine interviews and television and radio appearances. My classmates at Harvard may have been sceptical, but to our amazement and delight corporate executives and business school professors from around the world were lining up at our door to get a look at the place. It got so crowded around our plants that some factory committee leaders complained that all those visitors were interfering with production. To ease the pressure, we instituted the 'Semcotour' programme. We would save up the requests and once a month group together representatives from a dozen companies and take them through the company together. When we found we still couldn't handle the volume, we ran tours twice a month and increased the number of participants to 35. Even so, there was a five-month wait.

It was all so flattering, so exciting, that I suppose it was understandable that for a while we lost track of what had brought us all this attention and fame – our business. In time, I cut back my lectures to about 20 a year, and we discouraged tours and reduced our exposure in the media. But it wasn't soon enough to avoid making a series of mistakes.

We were so thrilled with the attitude of the workers at our food service equipment unit that we fell in love with everything they made. The plant was in the black, but we realized too late it was making less than it should have been. Call it the price of vanity, but we lost at least $3 million over four years by stubbornly sticking with the unit's mechanical scales, slicers, meat grinders, and potato peelers. They had just about run their course commercially, but we kept thinking we could make improvements that would set them apart, so they wouldn't be just another commodity.

Take the mechanical scales, for example. They were still selling at the rate of 1,300 a month, which represented about 20 per cent of our business from the food service equipment unit. But the product was so unsophisticated it didn't have much of a future, and because it was being knocked out by 20 competitors, its price had deteriorated and there wasn't much profit in it. So the scale didn't have much of a present, either. Even so, we spent hundreds of thousands of dollars changing the design, the materials, the suppliers, and the production process, frittering away managerial energy trying to fix something that was best abandoned. We all had such an emotional stake in keeping the scale alive. It had been the mainstay of Hobart in Brazil for half a century, and was a fixture in half the grocery stores and supermarkets in the country.

We finally recognized reality and offered the manufacturing machinery, patterns, and moulds to any employees who wanted to start their own scale business. But our workers were so convinced we were giving away the family jewels that it took us 18 months to shut down the line and transfer the equipment. They kept forming task forces and pleading for time to prove that a new process or a new assembly method would revitalize the scale market.

We also spent years clinging to an air-conditioning cooling tower for office buildings we made at our BAC plant. Our product was still made from steel long after the competition had switched to fibreglass or plastic. Steel was stronger and fire-resistant, we kept telling ourselves, but it would also rust – especially in buildings by the sea. We spent much time and money trying to convince customers to accept our superiority, before switching – much too late – to a fibreglass tower.

We had trouble as well with a piece of machinery called a fluid coupling, which is used in large conveyor belts. We made a deal with a British company, Fluidrive, to jointly set up a sales force in Britain and Brazil and started advertising, but our line never caught on. A German company called Voith had a vice-grip on the market and would cut prices every time we bid against them. Stubbornly, we tried to battle them head to head, when we should have lain back, biding our time. Then, when customers became tired of having only one supplier, we could have entered the business with a chance of success.

But we were impulsive and headstrong, and it cost us money and jobs. Perhaps we were taking our own press clippings too seriously.

At the Jabaquara plant, meanwhile, Fiasco and Rogerio had worked miracles. Productivity soared. Labour relations were exemplary. Sales of their electronic scales had grown from an average of 150 to 600 or 700 a month, and they had peaks when they sold more than 1,000. Our market share rose from less than 10 per cent to more than 35 per cent, and our profits rose along with it. It was marketing heaven.

There was no second-guessing the move from Ipiranga. The Kids at Jabaquara had ended the plague of late deliveries and solved the unit's chronic quality problems, among other things closing an opening in the scales' housing that enabled cockroaches to enter. (Once inside, they would eat all the bits of food they could find and then move on to the integrated circuits.)

When we saw we were making a bundle, we did what any shrewd company would do and invested heavily in the new plant. Then we hit another of those economic air pockets and everyone suddenly stopped spending money. Our distributors were loaded with electronic scales, and sales dropped to less than 200 a month and, during a few dreadful months, to 50 and even 30. At one of our Tuesday Partners' meetings a little later, Fiasco came in with a plan. 'We call it "The Mule Without a Head",' he said, passing copies of it around the table.

We all looked at the document while Fiasco sat there with a sardonic grin we didn't quite understand. First, there was a projection for the coming year that showed the unit would make a small profit. No mean feat, considering the difficult times the electronic scale plant faced. Then came a balance sheet that also forecast a recovery. Projected sales volume, however, was not optimistic, and investments in new products and production machinery were estimated at zero. So where was this profit to come from? we wondered.

The answer was on the next page, where there was a list of all the people who would be left at the unit after the 'Mule Without a Head' reorganization occurred. Absent were Rogerio, the purchasing manager, the sales manager, and several other key people.

'How will you run the unit without all these people?' Vendramin asked, assuming Fiasco would be willing to put in extraordinary personal effort, out of self-preservation.

'Do you see my name on that list, Joao?' Fiasco replied.

That's when we realized what the title of the proposal meant. There was an awkward silence around the table.

'What will you do?' Batoni asked Fiasco after a while. 'Do you have another job lined up?'

'Not at all,' Fiasco said. 'I'm at the company's disposal. I can't think of anywhere I would fit in now, but we can worry about that later. The bottom has dropped out of our business, and I can't try to preserve my job when I feel the unit can't afford me any longer.'

'This could all be temporary,' Clovis said. 'What happens if the business springs back? It has in the past, you know. Are we going to throw away all the investment we have made in you and your staff?'

'Today, Clovis, my recommendation would be "yes",' Fiasco said solemnly. 'If it were my money, I wouldn't put any more of it into a business with such a risky future.'

'Does that mean you don't believe in the scale business?' Vendramin asked. 'Do you think we should shut it down?'

'No, I believe in the business and in our product,' Fiasco said. 'What I don't believe in is Brazil's ability to pull itself out of its economic slump so soon. If you want my opinion, I'd move the unit back to Ipiranga.'

Everyone protested at once. The decision to split up our plants had been one of our great successes. It was inconceivable that we should abandon this approach.

The plant had made $1 million for us in its brief life. The trouble was, we had sunk half of it back into the building, the design consultants, the prototypes, and the specialized machinery. As we debated the future of the plant, Fiasco proved to us that we would have to spend more than $500,000 a year to keep the unit going as it was currently constituted until the economy rebounded. Cutting the payroll and folding the digital scale plant into Ipiranga would at least give us a chance to ride out the lean years without a heavy additional investment.

So we moved it back, but only under certain conditions. First, we would keep the unit configured just as it had been at Jabaquara, except on a smaller scale. An area of 15,000 square feet was set aside at Ipiranga for the new plant, and everything about it – all inventories, decisions, operations, even the entrances – were to be separate. Of the 28 employees at Jabaquara, 20 would move with the unit. Some of the other managers were transferred to other Semco plants. The personnel reductions, incidentally, cost us another $1.5 million, since most people left with the equivalent of half a year's pay or more.

And what of the Head of the Mule? It would be a shame to lose someone who had had such a successful career at Semco and so understood our culture. But we had nothing suitable for Fiasco and, given our opposition to stockpiling talent, putting him on the shelf was not an option. He stayed on at Semco for a few months, helping to organize the move and smoothing out the transition. Then, as destiny would have it, he became production director for Sasib, a subsidiary of the Italian giant Olivetti that made biscuit factories in competition with our Santo Amaro unit.

'*C'est la vie*,' a Frenchman might say. Or, perhaps, '*Merde*.'

twenty eight

ZERO TOLERANCE

You can run a successful business or be ethical. Take your pick.

You hear this a lot in Latin America, with good reason. Corruption wasn't invented on that continent, but it is rivalled only by Africa as the warmest greenhouse for its growth. Below the equator it is a daily affair, democratic in the broadest sense, since everyone can take part if they wish. And so many do. Passports ordinarily take weeks to arrive, but can be had within a day if the way is greased. Building permits? Speeding tickets? Tax audits? No problem.

How did I get to be such a nun at the brothel? I was born wealthy, which makes a huge difference. Having a family of means creates the opportunity for all sorts of idiosyncrasies. One of mine is proving that business can be conducted without blind obedience to established but anachronistic rules and traditions, including corruption.

Most large Latin American companies wouldn't survive the pressures exerted by crooked governments (which are the vast majority of governments in the last hundred years) had they not decided to trade commendable credos and cash for, say, a zoning change to build a factory or a licence to open a branch business. But about three years after I took over, an opportunity presented itself to test my conviction that Semco could be different.

Companies in Brazil are subject to routine inspections every so often, ostensibly to check compliance with building codes and other regulations. We received such a visit just after we renovated part of the Santo Amaro plant. The law said we had to have a covered walkway separating the factory from the workers' dressing area, but we didn't. I don't really know why, an oversight, I guess. The two inspectors decided on a

small fine and gave us 90 days to comply with the require-
ment.

But we were just too busy to get around to it. Alas, when
payoffs are a way of doing business, people rarely feel the need
to comply with arbitrary rules, since they believe all will be
certified in the end, one way or another.

The two inspectors came back and this time they said they
would have to fine us $200,000 and, if we didn't fix the build-
ing within 30 days, close us down. *Pause.* Or they could do
some 'consulting' for us, for $20,000 in 'fees'. There would be
no fine and no plant closing. Just business as usual.

Clovis and I discussed the matter at length. Paying the
inspectors the bribe was out of the question. But the possibility that the plant would be shut was too awful to contemplate,
and there was no way we could make the changes in 30 days.
So we decided to blow the whistle.

We knew the risks. We would instantly become a favourite
target for inspectors of all stripes. Retaliation was their forte.

We called the mayor's office anyway and were referred to a
high government official who, we were assured, was an honest
man.

Off we went to see him. We had the names of the two
inspectors and the last name of the man we believed was their
leader, which was Rota. The official received us warmly and
was extremely interested in the case. He was looking for
opportunities to rid the city of corrupt officials, he said, and
was thrilled we had stepped forward. 'I want the man who is
leading my team of corruption-busters to hear your story,' he
said, picking up his telephone to summon him.

Clovis and I exchanged a glance. 'Hello,' the official said
into the phone. 'Yes. Can you drop by my office right now? I
have two gentlemen here who are telling me about a payoff.'

Minutes later, a tall, white-haired man strode into the
office. 'Ah, here's our man now,' the official said to us. 'Mr
Semler and Mr Bojikian, I'd like you to meet Mr Rota.'

Visits from inspectors were more frequent after that, but we
weren't sure Rota had anything to do with it. Most of the

inspectors seemed honest, and we did all we could to stay within the rules.

We weren't especially worried when one day in 1989 a tax department official arrived at the Santo Amaro plant and began an audit. He was 60 years old or close to it, and more than a little arrogant. Later, we learned he had been a professor and a lawyer. Usually tax inspectors stay about a week and then, if they are honest and everything is in order, move on. This guy spent a week with us and found nothing. Then he spent another week. And another. He was still at the plant after five months. Five months! Through it all our people scrupulously followed his instructions and gave him everything he wanted.

Finally, the inspector had a meeting with our accountant and told him he had found 'several irregularities'. If he reported them, he said, Semco would be liable for $700,000 in taxes and fines. Our accountant looked through his report and found it outrageous. All the inspector had come up with were a few administrative and clerical mistakes, all of them minor. An invoice with one date would be listed with another date in our books: innocent errors, that was all.

'This is absurd,' said our accountant angrily.

To his astonishment, the inspector agreed. 'But if I levy these fines against you,' he added matter of factly, 'it will cost you a fortune in lawyers' fees to defend yourself. Sure you'll win, but at what price?'

So now we got the picture. For $150,000, he would save us all that trouble and a good piece of change, and give us a tax-audit that would keep us safe from other inspectors for three years. They all worked together, the inspector said, so we were guaranteed not to be bothered.

We had a quick meeting of top managers and unanimously decided to take another stab at whistle-blowing. I phoned a friend who had been Brazil's finance minister and told him the story. He referred me to a high government official, who explained what we would have to do. Brazilian law is sticky about entrapment; only the victims of a shakedown can conduct a sting. The police would have to wait until a payoff before moving in to make an arrest.

Off Clovis went to buy the recording equipment. Oswaldo Guimaraes, the engineer, would set it up. Violi would conduct the final negotiations with the inspector and make the actual payoff. The plan was to hold another meeting at which he would tell the inspector that we accepted the deal and set the time and terms for payment.

The meeting was arranged for 3 p.m. that Friday. 'I can laugh about it today, but I was really nervous then,' Violi recalled. 'The office where the meeting would be held was on the ground floor of our headquarters. The door would be closed, of course. But I was to turn the knob twice. That was the signal to Clovis and Oswaldo to start recording us.'

Violi must have seemed a little crazy that day, pacing up and down the hall and working his fingers into tight fists. But when the inspector arrived, he played his part perfectly.

'I said it wasn't going to be easy to pay him, since Semco didn't have an "unofficial" bank account for that purpose. He told me how to do it. I was acting like I didn't understand him, to make him repeat himself, because the more he spoke, the better it was for us. I said it would be really hard to get all that money at once. He said we could pay in ten instalments.'

The inspector even offered Violi a 10 per cent cut, saying it was traditional that the person with whom he did business got a share.

'I said I wouldn't take it,' Violi said. 'That made him nervous. He said that he only kept 10 per cent, too, and that the other 80 per cent stayed in the "system", which was the word he used for corruption. I had to say I would think it over.'

Violi set up another meeting on the next Monday, same place and time, and promised he would have the first payment ready. The inspector said he would write up a report citing Semco with a minor infraction, which we could easily contest. 'Don't worry,' he said. 'I'll show you how.' But Violi, ever a detail man, insisted the inspector give us a clean bill of health. The inspector got nervous, but Violi was adamant. 'Take it or leave it,' he said.

All this time, we were next door, listening to bits of the conversation. I say bits because the microphone wasn't working properly and at one point a compressor went on in the factory and drowned out everything.

By Monday we had perfected the recording system and arranged for the compressor to be silent. We also hid a video camera in a corner of the room, in some plants. At around 2 p.m. two police officers and two investigators arrived in an unmarked car. A little later, a reporter and a photographer arrived from one of Brazil's biggest newspapers. We had invited them to document the arrest, just in case the government officials let us down.

The payoff was set for 3 p.m. It was midsummer and unbearably hot in the un-airconditioned building, especially in the bathroom, where six grown men were now hiding.

We watched the clock: 3 o'clock came and went, then 3.10, 3.20, 3.30. The inspector had always been prompt. Was he on to us? To help calm his nerves, Violi called home and chatted with his wife. It was 3.40, 3.50. The police officers, stretching, looked at their watches and wondered whether they should leave.

Finally, the security guard rang to say the inspector had arrived. Everyone scampered into position. Adrenaline levels soared. The inspector apologized to Violi for his tardiness. His wife wasn't well, he said.

Violi got straight to the point. 'Are you sure you want to do this?' he asked, trying to make the inspector go through the scheme all over again, for the benefit of the recorders and, we hoped, the witnesses and eventually the courts. The inspector said he did and got out the audit papers for Violi to sign. Meanwhile, he told Violi how his wife had broken her leg in a fall over the weekend and was now hospitalized.

Great, Violi thought to himself. In a moment he will be arrested and his life will be ruined.

After they finished the paperwork, Violi turned over the cheque, announcing: 'This is the first payment.'

'A cheque? I want cash.'

Violi told him there was no way he could withdraw that amount of cash. The inspector wanted Violi to go with him to the bank. Violi said he wouldn't. Finally, the inspector took the cheque and put it in a little wallet.

It was over. Violi invited the inspector to have coffee on the third floor. That was the signal for the police officers to arrest him. Violi half-expected then to break down the door and burst in with guns drawn. Instead, the door slowly opened and a single officer calmly entered the room. When the inspector realized what was happening, he turned pale, then looked over at Violi and started cursing. The police officers got the video cassette and the audio tape and sealed them in an evidence bag. As they all walked to the parking lot, Violi tried not to look at the inspector. The inspector asked to talk with his son, who was waiting outside in a car. Then everyone went to the police station.

Violi, rattled by the episode, took some time off. I went on television to try to encourage other executives to help root out corruption. The inspector was eventually convicted of extortion and sentenced to two years in prison.

There was no reason to rejoice, though. The inspector's superiors, whom he cited in the tapes, were not even brought in for questioning. I got a few letters and telegrams of support, but when I proposed to establish a centre to combat corruption and provide businesses with legal advice, not one executive publicly supported me.

A little while later one of our clerks went to a government department for a document and was told, 'Tell your boss he doesn't just have one inspector to worry about, he's got 100,000 against him now.' And so it seemed. Shipments destined for Semco plants were held up for ages at airports and docks. Semco trucks were stopped at state borders for inspection. Certificates, approvals, and forms of all kinds took forever to be issued. It was the price of doing business honestly.

A year and a half later, while Sofia and I were on our honeymoon, several inspectors showed up at the house we were building and demanded a $6,000 bribe. Otherwise, they said, they would hold up the work for months. (They didn't know who the owner was.)

The contractor, long accustomed to paying, negotiated a sum. His plan was to pay them before I returned, knowing I wouldn't agree, and then bill me many months later, when everything was done. But we returned before the payment was made. On our first visit to the site, I asked a foreman if everything was going well and he enthusiastically agreed. 'Especially since those inspectors stopped coming round,' he added with a grin. Alarm bells went off and I asked the contractor what had happened.

I called the mayor, a woman known for her honesty, and told her the story. She asked me if I wanted to make another arrest. So we did it all over again. This time, Brazil's main television network covered it live. But I didn't take part in the proceedings or give interviews afterwards. The mayor's office handled everything and few viewers even knew it was my house.

But, of course, the inspector's friends did. During the rest of the construction we were visited by an unending stream of inspectors armed with electronic measuring devices and thick books of building codes, most of which they probably hadn't read in years. There was no end to petty bureaucratic obstacles. But it just hardened our will to build our home despite complex and unreasonable building codes that had undoubtedly been created to foster corrupt activities. In Brazil, we call this 'creating difficulties to sell simplicities'.

Now we are the proud owners of a home that should be a museum, since it is probably one of the few structures in Brazil that meets every regulation.

twenty nine

THINKING FOR A LIVING

Next to our Santo Amaro plant is a cemetery. Our silent partner, some of us call it.

'See that lawn?' my father used to say. 'It's filled with people who were indispensable to their companies.'

One day he too would be buried there, facing the factory at his insistence, 'to keep an eye on it'.

His spectral vigilance did not dissuade three of our most free-thinking engineers from making without doubt the weirdest proposal we ever entertained at Semco. They wanted to invite all the Partners to the cemetery, where everyone – dressed in black, naturally – would gather around a coffin emblazoned with a ribbon that read 'SEMCO'. It would be a symbolic burial of the company.

While others complained that Semco was moving too fast, these three instigators – Oswaldo Guimaraes, Marco Aurelio, and Rogerio Ottolia (of the late, lamented Jabaquara unit) – were annoyed with what they regarded as our slow, cumbersome, wasteful, bureaucratic ways. Laying all that to rest was their way of waking us up. We didn't hold the ceremony, but the engineers – who were also known around Semco as the Nucleus of Technological Innovation – had once again made their point.

The three had proposed the unit themselves at a meeting with Clovis, Laura, Marcio, and me. Their idea was to take a small group raised in Semco's culture and familiar with its people and its products – them, naturally – and set them free. Removed from day-to-day activities, they would no longer worry about production problems, billing, inventory, machines that didn't work, or subordinates who wanted a raise. They would have all their time free to think.

They believed that, thus liberated, they would invent new products, refine old ones, devise market strategies, unearth cost reductions and production efficiencies, even dream up new lines of business.

It seemed to us that the three engineers had the right credentials. Each had shown a combination of creativity and pig-headedness that constantly caused them to question nearly everything about the company.

The bearded, 30-year-old Oswaldo had twinkling eyes that lit up every time the 'Eureka' machine in his mind switched on, which was often. He had started as a draftsman at the French machine tool company Brevet and rose to assistant manager before we whisked him away to become our chief engineer and then engineering manager. In our Great Reorganization, he had become a Co-ordinator in charge of a sophisticated team that designed large machinery such as mixing equipment for bubble gum and rocket fuel. He liked to say he turned his subconscious on when he went to sleep, and had the answers upon awaking.

Marco, an electrical engineer, was a tall, awkward fellow, with bulging eyes, dishevelled hair, and a strong contrarian personality that threw colleagues and customers off balance. A brilliant technician, he would invent wiring schemes that no one but he understood. A line of biscuit machines he designed for United Biscuits had six miles of wiring, in fact, with hundreds of controls and thousands of switches. The company's engineers pronounced it 'worthy of a 747', confiding to us that they would have settled for something in the order of say, a 707.

After Rogerio left the digital scale plant, courtesy of 'The Mule Without a Head' plan, he became our chief electronic engineer. Like Oswaldo, he had often been courted by potential employers, but had spurned their lucrative offers. The NTI, it seemed, would make his loyalty worthwhile.

We all liked their idea for the unit, but added five ground rules. One, members wouldn't have a boss. They would report to no one at all. Two – the flip-side of one – they could not hire any subordinates. Three, they would be free to set their own schedules, write their own job descriptions, determine their own activities, and change any of it as they pleased, any time and for any reason. Four, they would report their activities twice a year to the Partners, who would decide whether they would keep their jobs for another six months. Five, they would continue to receive a salary, though it would be less than they had been getting as senior managers. But they would also share in the proceeds of the ideas and innovations they thought up, whether it was profit-sharing on products they designed, royalties on sales of new products they developed, or a percentage of the savings from cost reductions they came up with. (How big a cut would be up to them.) And they could sell consulting services to anyone else who wanted them.

The three had been making between $25,000 and $35,000. As NTI members they would earn more than that in a good year, but less than they might as independent entrepreneurs. Then again, they would suffer less in a downturn than if they were on their own, and would have the backing of a large organization with a well-known name. All in all, we figured their compensation could swing from $15,000 to $80,000.

They knew a good deal when they saw one. We all shook hands and our three newly liberated engineers went home to rest. The next day they would have to start thinking for a living. Well, Oswaldo would anyway, since both Rogerio and Marco went off on vacation.

The trio moved into a small suite of offices in our Santo Amaro headquarters. Partitions that separated work areas were removed and drafting tables were installed. Files started arriving from all over the company containing technical information on our products and processes. The engineers gathered all sorts of records and documents, probing for weak spots they might turn into opportunities. Soon there was a large collection of spare parts – bolts, bits of scrap metal, an odd motor shaft, a gear for a dough mixer – piled in the centre of their floor. To some it looked like junk. To the NTI it was inspiration.

Having thus feathered their nest, the team started to adjust to a life without routines. They arrived early, read the papers, and, well, thought. Then they thought some more. Like subjects in an isolation tank, they floated all day, unfettered by corporate gravity, undisturbed by bureaucratic distractions.

It was too much of a good thing for Marco. He missed running the wiring of his machines, redesigning and then testing his ideas, and, yes, having subordinates to do those little things for him. And he was too nervous just sitting around thinking, so he went back to his old department.

Laura de Barros, by then a Co-ordinator for training and organizational development, took his place. While Oswaldo and Rogerio concentrated on the industrial side, she would act as a counterweight on non-production issues, focusing on Semco's 'software'.

That was what we kept telling ourselves, anyway. But at first the three of them butted in all over Semco: 'Poking the wound', they called it. The marketing department wasn't aggressive enough, they complained. Why did human resources have to run the Semcotour programme? Shouldn't each department get to play host on a rotating basis? And they wanted the Partners to start a programme in which we would call customers at random and ask them how satisfied they were with our products.

'We interfered with everyone, from directors to workers,' Oswaldo recalled, barely suppressing a grin. 'There are still people who don't like us.'

One afternoon, Oswaldo, Rogerio, and Laura were sitting around studying one of our mixers. It blended paint and pigments in a tank, using a mixing arm that moved in a slow, circular motion. Laura, a mechanical neophyte, asked how the tanks were cleaned when the colours were changed.

'The arm is lifted and someone scrubs the tank,' Oswaldo replied.

'Someone should invent a giant toothbrush to clean the tanks,' Laura said.

So they did. The new product had a brushlike appendage

that, hooked on our mixer, swept the sides and bottom of the tank automatically, eliminating manual labour.

Soon our curious trio of thinkers started attracting attention from outside Semco, including an article in *Exame*, the big Brazilian business magazine. After that they were bombarded with inventions, including – this was my favourite – a device that looked like a miniature umbrella and opened up inside the nose, removing any obstructions.

They passed on the nasal cleaner, but even so had 18 new projects under way by the time of their first six-month review. They grew even more prolific after that. In just a few years the NTI has come up with such diverse items as a scale that weighs freight trains while they are moving at full speed, a fibre optic tube used by doctors to examine patients' throats, and electronic systems to control small assembly lines.

The team also formed an environmental consulting firm that advises clients on the recycling of waste materials and conducts audits to assess the environmental liabilities of companies being considered for takeover. This eventually became an independent business unit, Semco Environmental Resources, and has, besides a permanent staff of 25 professionals, another 40 biologists, geologists, hydraulic engineers, and economists on call.

The NTI has made internal changes at Semco, too, reducing downtime on machines, streamlining manufacturing processes, and cutting assembly times. It has redesigned our paint mixer completely, changing the steel casing and the motor's pulley system, which allowed us to cut its price by 32 per cent and enter an export market that had been closed because of its high cost. And it has revamped our dough mixer, which used to take ten hours and fourteen steps to assemble but now requires three steps that take less than an hour. The gears, formerly custom-made, are now adapted from off-the-shelf automobile gears, another cost-saving idea of the NTI.

We've even begun a junior version of the NTI. We call it Lost in Space. Every year (provided it's a good one), we choose at least one young person from among our applicants from business or engineering schools or even high schools. These extremely fortunate souls have no job description, no boss, no set responsibilities. They are free to roam through the company for a year, so long as they work in at least 12 departments and try to generate enough revenue to cover their salary. (Even a trainee can put together a financial analysis, gather marketing data, work in production, or sell.) At the end of the year, they are free to negotiate a more permanent arrangement with any of the departments in which they served.

We've unearthed some exceptional people through Lost in Space, including one young man who left us after two years to become, at age 25, the planning manager for Shell Brazil. He went on to land a job in Paris as European sales manager for Brown's, which owns 4,000 clothing stores.

We'll let the multinationals train him some more, and then bring him back from space.

thirty

RISE AND SHINE

Regimentation is the soul of the modern factory, and standardized shifts are the soul of regimentation. So what was that worker doing showing up at the darkened, deserted Ipiranga factory at 4.30 a.m.?

Given the traffic, the long commutes, and the usually inadequate public transportation many workers put up with, it seems utterly unreasonable to expect them to time their trips so that they will arrive at the factory at precisely the same time, day after day. Yet every company does, even in huge cities such as São Paulo, with 15 million people, most of whom seem to be on the road simultaneously.

We had long ago let our office employees decide when they would start and end their working day, becoming one of perhaps half a dozen companies in Brazil offering this freedom. In 1988, we tried to extend it to our factory workers. If they wanted to have breakfast with their kids or take them to school, who were we to stop them? Beyond that, flexible working hours demonstrated our belief that we wanted to pay workers for results, not merely their time – and we didn't care how those results were obtained. Our idea was to agree on our common goal, then let our employees loose to achieve it.

Anyway, if workers arrive promptly at 8 a.m. and leave at the stroke of 5 p.m. but are ineffective in between, what good is it? With flexible work schedules, we thought it would be possible to finish the year with the performance we wanted but without mind-numbing records of what time people showed up each day.

Such freedom was – is – unheard of in an industrial setting. At least we weren't aware of any other company, in Brazil or elsewhere, with factories running on flexitime. When Paulo

Pereira brought up the idea just about everyone at Semco was against it, including many of the plan's beneficiaries. We had grown so quickly that as much as 40 per cent of our work force had been at Semco for less than 12 months, and their experience elsewhere had convinced them that anything a company proposed was suspect, even flexible working hours. What's more, their union leaders, who like to make speeches about how employers ought to treat workers with dignity and respect, were jealous and insecure. When a Semco initiative appeared counter to common practice, they would drag their feet until they were sure they understood all the implications.

So flexitime had two strikes against it even before we considered the leery reaction of our managers. True, many of our products were being assembled by teams of workers in self-managing manufacturing cells, and workers were making many decisions bosses used to make. Even so, in many instances these workers all had to arrive at more or less the same time. Otherwise, production sequences would be scrambled and some would be idle, waiting for colleagues who were responsible for the preceding manufacturing steps.

For three months, Paulo conducted a feasibility study on flexitime, hoping to prove it would reduce absenteeism and poor performance. One of his best sources was our 'Good-Bye Interview', in which everyone who was laid off, fired or left voluntarily had a chance to give us a piece of his mind. 'I live too far from work and my commute is too long,' many would tell us, or, 'I haven't had breakfast with my kids in ages,' or, 'I constantly fought with my boss about tardiness.' From all this Paulo concluded that starting times were a major cause of conflict and misunderstanding between bosses and subordinates. He believed workers would let resentment over rigid schedu.es build, until they exploded at critical times.

Paulo called our top managers together and told them that with flexible schedules it would be possible to reduce almost to zero absenteeism and greatly cut overtime as well. 'There are very few activities with such a high degree of dependency that it is not possible to have an interval of 15 or 30 minutes between one production step and the next,' he told them. 'In those cases, we won't adopt the flexible schedule. You'll be pleased with the results. Conflicts with the supervisors will be reduced, the time clock will no longer be viewed as a monster, workers will feel more respected – and they'll produce more.'

No, they weren't convinced. In response to their objections, Paulo said we would form a task force to mediate disputes between workers over starting times (which, in fact, has yet to meet). The managers still weren't convinced, but at Paulo's urging they decided to go along, if only as an experiment.

The Nacoes Unidas marine products plant was Paulo's laboratory. Though it had only opened in 1988, some of our most veteran workers, the ones who knew us the best, had been shifted there. We called in the factory committee members and the union leaders, who naturally brought their lawyers, since our plan would require major changes in our contract.

Under the plan we had in mind, everyone would still work eight hours a day, but they could get to the plant any time between 7 and 9 a.m. and leave accordingly in the afternoon.

Now, when our workers arrived at the factory, most of them would go to the locker room, put on their uniforms, then go down to the cafeteria, have their coffee and rolls, and maybe read the newspaper, and *then* start their shift. They wouldn't be clocked in, though, until they actually started working. We didn't want to change this. But the union leaders' attitude to flexitime was: 'No one just suddenly lets people come in whenever they want. We don't know what it is, but there must be a catch.' And, failing to find it, they took the opportunity to demand that workers be clocked in as soon as they arrived at the plant.

We believed working hours were just that, and rejected the paternalistic notion that 'once you enter our gates you are under our wing'. We were pleased that our workers felt at home at Semco and encouraged them to play cards, lounge about, read the paper, and all the rest. But we weren't going to change our policy of clocking them in when they arrived at their machines.

After many meetings, neither side had budged. So the union did its best to convince the workers that, under the circumstances, flexitime was a bad idea. With a truck and a loudspeaker, they repeated the well-known refrain: 'Be careful, colleagues. Bosses don't do anything good for workers.'

But they didn't prevail, perhaps because the employees knew us so well. During a mass assembly in the cafeteria the workers voted to give the plan a try.

Most of them came in between 6.30 and 7.30, which was fine, since there wasn't an assembly line at the plant.

On to the Ipiranga factory. The union wasted no time mounting its attack there too, putting out the word to workers that they had a right under the labour law to be five minutes late a day, or thirty minutes a week. It accused management of trying to eliminate this grace period. We argued that under the same law workers could be docked pay or even suspended for arriving more than five minutes late, and that, besides freedom, we were offering relief from that ridiculousness.

We successfully countered the union's attack only to face resistance from the managers who wanted to scupper the programme before it started, believing that the workers were not capable of self-control. True, this had been a showcase plant, with inter-departmental teams and workers making all sorts of decisions, but don't forget that it had gone through the disruption of being divided into three units and workers there had a set of new bosses to deal with. And, of course, there were still scars from the strike.

But the factory committee, under the leadership of Soares, saved us. First, it convinced the workers to give the plan a try. Then it stationed a group of workers near the time clock to discourage colleagues from violating the new rules. At the end of the first month, the guilty parties were identified publicly and warned that if they didn't comply with the programme they wouldn't have to worry about what time they came in, since they wouldn't have a job.

It was at Ipiranga that Saulo Henri Fiorini, a welder, decided to come in at 4.30 a.m. But one worker alone in the dark could get hurt, so we asked him to readjust his hours, and he complied. Eventually, nearly half the shop floor workers decided to come in at the same time, 6.30, so that the dishwasher assembly wouldn't be disrupted. Many commuted along the same rail line, and there was a train that was nearly empty at that hour.

The programme was more of a problem at the machinery plant at Santo Amaro. Obstreperous and irresponsible union leaders persuaded workers to vote the plan down, again accusing us of trying to do away with the weekly 30-minute grace period for tardiness. But a year later, the members of the factory committee, impressed with the success of flexitime at other plants, called a plantwide meeting to reconsider the idea. Flexitime was adopted by a nine to one margin.

Alas, it was a different story at our air conditioner plant. The town of Diadema, where it is located, has a large concentration of metal workers, a contentious bunch who are represented by an avowedly Marxist union with links to the Workers Party, a political organization that comprises many far-left and militant groups.

Workers at this plant, and members of the factory committee, were much more radical and less trusting than anywhere else at Semco. Years later they eventually came around, and their leader, Vicentinho Da Silva, told a television audience that 'Brazil had only one trustworthy boss – Ricardo Semler and Semco.'

But back then they didn't want to try flexible hours. In fact, it wasn't until 1991 that they finally accepted it.

In high school I was fascinated with the high jump, maybe because no one else was. It was as if I was always measuring myself against the bar. Perched atop two supports, it seemed to enjoy thwarting my efforts to surmount it.

In the beginning, five feet was a grand obstacle. Observing the intensity of my interest, the coach decided to teach me the then-radical technique of jumping backwards. After almost a year of practice, I was clearing 5' 8". Every inch became an obsession. The bar and I had long, solitary matches. Sometimes I would take the school bus home frustrated beyond words. Sometimes it would be the bar's turn to brood. Making it over 6' 0" was the most important goal in my life. I would barely scrape the bar and lie breathless on the mat, peering up to see if it would roll over on to me. Then after one jump it held fast. A silly grin formed on my face and stayed there for days.

A few years ago, I struggled with an opportunity to acquire a company with five plants and 2,000 employees. 'Why do we want to grow more?' I asked myself. 'Are we going to be better for it?' It reminded me of a feeling from an earlier day. 'Why do I constantly throw myself at the bar? Is there no limit?'

It's all about persistence, isn't it? But where does persistence end and obsession begin? How high is too high? How big is too big? Of course, some growth is necessary for any business to keep up with competitors and provide new opportunities for its people. But so often it is power and greed and just plain stubbornness that makes bigger automatically seem better.

thirty one

COLLAPSE

In the first 11 years I led Semco, Brazil had two good years, three transitional years, and six dreadful years. Inflation, the scourge of Latin America, averaged more than 400 per cent a year, swinging from yearly highs of 1,600 per cent to lows of a mere 100 per cent (with some months of deflation in between). From 1986 to 1990, the country endured five economic shock plans, knocked three zeros off its currency twice and on two occasions changed it altogether. The stock market soared during the country's worst recession and went bust during a boom; banks made billions when inflation rose, then fired 150,000 clerical workers when it fell.

Given this almost unimaginably complex and difficult economy, 150 million people were nearly always unsure what to do. A 10 per cent wage hike might look tempting one month, then prove inadequate when the official statistics showed that inflation had been 15 per cent. The tension between suppliers and customers was intense, as each sought to change the payment terms to their own advantage. Competition to sell anything was fierce, but Semco endured the dangerous oscillations with the help of our workers. We had years in which sales grew by 80 per cent and even 120 per cent, in real terms, but also years in which they dropped by 20 per cent and then 35 per cent the next year.

As the 1980s – 'the lost decade', the experts called it – ended, the economy fell off a cliff. Industrial output plummeted by 9 per cent in 1990 and the gross national product was heading back to levels not seen since the 1970s. In São Paulo, there were half a million people unemployed, a number that would nearly triple by 1992.

And just when we thought it couldn't get worse, it did. A

new President, Fernando Collor de Mello, assumed office and appointed a young economist, Zélia Cardoso de Mello (no relation to the president) as finance minister. She proceeded to test some new theories, including one that held that there was too much money in circulation, that it belonged to too few people, and that they were doing too much speculating with it. Because of this, her theory went, not enough money was being invested in industry. This was generating inflation and stagnation.

So, she thought, let's take some of that money and give it to the government (which doesn't have enough, right?). On a sunny spring day in 1990 she went on television to declare a bank holiday and seize 80 per cent of the cash in the country. The government laid hold of savings accounts, cheque accounts, certificates of deposit, company funds, the works. Every Brazilian, no matter what his assets, was left with $800 or 20 per cent of his holdings, whichever was less. If someone had, say, $1,000 in a cheque account, he now could spend $200. The lady said she'd give the money back, corrected for inflation by an official index, in 12 monthly instalments, starting in a year and a half.

Chaos doesn't begin to describe the reaction. Industrial output sank another 14 per cent in the next 12 months. Companies didn't have money to meet their payrolls, much less to conduct business. At Semco we struggled through several months of zero sales – what company was going to buy machinery that took ten months to deliver when it didn't know if it would survive the week – and then the government decided to open the country to imports. The duty for foreign machinery, which had been 45 per cent, was cut to 35 per cent, then 30 per cent, and by the end of 1992 to 20 per cent. So we had to contend not only with a market that had lost nearly half its volume but also with increasing competition from abroad.

Thrashing about in precarious waters, we started discussions with our factory committees to find ways to keep Semco afloat. It struck most of us as obvious that we could no longer employ the same number of people as we had. Not with so few sales. The question was, how could we all work together to minimize the pain?

Nothing is more corrosive to motivation and productivity than layoffs, and over the years we had tried mightily to insulate our workers from the wrenching volatility of the Brazilian economy. For starters, we refrained from hiring people to work on products we knew would have a short life span. Opening a hula-hoop division without knowing what to do with all those hula-hoop makers when the fad inevitably wanes might make you rich in the short run, but it is a strategy for adventurers – and adventurers have no future, only a present.

Also, we never promised anyone job security. In fact, we refrained from hiring good executives if they demanded a job contract. There is no such thing as a sure thing, and one side or the other will necessarily suffer. Look at the damage those golden parachutes have done to corporate morale, not to mention balance sheets.

Nearly everyone stops putting people on the payroll when business is down, and almost everyone eases up when it improves. This is another error. Sales start going up and soon secretaries, office assistants, chauffeurs, analysts, receptionists and an army of others are streaming through the doors. Sales slow, and they are all 're-evaluated', depressing the lucky ones who survive the inevitable purge. Even when the government stimulated the economy and orders abounded, Semco controlled hiring with the same iron hand it used during lean times. We possibly lost market share as a result, but when demand sank to its original level we didn't have to let scores of the new people go. Any alley cat can stay lean when food is scarce; the trick is to stay lean during the good times.

Yet from 1989 to 1991 Semco suffered a 40 per cent drop in sales. We had come to rely on our work place initiatives for at least partial immunity against economic turbulence, but there's only so much you and your people can do when you lose almost half your business. For some of our plants, there was no way out.

*

In the late 1980s, our marine division at Santo Amaro enjoyed a huge $14 million backlog of orders. Since it only produced $5 million worth of products a year, it had three years of work already secure. We decided to invest more than $500,000 in the building, which had an innovative layout the workers helped design and new pump-testing facilities that cost a bundle. It all seemed worth it, though, as productivity ascended to unimagined heights.

Then Hurricane Zélia hit and the shipbuilding industry took the blow head on. Emaq, the shipyard that had saved us in 1981 with the Petrobras order, foundered. Then Verolme, a yard that had ordered pumps for five years from us, followed. Only three shipyards were left, and they were months behind in paying their bills. Semco was left with $1.5 million of receivables that were no longer collectables, and, even worse, $4 million worth of products ready for delivery that the shipyards could no longer pay for. We needed 20,000 square feet just to store all the unwanted pumps, half-ready casings, and 300-horsepower motors. The stacks were 15 feet high.

We called the workers together and discussed what we all could do. One proposal, designed to avoid layoffs, called for salary cuts of 20 per cent across the board, until the business revived. But many workers, already struggling with their bills, felt they couldn't afford even a small cut. They also thought it would be like 'using a sieve to block out the sun'. These employees wanted us to take our losses and lay off part of the workforce at once, and they had enough votes to turn our proposal down.

We tried all the cost-slashing measures we could think of – coffee breaks were cut to once a day, copying machines were locked away, electricity consumption was monitored, new uniform purchases were suspended, and all expenses were looked at by many sets of eagle eyes. But I didn't hold out much hope. I'm not a big proponent of cost-cutting programmes. I like to think we don't spend money unnecessarily even in good times. And how do you measure how many sales were lost because the reps had their gasoline allowance cut, or what the cash flow might have been if the clerks in billing had not been saddled with a cut in telephone expenses, or even how many little mistakes and miscalculations could have been avoided if engineers hadn't cut back on photocopies of blue-prints? When the foolish penny-pinching is over, everyone goes back to business as usual – until someone thinks expenses are excessive again and begins a new round of cuts, starting with the expenditure needed to make up for the shortsighted-ness of the previous cost-cutting campaign.

Our people at Santo Amaro scrimped and saved, but it was far from enough. So we got serious. We organized the factory workers into teams and sent them out to sell replacement parts at the docks. This was a steady market, since incoming ships needed to change worn impellers, shafts, and wear-rings, boom or bust. But lots of smaller machine shops had already realized this. We called these shops pirates because they made cheap, shoddy copies of Semco parts and gave 'friends' on the ships fat commissions to buy them. Our workers did their best to compete, but they were no match for all these Captain Hooks.

Meanwhile, at the marine products plant, a worker assembly was called at the cafeteria and we repeated our proposal to cut working hours and pay to keep everyone employed. This time, we said, we would implement the wage reduction in a Robin Hood-like manner, so those with lower salaries wouldn't suffer as much.

Labour law has always been paternalistic in Brazil (and justifiably so, given the greed of some Brazilian businessmen). If a worker is paid, say, $250 a week, his company has to pay him another $1,000 at Christmas, $1,300 at vacation time (four weeks paid, plus a $300 bonus), and deposit a sum equal to 8 per cent of his wages each month in a savings account. If an employee is dismissed, he gets whatever is in that account, plus 40 per cent more, plus double pay for vacation days that haven't been taken. Then there is severance pay that, for employees such as ours, many of whom had been with Semco 10, 15, even 30 years, would add up to two years of salary.

It wasn't a golden parachute but, given the belief of many workers at the marine products division that our business was not likely to revive soon, it wasn't a bad deal, either. Why work for one or two years at reduced wages, only to be laid off anyway? So like the workers at Santo Amaro they voted down our salary reduction plan, in the process consigning some of their colleagues to walk the plank.

About this time I went to Ipiranga to see Alipio Camargo, then its Partner. Sales of our big industrial dishwashers had dropped from 40 a month to 25 and then to a measly 5, and inventory levels and factory expenses were killing us. If the situation didn't improve, I didn't have to tell him, the plant would have to shut.

I was so absorbed in my thoughts as I left that day that I didn't notice João Soares, the factory committee leader, standing in front of the welding booth. But he saw me.

João knew things were bleak, but he was adamant. The plant, which had been proof of what can be achieved when workers are treated as adults and encouraged to make decisions, could not be shut. Not now. Not after what we had accomplished.

'Tell me, João,' I said, 'if this business were yours, and you knew that over the next quarter you were going to sell only a handful of dishwashers a month, not the 40 you used to sell, what would you do?'

'That's the trouble with you,' he replied. 'You're only thinking about the next three months. What about when we start to grow again? Or do you believe we're never going to grow again?'

'No, João, it's not that. But it's been a while since this unit has made any money.'

'But there are things we can do,' he said.

The machines were down. In the background I could hear the murmur of the workers as they said their goodbyes and left for home.

'I'll leave it to you,' I told Soares after a while, 'and the factory committee. Come up with a plan, go over it with Alipio and the others, and we'll try it. But think it over, João. If you have the capacity to produce 40 dishwashers a month but you sell only a handful, what are you going to do with all those people? The economy could take years to recover.'

It's so much easier to throw the stone, I thought to myself, than be the window.

João went to his house just outside São Paulo – a house he could not have imagined owning when, as a nine-year-old, he sold iced tea and peanuts at the Maracana soccer stadium in Rio. He stayed up long into the night worrying about the plant. He thought about it all through Saturday and Sunday, too. Semco was his life. Too much so – his constant presence at the plant was one reason why, a year earlier, his marriage had failed.

João thought about the succession of grim factories in which he had worked before joining us. One had toilets with half-doors, so workers couldn't hide from foremen. At another, he would lose a whole day's pay for being one minute late. Pacing up and down his small bedroom, he thought about how different his life now was. He remembered his first factory committee meeting, how he and his co-workers had been too scared to talk. And the benefits they had acquired: health insurance, free breakfasts, flexible working hours, and, most important, the intoxicating feeling of self-determination that is all but non-existence in conventional factories. The workers at the food service equipment unit had achieved so much, João thought. Then it struck him. That was their way out.

When he arrived at Ipiranga on Monday he gathered all 150 workers in the middle of the shop floor, telling them he had an idea that might save the plant and their jobs. The workers would voluntarily reduce their wages by 30 per cent and forgo a 10 per cent raise they were due. They would also give up subsidized meals, their transportation allowance, and other benefits. That was the conventional part of the plan. Then came the twist: the workers would take over all the services at the plant provided by outside contractors and third parties and perform them themselves, slashing the company's costs. At the cafeteria, Soares said, the workers would buy the food and prepare it. They would guard the factory gates and clean the offices and the shop when the working day was over. They would transport finished goods to customers and sell replacement parts to restaurants and hotels.

In return, the workers would share with management the authority to run the plant, making all business decisions jointly – a guarantee that their sacrifice would not be wasted. All strategies, policies and investments – every check – would require approval from both the bosses and the workers. Oh yes, and the bosses would consent to a 40 per cent pay cut.

When he had finished explaining his plan, his colleagues were silent. Then a woman spoke.

'Clean the bathrooms? No way. I've never done it, and I'm not going to start now.'

'I'll be the first to clean the bathrooms,' João said. 'There's nothing wrong with spending half an hour a day cleaning bathrooms. And the offices, too. Look, with this plan the company won't have to send anybody away. We won't have any layoffs.'

When he called for a vote, more than 100 hands were raised in approval.

The plant managers, as might be expected, were hardly as enthusiastic about Soares's idea, but slowly they warmed to it. Alipio was already thinking about starting his own business and would soon implement a 'Mule Without a Head' plan of his own, essentially putting himself out of a job for the second time in just a few years.

Some changes were negotiated. Management accepted the 40 per cent pay cut for two months only, with a 30 per cent reduction after that. The cuts were applied in the Robin Hood fashion, to protect lower-paid workers, and – ever the optimists – employees were granted an extra profit-sharing payment of 15 per cent, on top of the 23 per cent provided by SemcoPar. And with that, Semco had its first experiment in co-management.

*

After just one month, we could hardly believe the results. The workers had saved so much that the extra profit-sharing clause was actually invoked, which helped compensate for reduced salaries.

The second month was even better. And by the end of the third month, the employees' salaries had been fully restored. Sales of dishwashers stabilized at a hardly spectacular 12 a month, but the plant was selling more spare parts than before.

Even so, co-management, though a noble experiment that helped stave off a deep round of layoffs, wasn't a permanent way to run the Hobart plant, or any plant. Profitability depended on an extraordinarily low level of expenses, which in turn depended on exceptional efforts of workers that couldn't be sustained forever.

And there are other reasons why I don't believe in co-management. Take that second signature on the cheque, the one that belongs to the workers. Do they get to appoint anyone to sign? What if they choose someone to lead them who won't work with management? João Soares was particularly well suited to deal with the problems we had at the food service equipment unit, but what if the workers there decided they wanted, say, a radical union leader or someone who asn't versed in our corporate culture?

Co-management requires two sides, which is one more than is necessary to run anything efficiently. Too many leaders may be worse than too few. We had proved that at Semco as we eliminated extra levels of management. This was no time to turn back.

All in all, we withstood the downturn better than other companies in our fields, most of which laid off 30 to 40 per cent of their workers. We had endured a 40 per cent drop in sales and hadn't even increased our borrowing. But carrying many surplus workers on the payroll and finishing new orders without the inflow of cash from old ones had cost us nearly all of our retained earnings.

After months of debate, we concluded that Brazil's economy wasn't going to get better soon, so continuing along this

path was dangerous. We didn't want to change our philosophy, or even our long-term strategy, but we needed some new
tactics if we were going to survive.

Well, we had created a company as flexible as any we knew.
If nothing else, Semco had been redesigned to adapt to
change, and to do so quickly and without pre-conceived, 'this-
is-the-way-it's-done-here' solutions. Now we would put that
adaptability to the test.

thirty two

LAUNCHING PAD

Pedro Miranda de Oliveira paced up and down, wearing out the linoleum in the hall outside the cafeteria at Santo Amaro and demonstrating why he was called 'The Bullet'. He was facing the biggest decision of his life, and he had only an hour to decide.

Pedro, a short, muscular man with dark, tousled hair and eyes that darted all over the place, had joined Semco in 1979 as a lathe operator, running the big machines that cut metal bars into shafts for pumps, mixers and motors. It required considerable skill, since a wrong move would turn dozens of pounds of valuable bronze or stainless steel into scrap. Pedro became one of our best operators, then went through a nine-month training programme studying machining and learning to read engineers' plans. After that, he moved up to our most demanding lathe, which could cut cylinders of steel five metres long into shafts for agitators used for refining gold, among other things.

In 1987, Pedro became a Co-ordinator, supervising more than 50 co-workers who cut and polished sheet metal for mixers and pumps. We weren't surprised when he proved good at it, for he made the quick decisions blue-collar workers prize.

But now, despite our efforts to keep the payroll tight, our success in cutting unnecessary expenses, and our astonishing gains in productivity, Semco was in trouble. We had too many employees making too many products at too many factories – or maybe just too few customers. Either way, we had to change. We had achieved a true partnership with our workers – er, I mean our Associates – based on trust and a mutuality of interests. But in this excruciatingly harsh economic climate, we needed a divorce – an amicable divorce, of course, with community property.

During our 'Chats at Lunch' sessions, at assemblies with workers, in interviews company officials gave to magazines and newspapers, Pedro had heard the phrase horizontalization. We were constantly discussing and debating what functions Semco should continue to perform and what activities it should farm out to others. As we thought more about it, we became convinced we no longer wanted to do anything that could be done just as well elsewhere.

But at Semco there is always a wrinkle, isn't there? Instead of contracting out business to strangers, we decided we wanted to contract it out to the people we knew best: our workers. We would help them to start their own companies, transforming themselves from employees to partners. And so the Satellite Programme was born.

'If you want something done well and cheaply, do it yourself.' That was the mantra of the-bigger-is-better companies. But how many businesses have lost their way as they grew? Henry Ford was so fond of verticalization he raised trees to make the sideboards of his Model T's, bought iron mines and cargo ships, even searched the Amazon for a site for a rubber plant for tyres. The company's official history doesn't play it up, but Ford had to fire 60,000 workers because of rampant do-it-yourselfism.

Farming out work to specialists, sub-contractors, consultants, and assorted third parties can avoid a host of problems. For starters, it reduces fixed labour costs. It also helps empty the shelves of inventory, since the raw materials and spare parts a company would normally stock are spread out among its new suppliers. Companies like ours, which make products requiring complicated and sophisticated manufacturing processes, tie up a lot of capital in stockrooms and warehouses. This is not good when the economy takes a downturn.

Above all, people act differently when they own their own businesses. Workers who fight for every extra minute of a coffee break will toil late into the night and on Saturdays and Sundays if it means keeping their own company alive. At Semco, we had succeeded largely because we had increased our employees' stake in their jobs. Our people already worked late and on the weekends of course, and they didn't need any prompting from bosses. But by encouraging them to start their own businesses, we would raise their sense of involvement even higher.

Theoretically, farming out work means a loss of the profits of verticalization. But just ask Henry Ford about that. So as Brazil's economy foundered, we decided to heed lessons old Henry ignored. Few companies could match our five-metre lathe, a rare machine that can cut down huge metal cylinders, or our vertical mills, which are used for creating perfectly polished and symmetrical surfaces on steel casings and housings. Few companies had the expertise to solder the huge internal coils of our cooling towers, fabricate special gears for our mixers, or coat couplings with titanium. These operations would be expensive if not impossible to sub-contract, so we would continue to perform them. We would also keep our staff of highly specialized design engineers, who adapt our products to suit customers' specific requirements, whether they need mixers for soup or bubble gum. Same with the people responsible for computer-aided design work that not only entailed expensive equipment but also crucial trade secrets.

But drafting in ink? There were thousands of drafters in Brazil as skilled as ours. And sheet-metal work? There were hundreds, if not thousands, of Brazilian companies that could roll steel plates for mixer bodies. And what about legal work and software development? Weren't these candidates for sub-contracting?

Sub-contracting has its problems. Third parties need to learn a lot about a client company's business, and that isn't easy at an idiosyncratic company like ours. There's also the 'brain-drain' factor, and the risk of letting outsiders know your know-how. But in our case, both worries were unfounded: under the Satellite Programme, we would be working with people we already knew and trusted, and vice versa.

But how would we convince employees by the hundreds to become entrepreneurs, leaving a secure nest at Semco in the midst of an economic storm? That's where those paternalistic Brazilian severance provisions came in. The six- ten-, even twenty-plus months of salary we were obliged to pay employees when they left, plus additional benefits Semco added over the years, would be their seed money. Of course, no employee would have access to this nest egg unless they were fired. So we would offer to fire them, then help them use their severance to establish their own businesses, which would supply materials or services to us. To clinch the deal, we offered to lease our workers the very machines they operated in our plants, at no cost to start with and extremely reasonable terms later on, as their companies became profitable.

Once they set up their own shops, our workers would have the possibility of making many times what they could earn at Semco if the economy straightened out. Yes, that was a big if. And if the recession persisted they might make less than they would at Semco – but only assuming they continued to have a job at Semco, which was, for a distressingly large number of our people, becoming more doubtful with every day.

Pedro wasn't surprised when he and the other Co-ordinators at Santo Amaro were called in for a 'serious conversation' with top management. He knew business was bad.

He had already been through one round of layoffs, going over the numbers with executives, helping draw up a list of colleagues to be dismissed, discussing the choices with the factory committee, and then breaking the news to the employees, one by one – leaving time in between to recover his composure.

Pedro was expecting to go through it all over again now. He knew about the Satellite Programme, but he thought it was one of those things that only happened to other people. So he was taken aback at the proposition we made. Out of the dozen employees who had endured through the hard times and were still under Pedro's supervision, we suggested that half would remain at Semco. They performed sophisticated operations that were part of our technological core. We hoped many of the rest of the workers would be employed at a company that might be called Pedro and Friends, Ltd.

Pedro was so stunned he uncharacteristically asked for time to think it over. After an hour or so, he stopped pacing and returned to the board room, where the managers were waiting. As he entered, he felt, he said later, 'like a bride-to-be'.

'All right,' he said, taking a deep breath. 'I'll do it.'

The actual name of his company turned out to be JBL Machining and Sheetmetal Ltd. The J and the L were for José Maria and José Lima, two Semco colleagues. (The B was for Bullet.) The three of them spent several long days searching before finding a suitable building a few blocks from the plant. They drew up the list of machines, all of which we delivered to their new address, and, after squeezing them into the small shop, Pedro and his colleagues began supplying us with couplings, gearboxes, drives, metal shafts, turbine blades for mixers, and machine casings for marine pumps.

Their lives changed drastically. At Semco, Pedro was always home by 5.30 p.m.; now his wife sometimes takes him coffee at his little shop at night, and when Pedro finally does get home he often brings paperwork with him. Semco set up a team of executives to teach our mini-entrepreneurs to control costs, set prices, manage inventory and maintenance, and take care of all those bureaucratic details. There was no end to their problems, as we knew, since we did business with them. 'I would send them the same invoice twice,' Pedro recalled, 'and they would call asking whether I had doubled my price without telling them. Then I would hear laughing on the other end of the line.'

But we never tired of helping him and the others. And we were only too happy to call their other prospective customers and provide recommendations.

Like other Satellite firms, JBL has had good and bad times. Its payroll has soared to ten employees – God knows where they put them – only to sink back to five. But they haven't lost their enthusiasm or their optimism. In fact, they've just started a profit-sharing plan.

*

No one was forced to start a Satellite company; all our employees would get severance with no strings. Some took the money and simply left. Others tried to hang on to the payroll as long as they could.

But our offer was almost irresistible. I know companies that tell suppliers that they can't sell to competitors, or that dictate the price or profit margin. We told our people they were free to sell whatever they made to whoever they wanted, even our competitors. Then again, we would be free to buy from any company we wanted. There were no guarantees for either side, which ensured that we both would be competitive and innovative.

The Satellite Programme spread quickly from plant to plant and office to office. White-collar employees actually took it up first, especially our tax people, human resources staffers, and draftsmen. We dissolved our legal department and farmed out the work to several firms with different specialities, including one formed by one of our ex-lawyers. Some of our accountants formed a firm, too. And computer programmers went off on their own to make our software.

Starting with Pedro and his colleagues at Santo Amaro, the Satellite movement caught on with blue-collar people at the food service equipment and refrigeration systems plants. I won't say it was utterly painless. Let's say we had a business unit with five manufacturing cells, and four detached from the mother ship and went into their own orbit as satellites. It didn't make any sense for us to keep the remaining cell; we'd just be competing with the other four.

There were some surprising converts, as well. Tired of pollution and traffic, Paulo Pereira had long wanted to move his family from São Paulo to his native Bebedouro, a small town 150 miles away. But we didn't want to lose Paulo, who was the architect of some of our most innovative programmes. The Satellite Programme was his chance and ours: Paulo set up his own consulting and recruitment firm in Bebedouro, and commuted to São Paulo to work for us from Tuesday to Thursday each week.

Laura de Barros went off on her own, too, to become a

human resources consultant. Simpliciano Domingos de la Sierra hung on, although at one point the young entrepreneur had to drive a minibus in order to support his family. And Alipio Carmargo, with a handful of Semco colleagues and a pair of mechanics, started a company to sell and service Hobart products in São Paulo. He's doing well.

Semco has so far helped form more than two dozen Satellite companies. About half the manufacturing we had performed in-house has been turned over to them, and we believe we can farm out another 10 per cent or even 20 per cent in the coming years. To this day, no Satellite has closed. Some are looking for partners, others struggling to expand product lines. Some are little Semcos, organized around the ideals of democracy, transparency, and trust. Some are utterly traditional, tiny Fords or IBMs (a temporary affliction, we hope). Almost all have customers besides Semco, which is fine with us. It's their business.

The Satellite Programme works because it is based on the principle that people who have a stake in their company are bound to be more involved in their work. As a result, only good things will happen: costs will fall, quality will rise, innovation will bloom. People will look at a part and say, why does it have to be like this? Why can't it be made better? Or cheaper? Or faster?

For Semco, the Satellite Programme has meant tremendous flexibility. We buy only what we need, when we need it. Freed from the distractions of manufacturing, we can concentrate on designing, engineering, and assembling better products. And we no longer have all those expensive machines sitting around that we feel compelled to use, so we're not locked into procedures and processes.

In a more fundamental sense, the Satellite Programme is an extension of our philosophy of empowerment. After all, our new entrepreneurs have complete control over their work place – at least the control any owner has. They make all the decisions, including deciding how many decisions their workers should make. They are almost always even more productive than they were at Semco.

Implementing the Satellite Programme wasn't easy or quick. But I think it has helped us remake Semco into a company that can float on the roughest seas, without taking on water or having to force the crew to abandon ship.

thirty three

REBIRTH

Suddenly, the plants where we all had worked so hard to work together were half-empty, the machines and the people who ran them scattered all over. We looked around and asked ourselves, 'Do we need all these factories any more?' It was time to move out.

None of the plants was easy to close, but the most difficult was the food service equipment unit, where in the years since we took it over billings and sales had more than quadrupled, even as management was pared in half. We lost close to $1 million, an horrendous sum, closing the plant and moving what was left to Santo Amaro, which made the decision that much less comprehensible to some workers who had been based there. 'What company buys a plant, spends money to re-do it, introduces programmes that improve productivity and turn the place around, and then walks away from it?' we were asked more than once. But moving the food service equipment operation would cut expenses to a level they couldn't match if they stayed. Rent on the old plant alone amounted to 6 per cent of sales, which was about three times the usual percentage.

The BAC unit in Diadema, which made refrigeration equipment for the food and beverage industries and cooling towers for air-conditioners, was also hard to close, since its business was holding up much better than our other plants. Its main customers, beer and soft drink manufacturers, were relatively unscathed by recession; they weren't subject to much competition from abroad and their customers, though pinched, still had change for a soda or a beer.

But as the Satellite Programme caught on at the refrigeration systems unit we saw that there was the potential to farm out 60 to 70 per cent of the plant's production, without a drop in quality. The move to Santo Amaro was inevitable, although we took it as a great compliment that leaders of the union there, a radical organization if ever there was one, tried to talk us out of leaving. The region was home to Ford, General Motors, and other companies with tens of thousands of workers, so the union was hardly worried about the 100 jobs we were transferring. But it had been using Semco and its programmes as examples in its negotiations with other companies. With us gone, it would lose a bargaining point.

Clovis and others felt that closing the plants was a step in the wrong direction. Rationally, he could see the Satellite Programme was our best strategy, but his heart was with those odd factories with coloured walls and shrubs between the machines and workers who hardly needed bosses.

The decision wasn't as wrenching for me, because I was farther from the day-to-day management of the company. Unlike the workers, I didn't have to help cart off the furniture and the fixtures. That's the difference being a general who never sees the front line. Although it can lead to disasters like Gallipoli, often officers who aren't close to the shooting make better strategic decisions.

The truth is, I had been thinking about closing the plants and consolidating our operations at Santo Amaro for several years. The idea was initially dismissed by just about everyone – Vendramin, Violi, Batoni, and Clovis. Even as the economy sank and our fate became apparent, it took months to bring everyone around. I know many people feel we at Semco talk too much before making decisions. They assume a company our size should turn on a sixpence. I admit it: we can take longer to make a decision than General Motors, which is 10,000 times bigger. But if we debate a decision forever, once we make up our minds we usually implement it much faster, since everyone is totally committed to it.

Which is what happened when we closed our plants. Even Clovis came to agree it was the best way to preserve our idiosyncratic culture. We wanted a company built to last decades, one that could withstand the ups and downs of many business cycles. We would never achieve that stability if we had to maintain a certain sales volume or depend on desperate, last-minute cost-cutting to cover the fixed expenses of a large work force and machine-filled factories.

Semco went from 830 employees and nine business units at five locations in 1987 to a little under 300 employees in six business units at two sites (plus some 200 workers in Satellite companies and full-time consultants) four years later. We rebuilt and expanded our original plant in Santo Amaro to house our divisions, each in its own area, and used part of the Nacoes Unidas plant to test marine equipment and as a warehouse.

But the consolidation of our plants didn't affect their structure one bit. We're still a decentralized company. We've retained the essence of these units – their autonomy, their individualism, their separate factory committees, their inter-organizational teams, their personalities. We've divvied up the space so there is no interaction between them. Each unit has its own turf, entrance, storehouse, and shipping dock. Only their addresses have been changed to protect the transplanted.

The units can negotiate among themselves to change the layout any time they want. They are even free to move away, if it makes business sense. Recently, a small start-up unit called Difitex, one of the two or three embryonic operations we usually have in our orbit, concluded it was being charged too much for its space at Santo Amaro. (Each unit pays a share of the building's costs, including security, cleaning, electricity, water, and insurance, based on its square footage.) So the leaders of the unit, which imports textile machinery, decided to move somewhere in downtown São Paulo. They didn't tell me, and I still don't know where. It doesn't matter. I send a fax when I need to talk to them. They fax me back.

Although we've shrunk Semco to a core of sales, engineering, design, materials handling, purchasing, and assembly people, our plant looks as bustling as ever. Santo Amaro is always overrun by former employees who sell software, tax advice, audits, ball bearings, welded components, and slicers and fan scales we sell under our name. There are hundreds of people wandering around, many of whom I've worked with for years and a few I don't know from Adam. They can use our desks and phones and computers and park their cars in our lot.

When some of the consultants whose advice we seek from time to time on strategy, organizational behaviour, and marketing heard we were going to consolidate, they advised us to pare down our product lines at the same time. Retain only those goods and services that make money, they said, such as marine parts and pumps, large dishwashers, food and beverage cooling equipment, specialized biscuit machines, high-tech mixers, and our environmental engineering and auditing team. Eliminate weaker products such as Hobart slicers, fan scales, potato peelers, and meat grinders, and oil filters and air-conditioning equipment. But we decided these were still good products; we just weren't making them at competitive prices. Which is where the Satellite companies, with their inherently lower overheads, come in. We take their products – sometimes finished and ready to be sold, sometimes parts in need of final assembly – tack on our brand name and use our sales force to market them, at a comfortable margin.

Consolidation has also enhanced our ability to innovate. We still perform the final assembly of most of our products, and that is when you sense the problems and opportunities in a production process. And we still control the critical interaction between engineering and assembly. We can change from sheet metal to ceramics or from stainless steel to plastic at any time, and no machines will become obsolete because of a switch.

Similarly, for 20 years we had made a pigment mixer for paint manufacturers that consisted of a large steel plate with teeth to do the blending. Our competitors switched to mixers made of ceramic material, which didn't rust and were much cheaper, but we didn't consider a switch because we owned the machine that made the steel blender. Once we leased it to a Satellite company, we were free to change.

(Cynics might accuse us of palming off obsolete equipment on our new suppliers. But most of it isn't. And don't forget, they were getting the machines at bargain prices.)

The consolidation cost Semco more than $2 million. That, coupled with the loss of more than $4 million from cancelled shipyard orders, should have been enough to throw us into a lion's cage of bankers. Brazil's economic crisis brought down lots of fine companies – an average of 800 went broke every month. Semco not only survived, but also paid the huge cost of plant closures and employee reductions and re-adaptation without taking on more debt. We managed to break even in the very worst years and made good money in middling ones. Our employees, who each produced an average of $10,800 worth of goods a year in 1980, now produce $92,000 worth of goods a year (adjusted for inflation), four times the national average. And by the value-added standard, productivity rose six and a half times. Sales volume grew from $4 million a year to $20 million or so a year, with *one-third of the workers*. Yes, we're down from a peak of $35 million in 1987 (with 830 employees), but it's still a hell of a growth rate for such a miserable economy. Indeed, by the end of 1992 we had six months of working capital in the till, without a single outstanding bank loan. (Violi had a list of nearly a dozen bank executives who were seeking an appointment to try to talk us into correcting that situation.) We were prepaying suppliers and had increased our people's real salaries – that is, above inflation – by more than 7 per cent. Moreover, almost all our Co-ordinators received fat bonuses in 1992, and we had begun launching two new businesses, a factory maintenance service and a waste disposal and recycling operation for offices, including container systems on every floor that separate glass, paper and plastic and then automatically recycle it.

We should have seen it coming, you say.

We did. Some of us did, anyway.

Three years before Brazil's economy collapsed and Semco launched its Satellite Programme and then consolidated, we held a weekend retreat for 40 of our top managers. It was a typical Laura de Barros production: the lights were low and Debussy's 'La Mer' was playing. Everyone was asked to lie on the floor, relax, and disconnect from day-to-day concerns. I was surprised how even hard-boiled engineers got into the spirit of it, kicking off their shoes and stretching out in all directions. I should have known not to underestimate Laura.

The key exercise involved 'visioning' the future of the company. Each participant was asked to imagine what Semco would be like in the year 2010. What would the plant look like? How many people would work there? You get the idea.

The managers pondered and then, when the lights came up, wrote down their individual predictions. Then they were asked to share them with a colleague and together meld them into a single portrait.

Walking around the room, I overheard a snippet here and there.

'I see myself going to work in a train that has fax machines and computer terminals,' one man said, as his partner grimaced.

'My office is full of greenery – it looks like a rain forest,' said another.

'The shop floor is polished like a ballroom,' someone else says, 'and the assembly-line workers are all in bright white overalls.'

Then each pair of managers joined another pair and repeated the melding process. Then those four met with another four, and so on until all the crazy ideas had been screened out and what remained was a collective, integrated vision of what our top managers thought Semco would be like.

What was that vision?

We expected that, because of our annual growth of 40 or even 50 per cent in the mid-eighties, our managers would picture Semco with perhaps 15,000 employees by 2010. But the company they described was not much larger than the Semco of the present, although the quality of both our products and the lives of our employees was much higher. Our people did not want a bigger company, they wanted a better company; a

company in which people could work at home, liberated from
conventional structures and schedules; a company in which
there was such fluid movement on to and off the payroll that
it wasn't always clear who was an employee and who wasn't.
They didn't want our business to cause pollution; they
wanted our plants to be safe enough for them to bring their
children to work.

Somehow this vision of a smaller, more fluid, more flexible,
less defined company has mostly come to pass. No more are
we victims of the adolescent urge for more people, more
plants, more products, more revenue. We have outgrown the
allure of growth, albeit after paying the price in money, time,
and gastritis.

To want to grow just to be big is an idea that comes from
the sandbox. Sure, some growth is necessary for nearly every
business. It allows for diversification of products and markets,
which is one of the best ways for a firm to guarantee its survival. It creates additional opportunities for employees and
improves motivation and productivity, since it creates change
all over a company.

But beware. Growth opportunities are always springing up
and should be regarded the way Ulysses regarded mermaids.
Much about growth is really about ego and greed, not business strategy. At Semco we initially pursued the acquisition of
companies because a good part of our own potential had been
fulfilled. We studied more than 100 firms, negotiated with 15,
and bought four. I can summarize in three sentences the hundreds of hours and millions of dollars we invested:

*Growth through acquisition is exciting, glamorous, and ulcer-
inducing.*

*The company you buy is not very similar to the one you thought
you were buying, and never like what they told you.*

*Buying small, family firms is a certain way to skip the ulcers
and go straight to bypass surgery.*

In our case, we incorporated subsidiaries of multinationals,
which mostly honour commitments, God bless them. They

usually have accurate books, unlike family-owned firms, where the closets are typically full of skeletons. But when you buy any company, you must be willing to watch it and learn from it, at least for a year, before putting your paws in the soup.

Most of our acquisitions eventually worked out. But now we've consciously made the decision to stop growing. Our people want to be convinced that the products they make are necessary and want to like making them. They want to end their careers with a feeling of accomplishment.

The vision our managers shared with us was surprising at first, but it gave us the confidence we needed to consolidate. Simply grossing $40, $50, $100 or even $200 million a year means nothing. If you're willing to take risks, it's easier to pile up revenue than build the kind of organization our managers told us they wanted. Today we are still expanding. Remember those 1,400 résumés I told you we had received when we placed an ad for Engineering Associates? We're expecting to sign contracts with more than 150 of them in the coming months. But most won't be full-time employees, they'll be our partners. Similarly, we will grow our sales force through our new network of Satellite companies, consultants and partnerships.

I've seen countless companies grow tremendously and then flame out like a comet. Those once-in-a-lifetime propositions occur all the time, don't they? Whenever I'm tempted by a deal, I remember what Ray Krinker of Price Waterhouse used to say: 'A small hole can sink a big ship.'

thirty four

WHO NEEDS A NO. 1?

Most companies, even conventionally pyramidal ones, practise at least some form of consultative democracy, which means key executives can speak their minds, if only to one another, before the CEO decides.

This is better than Stalinism, since he didn't listen at all. But it falls well short of democracy, in which all employees – not just managers – have a say in corporate decisions.

Why do so many companies believe it is necessary or even desirable for one person to have the last word? I suppose they think it's more efficient. But centralized power is a high-risk proposition. Henry Ford may be known as the man who pioneered the manufacture of automobiles (even though other companies were making them, on a smaller scale), but he was also a hard-headed dictator who had to dismiss thousands of workers because he mistakenly insisted on continuing the Model T well after its market evaporated. Alfred Sloan of General Motors may be regarded as one of industry's most able organizers, but he was also a short-sighted structuralist who created a company so inflexible it failed to react to the threat of economy cars from Japan.

Ford and Sloan, like Stalin, knew how good it feels to wield absolute power. But is it good for a company and its employees to have a single strongman do pretty much as he pleases, with a disproportionate amount of attention to his habits and with the instability that reigns when his successor needs to be chosen?

Nothing is harder work than democracy, I keep telling myself. I don't remember the last time I made a corporate decision alone, nor can I count all the times I've been voted down. But I'll gladly bite my lip when I disagree with a judgement made by consensus, because I believe that unfettered democracy is much more important (and even more profitable in the long run) than prevailing over our managers in a way that takes you back to the days in which seesaws and sandboxes were important parts of the world.

There is an added benefit to having a democratically minded No. 1: the No. 2s, No. 3s, No. 4s, and No. 5s can play meaningful roles right away. Too many vice-presidents in traditional companies are made to feel like also-rans; when they can't move up they have to leave. An inordinate amount of talent is lost this way.

With this in mind, and with Semco restructured in a way that made it much less vulnerable to the economy, I decided it was time to virtually eliminate another level of our hierarchy: mine.

Instead of one person at the top, Semco would be run by a committee of our Counsellors. They were, I believed, a particularly well-balanced team, professionally and personally: Clovis, a father figure who had been influential in my thinking; Vendramin, an economist, industrial manager, engineer, and, above all, a thoughtful man who took his time about everything; Batoni, who pushed hard for results and was much less forgiving about people than either Clovis or Vendramin; Violi, who had a first-class financial mind and two feet on the ground; and José Alignani, a talented engineer and natural leader. They ranged in age from their 40s to their mid-50s.

They also own 1 per cent of the company each, and share in the year-end dividends. This wasn't just an expression of gratitude. I wanted to foster the entrepreneurial spirit of capitalism in our top management. I chose 1 per cent because it is a large enough share of the company to be meaningful to each o. the executives, and because their joint holding of 5 per cent is also an important block.

They use their Tuesday meeting to discuss and make all major operating and strategic decisions – that is, those that haven't been made by the Associates or Co-ordinators or resolved at the Monday meetings at each unit. Sometimes there is precious little for the Counsellors to do. Other times, it seems as if everyone else has decided to stop deciding.

Every six months, one Counsellor takes a turn as acting chief executive, co-ordinating the activities of the Partners and their business units, representing the company in legal matters, and sometimes meeting with customers who insist on speaking to the top dog. This system avoids the excessively collective thinking that characterizes government agencies and gives each Counsellor a chance to put his mark on the company (although the time any one is in office is short, so that mark won't be indelible).

So now I'm just another Counsellor. But my job hasn't changed – I try to make things happen, like a catalyst. I lobby for what I believe in. I step in when I think I can do some good, and step out when I'm tired of an issue or when the other Counsellors are tired of me. I attend the Tuesday meetings only when I'm invited, which is about every two or three weeks. Otherwise, they're on their own. I'd probably be asked to more meetings if I didn't have a habit of throwing out wild ideas. Also, I tend to have a hands-on approach that disrupts the system. When I become obstreperous, they just screen me off from the rest of the company. Like Mafiosi, none of them will talk to me about new developments unless he is accompanied by one of the others.

It's just as well. At the risk of sounding immodest, I've been concerned that I'll exert an undue influence on Semco. It's important to discredit the belief that the company will survive only as long as I'm there.

What if they make a decision I don't like? I'd say at least 20 per cent of the time I disagree with them, maybe 30 per cent. This includes some major decisions in the last year or two. In 1991, for example, our books showed us in the black in spite of what had been, according to Brazil's biggest business magazine, the worst year ever for machinery manufacturers. Just before our balance sheet was to be released to the newspapers, Violi called to say that an adjustment in a customer account was going to turn the nominal profit into a $90,000 loss.

'It seems so silly to report a loss when it's such a ridiculously small number,' I told Violi.

'But the profit would be small, too,' he countered.

'I know, I know,' I said, feeling a bit exasperated. 'But they're different categories. A loss is a loss, and a profit is a profit.' As I said it, I realized that this sounded like 'a mother is always a mother'.

The Tuesday meeting was the next day, and the annual report had to be ready the day after. Clovis asked whether I wanted to participate in the meeting, at which a final decision would be made.

'Were you going to invite me anyway, or is it because of the balance sheet?' I asked.

'Well, we wouldn't have called you for anything else,' he said.

'Then have the meeting without me. I'll fax you all a memo from home giving my opinion.'

In my memo, I noted that there was a series of adjustments concerning our shipyard accounts as well as an import payment that our auditors said we could include either in this year's or next year's budget. I didn't see why we shouldn't use one of these perfectly legal adjustments now to offset the small loss and get back our profit. After all, a profit in such a bleak year would look better to the vultures in the business community who were constantly circling overhead, waiting for Semco to slip up. I reminded my fellow Partners of the time we had laid off 60 workers at the marine products plant, and were accused in the newspapers of firing '1,500 employees in one bloody afternoon'. No amount of press releases could undo the damage that caused. So, I told my colleagues, let's not leave ourselves open to mischief for so little.

I sent the fax off, confident my arguments would prevail. They held their meeting and decided in favour of reporting the $90,000 loss. They had already told our employees about it, they reasoned, and to report anything else risked looking as if they were cooking the books.

Violi called to tell me the news. He said the Partners would meet with me to explain the decision. I asked him whether my arguments had been aired, and he assured me they had. That made me feel better. And when the Partners asked me to write the commentaries on the balance sheet for the annual report, I readily agreed, explaining why *we* had decided to show the small loss.

There were no hard feelings. It was just another day at a democratic office.

Besides the money and the perks, I'm sure most CEOs enjoy the sport of running a company – devising strategies and products, crunching numbers, taking risks, screwing around with other people's lives. It's like being a five-star general.

If I wanted to go to work every day at 7 and leave at midnight, I'm sure I could keep busy, as I did before my detour to the Lahey Clinic. But while most CEOs insist that they enjoy 70 or 80 per cent of their jobs, I suspect a more accurate percentage is about 30. There are so many meetings, phone calls, boring luncheons, administrative headaches.

That's about how much of my time I spend on Semco now, 30 per cent. I like to think it's a gratifying 30 per cent, since I hardly ever do anything I don't enjoy. I have no more than two or three business lunches a year, never leave the office (at the plant or at home) after 6 p.m., and return fewer than five of the 20 to 30 phone calls I get each day.

I respond to the rest and most of my mail with handwritten notes that I fax from my home machine. When I first started working at home a half-day a week, I imagined everyone thought it was an excuse for the boss's son to spend the day by the pool. I did nothing to discourage this suspicion, letting people who came by my house to pick up a report find me in my shorts. But the flow of documents from my house soon made it apparent that I was, in fact, working at home, and rather efficiently. Today I work there from three to five mornings a week.

Sometimes, just by sticking my nose into some issue, I'll find myself straddled with half a dozen phone calls, faxes, and memos. So unless I'm the only one who can handle a problem, I'll steer clear. I hate it when I make myself needed and then can't pull away. I'm proud to say I no longer know what a Semco cheque looks like. I haven't signed one for almost eight years.

The truth is, the company hardly needs me now in its day-to-day operations. And the ideas Semco is built on aren't mine, either. They flow from the company's culture, and that belongs to everyone at Semco. I don't have anything against capitalism, despite what my critics say. I value my shares in Semco. But it's really not my company any more. I am not Semco. Semco is Semco.

I have even gone so far as to ensure that this separation will extend to the next generation. I feel the company is too precious to run the risk that one of my children or grandchildren will badly manage it. And anyway, I don't believe in the family business in the long term. Family companies have a harder time attracting talented and ambitious professionals, who realize that at the very least the criteria for promotion won't be straightforward. Indeed, anyone who has the time to calculate the percentage of family businesses that have survived for four or five generations will soon be encouraging his son or daughter to go to medical school. So my children will not have an assured place at Semco. I know all business owners say this. But I mean it. I've already seen to it that none of my offspring can be promoted without the approval of three-quarters of the Semco board.

Not even my death will change their circumstances, since outstanding shares in Semco will revert to the foundation that Irene Tubertini helped start, which will be managed by another, 21-member board that will include employees and outsiders but not family members. It is through such mechanisms that Semco will finally have its own personality, completely independent of any Semlers.

When I think about the traditional CEO, I often think about my father. And when I think about my father, I recall a line from a James Taylor song: 'The secret of life is to enjoy the passing of time.' Most people live either in their memories of the past or their hopes for the future. Few live in the present.

I always wanted my father to enjoy the money he made. He never did. He was always worrying. Late in life, after his cancer had been diagnosed, he would walk through the park after radiation therapy and tell my mother that he had never really noticed the flowers and the ducks before. It took 73 years and a terminal illness to make him see the small but fascinating details of life.

When I was a teenager, my father would take the family on a long European holiday at the end of each year. For him, it was half-skiing, half-business. I remember we would always have dinner in the hotel restaurant. There was a sign on the wall on which room numbers would flash, indicating a phone call. Our room number appeared constantly. When it was eight o'clock in Europe it was four in the afternoon in Brazil, and people at Semco would be calling him, one after the other, to discuss that day's crisis. They were delegating up, because he made it clear he wanted to know everything. No matter how far he was from the office, he couldn't leave it.

He had a stroke, caused by cancer of the liver, while on a ship off the Italian coast in 1985. It was the first time he had been on a long cruise. He thought he was finally removed enough from the business to be out of touch for a while.

Looking back, I should have moved away from Semco earlier. But to its owner, a company is like an adolescent child. You want it to grow up and face the world on its own, but you lie awake worrying about whether it is going to smash up the car.

I admit I still worry a bit when I am away for long periods. So much can change so quickly in Brazil, usually not for the better. But my fears have always been unfounded, and I work hard at suppressing them. Persistence is a virtue only when it is pointed in the right direction.

What do I do with the other 70 per cent of my time, when I'm not working at Semco? I write a weekly newspaper column every Sunday, for 1.1 million readers. I talk about Semco to companies and business groups around the world. I am interested in politics and am a member of the executive committee of a large political party, the Partido da Social

Democracia Brasileira. I watch a minimum of three movies a week, buy the recordings of Beniamino Gigli, Billie Holiday, Philip Glass and Shostakovich, and take piano, golf, Chinese, and cooking lessons. I also read 50 books a year, mostly histories of war and empires. Centuries of blunders and successes are there for guidance. For a handful of dollars you can buy an explanation that would have spared Napoleon thousands of lives. For little more than the price of a Big Mac you can discover the mistakes of the Tokugawa shoguns in leaving their camp at Nara unguarded. For less than it costs to fill your tank with gas you can find out why Winston Churchill couldn't manage to get himself elected after World War II. I also read four newspapers a day – they're even cheaper. But I don't spend much time on the front page. The causes of great wars, early signals of stock market collapses, and the advent of innovative technologies are not found on the front page – not at first anyway. Often the most important news is buried inside.

Then I have this list of goals. I chanced upon a television programme about 15 years ago that, as people so like to say, changed my life. It was an interview with a 61-year-old American named John Goddard. I never found out who he was, or heard his name since. Anyway, Goddard had made a list of more than 100 goals and set out to attain them. He only had 19 to go. They included landing on the moon and living to the year 2000. He had already piloted a plane at the speed of sound, driven a submarine, descended the Nile in a canoe, navigated the length of the Congo River, and climbed Chile's Aconcagua Peak.

I decided that what worked for him would work for me, if on a less ambitious scale. I picked 16 goals, about half of which I've already met. I believe I have turned Semco into the most sought-after work place I know. I have created a foundation to provide opportunities for poor Brazilians. I am five-sixths of the way towards speaking six languages fluently.

And, like Goddard, I travel incessantly, and always with eyes open. I shudder when I think of those awful trips in the early 1980s, when Harro and I were desperately trying to keep Semco afloat. Now Sofia and I set out for Xi'An to see 6,000 terracotta soldiers buried hundreds of years ago, take balloon safaris in Kenya, camp in Tanzania, scuba dive in the Seychelles, cross the Sahara, comb beaches in Thailand, and float down the Nile.

It's a far cry from three cities in a day, then back on the red-eye.

thirty five

WILL IT TRAVEL?

I had just finished speaking to a group in the south of Brazil when a man in a white suit and white shoes approached the microphone for the last question. 'This story of yours is all very interesting,' he said, 'but I've been sitting here for two hours waiting for something that I could use at my hospital and pharmacies, and I don't know that I've heard anything that's applicable.'

Twelve hundred pairs of eyes turned towards me, and I could see that some people who were already on their way out had stopped. What could I tell this good doctor so that he wouldn't have to go home disappointed?

'Let's take one of the pharmacies as an example,' I began.

'But they're much too small,' he interrupted. 'Two or three employees, no more.'

'That's big enough,' I said. 'Who determines where the containers of medicine are placed on the shelves?'

'My partner.'

'How?'

'They're arranged alphabetically, of course. So they're easy to find.'

'I'm not so sure,' I continued, 'but indulge me with a few more answers, and then I'll make a proposal.'

Everyone settled back to see how it would end.

'How are the employees' schedules made up?'

'Our personnel department does that. It's very simple: a rotation schedule, so someone is always in on Saturdays, and during the night and on Sundays and holidays when it's our turn to be open,' the doctor explained.

'These people are paid fixed salaries, right?'

'That's the way it's always been done,' he answered, a bit warily.

'Well, here's the deal. Give me the phone number and I'll talk to your employees. And give me leeway to provoke their imagination.' He had a sceptical expression. 'Then give them time to decide how to run the pharmacy as they think best, and tell me what they did.'

There were groans as people in the audience realized there wasn't going to be a quick end to our little drama.

'And,' I added, 'we will tell all the people who are here today of the results.' I turned to a reporter I had recognized in the front row. 'Would you agree to write a story about it?'

She nodded.

'Now, we only need the doctor's consent.'

'I'll take you up on it,' he said. 'Let's do it with our smallest pharmacy. Its sales are less than one per cent of our business.'

'So I have your trust for that one per cent,' I said, as the audience laughed.

We met after the conference and I learned a bit about the pharmacy business. Then I called his employees and told them about Semco. I spoke to them a few more times in the next week and sent them a copy of my book. The doctor, true to his word, gave them the freedom to try anything they desired. They talked to me about a few ideas, but then I lost touch.

About six months later the doctor phoned me with his report. There were three employees in the pharmacy: two women with shopkeeping experience and a young man who was the pharmacist. All were single and disliked the irregular working hours, which put a damper on their social lives. So they started their experiment by asking that scheduling be transferred to them. They each worked the same number of hours, but devised a rotation that made it easier to plan their leisure time.

Soon, they had re-arranged the boxes of medicine. The alphabetical arrangement, it turned out, often required them to climb tall ladders. In the new system, boxes were stacked according to how often the pills in them were requested. That meant aspirins were next to vitamins and heartburn tablets on a low shelf.

Then they gave each product a number and bought an inexpensive computer to keep track of stock. They would take inventory at night and on holidays, when few customers came in, and re-order supplies themselves, in the quantities they felt necessary, with a goal of maximizing profits. They also suggested that the pharmacy stock more products, including cotton swabs, bandages, sunscreen, dandruff-fighting shampoo and other items not normally carried by hospital drug stores, which usually stick to the basics. In the beginning the employees were a bit pushy with customers and even scared some away. But eventually they found an appropriate level of salesmanship.

The last I heard was that the employees had proposed a profit-sharing plan, and the doctor was spreading the Semco gospel at his hospital.

Of course, the doctor, like me, owned the business. I get many questions from people in the middle or even at the bottom of their companies or organizations. They can't just decree that things will be different. So, they want to know, what can they do to change things?

I found myself in the middle not too long ago, when I was invited to join Brazil's imperious Federation of Industries of the State of São Paulo. And I discovered that, with perseverance and courage, Semco-style management can flourish in the most hidebound of environments.

The Federation counts among its members the nation's most powerful industrialists, traditionalists all. It is unwise for a Brazilian President to appoint a finance minister without consulting this 60-year-old club, and positions such as labour minister and the presidencies of the Central Bank, the Bank of Brazil, and the National Bank for Social and Economic Development are rarely filled without its benediction.

As Semco became more prominent, I had begun writing articles in Brazil's largest conservative newspaper, with 400,000 readers. The paper is a mainstay of the elite, so it seemed an ideal place for me to rail against them and their Federation.

I imagined what the Old Guard must have been thinking, sitting in their leather club chairs and smoking cheroots: '*Such a small company, you know*', '*He inherited it from his father, didn't he?*', '*He'll grow up to be like the rest of us one day. It's the only way to stay in business in this country.*'

But at first my columns provoked the worst of all responses, which was no response at all.

So I was truly startled when, having never ever set foot in the Federation's imposing 16-storey, pyramid-shaped (what else?) building, I was asked to become an officer of this regal group. The invitation came from Dr José Mindlin, a friend and one of the few Federation directors who believed that it would have to emerge from the Stone Age. Mindlin commanded and deserved respect – a former secretary of culture, he was one of Brazil's leading intellectuals, owned the nation's largest private library (with more than 20,000 rare volumes), and ran a $200-million-a-year auto-parts business. The election of Federation officers was approaching, Mindlin told me, and he had recommended that the organization's president, Mário Amato, invite me to join his ticket. Amato agreed, but only, I later learned, after Mindlin had lobbied him and some other, less resistant directors. Maybe these other directors thought that, once enshrined in the Establishment, I would shut up.

'I know what you think of the Federation,' Mindlin said. 'But no one will listen to you while you're on the outside.'

I was dubious, until he mentioned that I would be the youngest director in the Federation's history and that we would work closely together to change things. I accepted immediately.

My job was to oversee the technology department, which was responsible for such diverse activities as the development of industrial design in Brazil and the negotiation of international trade agreements. I soon learned that delegation was unheard of at the Federation. I had to personally approve purchases of office supplies, cash advances, absence forms – everything. There were always so many letters, memos, and forms awaiting my signature that I never got round to planning anything. When I would ask Federation officers why Joyce Leal, the department's feisty full-time executive, couldn't sign them, their eyes would roll heavenward. 'And let ordinary employees make decisions?' they would say.

One day I took some paperwork from my pile and gave it to Joyce. 'You sign these,' I told her, 'and I'll enclose a note saying this is the new arrangement in the technology department.' Joyce was a subversive at heart, too, so she agreed.

We kept getting the documents back, unapproved, in the inter-office mail. Mindlin and I even had to dig into our own pockets so the department's employees could travel, since our cash advance forms were bouncing along with everything else. But we didn't give in. In fact, my war with the Federation bureaucracy escalated. The department needed a new typewriter, but we knew it would take months of paperwork even if we played by the rules. So Mindlin sent us one from his company, while we waited for our request to come through. The borrowed typewriter broke while we were waiting. We had it repaired and sent the bill to the Federation, which had the nerve to send it to Mindlin.

Under the Federation's rules, employees who arrived late lost a chunk of pay. Was it any wonder that many were loath to stay even a minute late? We wanted our department's employees to come to work at a time that suited them, so we changed their contracts to make them part-time workers, exempting them from the Federation's time cards. Of course, they still worked the same number of hours and were paid the same salary. But now they could start when they wanted. Just as with our workers at Semco, their motivation and their productivity grew.

Even within our department, communication was a shambles, in large part because almost everyone was tucked away in small offices and cubicles and had only a vague idea of what colleagues were doing. So we tore down all the walls and introduced everyone to each other. Then we transferred some employees who didn't fit with our new style to other Federation departments, and dismissed a few who weren't up to par. But we didn't replace anyone. That gave us more money to pay those who remained, who were so productive they more than made up for their former colleagues.

These and other changes were provoking much gnashing of teeth within the pyramid, but the Federation couldn't get rid of me. What I was doing was working. Companies all over Brazil were telling Amato how much our department had helped with this or that problem. Seminars we staged with international experts on technology management filled the Federation's meeting rooms. Our departmental reports and position papers were being quoted by government policy-makers and legislators.

Meanwhile, I followed my usual approach to leadership and backed away from the department as it revived. There would be no cult of personality here. After a few months I no longer signed any papers. I started coming in only once a week, then every other week, then once a month. Of course, no one noticed. Once I had got the bureaucracy off their backs, Joyce and the others didn't need me.

Two years later, it was time for new elections at the Federation. Several directors tried to convince Amato to remove me from my spot at the bottom of the ticket, but he again stuck with me. I ended up as a vice-president, which confirmed a lesson I had learned through the years of change at Semco: it's always better to seek forgiveness than to ask for permission.

A bit later, I received even more of an endorsement from the business community. Each year, *The Gazeta Mercantil*, Brazil's *Wall Street Journal*, and a group of leading magazines polled 54,000 companies carefully chosen to represent the Brazilian economy, asking executives to vote, secretly, for Business Leader of the Year. It is a respected survey – or at least it was until 1990, when I finished first.

From outcast to Establishment in a single bound.

I give 15 to 20 lectures a year – it would be more, but I charge an exorbitant fee to keep down the number – to audiences ranging from executives at such giants as General Motors,

IBM, Lever Brothers, and Philips to partners of two-person franchising firms. I also speak at events as diverse as a Canadian Telecommunications Convention and a Gastro-enterologists' Congress in Rio.

Almost every lecture is followed by a stream of questions, about half from people who, like the doctor, are looking for lessons to apply. That's also what brings so many executives to our door.

We don't disappoint them. The programmes we have developed at Semco can be instituted in supermarkets, ad agencies, steel mills, baseball teams, and universities. Banks have implemented the reverse evaluation. In Brazil state-owned power utilities have begun to consult with employees before filling mid-level jobs. A bank in Rio has profit-sharing, Semco-style. A General Motors subsidiary, Delco, practises reverse evaluation. A museum has democratic decision-making. A hospital has open offices for administrators. And a classmate of mine at Harvard, Noel Ginsburg, reorganized his company, Container Industries Inc., of Denver, Colorado, on the basis of discussions we had in our dorm. Noel gives his workers the same kind of information and freedom we do, and has been delighted by the results.

Moreover, I believe military leaders would gain much from open discussions with the troops, although I am obliged to report that there were some frowns in the audience when I spoke to a group of many-starred generals at Brazil's Superior School of War. Cutting bureaucracy would give religious leaders more time for their flocks, too. And, of course, industries in the burgeoning service sector could benefit from the increased efficiencies that follow when employees have a say in their working lives. My stint at the Federation proved that.

But flattered as I am by all the companies that have imitated us, it makes me a bit nervous. For starters, I'm the first to acknowledge that Semco has a long way to go. We need to push decision-making deeper into the organization, especially on matters of business strategy. Our employees need to understand our balance sheets better, too. We would like to have worker representatives on our corporate board, with full voting power, not as second-class citizens, as in some European countries. And we want everyone at Semco to set his own salary.

Even if we were perfect, no company should set out to copy us, programme by programme. Yes, headline memos cut paperwork and flexitime improves productivity. Programmes like job rotation, self-set salaries, and reverse evaluation will, I believe, improve any company, but that isn't all there is to Semco. It would make me less like a snake oil salesman if, along with our programmes, companies also adopted the philosophy of freedom and trust that inspires them.

Modern managers are searching. Small companies are emulating large ones on the assumption that they must have done something right to get that big. Huge corporations, for their part, are envious of small and agile competitors. Entire American industries look with both angst and hope to the Pacific Rim, even as Asian companies become more Westernized.

In their desperation for quick fixes, too many executives are too quick to jump on the latest managerial fads and fashions, as if they will be panaceas for sagging productivity. Quality circles, just-in-time deliveries, Kanban production systems, networking, direct costing, total quality – you've heard all the buzz words.

Transporting Asian values to, say, Smyrna, Tennessee, is like wearing a kimono to a Tupperware party. Nothing is less Western than the notion of total loyalty to a company, except possibly the belief that age should come before competence. If you must borrow from Japan, don't forget to fill a 747 with enough Japanese to populate your factory.

Very early one morning I visited the Ishikawajima-Harima shipyard in Rio and found all the employees in the yard, singing the company song and exercising together. I pinched myself to make sure I wasn't in Kyoto. They had transplanted an activity that had taken 2,500 years to evolve to a young plant on another continent. If by succeeding you mean that half the people at the shipyard were exercising because they thought it was the best route to a promotion, then it was a success. If the goal was to integrate the employees, build respect for their leaders, and meditate on the importance of the company in each worker's life, then they are all on the wrong side of the ocean.

thirty six

MODERN TIMES

I know a textile company that wove fine English woollens. Its 200 employees worked in a machine-filled factory set in what might be called an ex-urban industrial park. The chief executive was definitely performance-oriented, starting with his own: he arrived early, left late, and made all the important decisions in between. The factory was sub-divided into specialized areas of production, each with its own boss. Each boss, in turn, had a group of foremen to watch the workers. Accountants and salespeople were on the mezzanine above the shop floor and reported to their respective department heads. Everything was strictly hierarchical and pyramidal.

As I described this company to an international telecommunications convention not long ago, I could see people in the audience becoming more and more puzzled. What was the point? they seemed to be wondering. It was just an ordinary business. There didn't seem to be anything distinctive about it.

Except that this textile factory existed in 1633. And the moral of the story: our advances in technology have far outstripped our advances in mentality.

It was a particularly appropriate message for an audience of people who turn over our technology base every year or so. They have made it possible to tele-conference instantly with China, and call home from the belly of a 747 over the Pacific. And yet most businesses today are still organized in much the same way as they were in 1633, with stultifying top-down management, close and distrustful supervision, and little room for creativity. The conflict between advanced technology and archaic mentality is, I believe, a major reason why the modern work place is characterized by dissatisfaction, frustration, inflexibility, and stress.

If only minds were as easy to change as machines. I'll wager that it's easier to invent a new generation of microchips than to get a generation of middle managers to alter the routes they drive to work every day. Technology is transformed overnight; mentality takes generations to alter. Who can blame us for thinking technology will cure all that ails the workplace. It's so much easier to acquire.

Computer networks, automated machinery, rapid new product development, and quick and efficient communications all make a business up-to-date, but nothing more. And what is up-to-date? Rushing to the Caribbean for a one-week break, sharing sardine-can passenger compartments with 300 overstressed office workers, all eating from plastic containers, calling the company on the airphone, and dreaming of the languid turquoise waters and pristine beaches they will have to share with the occupants of ten other jumbo jets landing ahead of theirs.

There's no doubt in my mind: technology has gone through the roof since 1633, but quality of life has gone down the drain. All we have done is accelerate our malfunctions and increase the intensity of our mis-communication.

Let me propose a new definition: the truly modern company avoids an obsession with technology and puts quality of life first.

It took us a while to see it clearly, but at Semco we now focus on innovations that will enable us to work better together, rather than simply trying to acquire the next generation of plasma welding computers or CAD/CAM machining centres.

While I am pontificating, let me go a step further: no company can be successful, in the long run anyway, if profits are its principal goal.

It has got to the point where business people forget their own identities and become what they invoice. I recently attended a luncheon in São Paulo with 30 industrialists who wanted to form a committee to elect an alternate candidate to the Federation of Industries board. As all these powerful men were settling around a U-shaped table, someone suggested that we introduce ourselves.

The first rose and said: 'My name is so-and-so, from company such-and-such, and we sell $200 million a year and employ 2,000 employees.' Then he sat down. Then the next person followed suit. And so it went. It was funny to watch these small men with large cigars getting up to announce proudly that they had doubled the sales of the person before them, or dejectedly acknowledge that their predecessor had beaten them by a few hundred million. You can imagine the discomfort when the smallest of the lot, barely a five-footer, declared that his company's sales had been $2.5 billion. It was all I could do to keep from giggling as I watched the awe and envy on my colleagues' faces. Moments later someone with a calculator declared that together we represented sales of $5 billion. Never mind that our candidate for the Federation board lost.

How important is money, anyway? Entrepreneurs say profits are their *raison d'être*. In the months I spent at Harvard, I met many industrialists who, like me, were taking the course in yearly instalments. During the first session I noticed that some of them paid close attention to the personal finance course. They clearly had thoughts of selling their businesses.

In the intervening year a few did cash in, trading their companies for a chance to realize dreams of an island, a sail-boat, and maybe even golf every day. But by the time the second session at Harvard came along a few of these liberated souls were already a bit bored. And by the third session nearly all those who had sold their businesses had started or acquired new ones and were happily back on the job. They were never in business for the money.

Neither was my father. He had long planned to retire at the age of 55. As it approached, however, he moved the deadline to 60, then 65. By the time I started working at Semco he had slipped the date to his 70th birthday.

Nothing is more comprehensible (although I didn't understand it at the time). Income, though vital, isn't a satisfying end in itself. As my Harvard classmates discovered, you can sell your company for 12 or 16 times earnings and not be happy.

At the risk of sounding patronizing, money isn't the only goal of workers, either. We try to pay people at Semco more than they would receive elsewhere, and of course there's profit-sharing. But that isn't why so few of our people leave. We offer employees a chance to be true partners in our business, to be autonomous and responsible. That's why many of our key people regularly spurn lucrative employment offers.

If money isn't all it's made out to be, information is, I believe, a most under-valued commodity. There is power in knowing something someone else doesn't, which explains why executives are so often loath to share information with employees.

You don't believe me? Try this test at your next meeting. When some important item comes up, say that it's better not to discuss it now because a related issue was decided that same morning that will change things considerably. Then, after a few moments of apprehensive silence, say that you just can't discuss it now.

I'd be surprised if you haven't just become the most powerful person in the room. You know something the others don't – at least that's what they think.

But when cards are held close to the chest, communication will be faulty and anxieties, misunderstandings, insecurity, and eventually hostility will manifest itself. No amount of 'we're-all-in-this-together-because-we're-all-one-big-family' sloganeering will compensate.

Which is why when we started sharing information at Semco it had such a profound effect. People in the higher echelons could no longer rely on the conventional symbols and had to develop leadership skills and knowledge to inspire respect. The centres of power shifted, as people who were formerly quiet and apolitical rose in stature and the people who were good at hobnobbing and gossiping eventually left. (And, yes, when they did, despite some perturbation from those who remained, we posted honest bulletin board notices explaining the reason for their departure.)

*

One of the biggest misconceptions about modern man is that he is somehow different from his ancestors. Man has always lived in tribes and I daresay always will. Whether these groups are ethnic, religious, political, or vocational, they are our anchors. Being a Buddhist, a member of the National Rifle Association, a bird-watcher, a Nintendo fanatic, a Rotarian, or a knight in the Ku Klux Klan gives us an identity, for better or worse.

People derive identity from their companies, too, wearing Mitsubishi or Motorola like a surname. And within companies they can belong to sub-tribes, each with its own norms of dress and conduct. Just as you will never confuse an orthodox Jew with a Hari Krishna follower, never will finance executives, with their suspenders and Ferragamo ties, be mistaken for production guys, with their multiple pens safely tucked in plastic shirtpocket protectors.

Companies and organizations must be redesigned to let tribes be. They must develop systems based on co-existence, not on some unattainable ideal of harmony. Different tribes will never fully integrate, which is why it is folly to try to create a 'we're-all-one-big-family' atmosphere in the work place. Fixed working hours, organization charts and policy manuals are all so negative. They strip away freedom and give nothing in return but a false feeling of discipline and belonging. They elevate bureaucrats and ennoble conformity. By all means establish and promote a common goal, but recognize divergence and let people determine their own ways of achieving it.

The issue of tribal co-existence is, I believe, critical for survival in modern times. Up until now it has been easy enough for the First World to keep its distance from the Third World and view the Southern Hemisphere as very far away. But technology is drawing everyone and every place closer together. Like lava from a huge volcano, tribes are moving towards areas where the standard of living is higher. In a few decades all that will be left of the First World will be a few ghettos of the super-rich, islands of luxury surrounded by misery. There will be a lot of Cairo in Paris, Mexico in Colorado, and Syria in Switzerland. And as the Third World makes its glacial movement north, it will leave behind places like Somalia, Bangladesh and the Ivory Coast, which will become an even more abject Fourth World.

Most companies and organizations are unprepared for this new world order. Their first impulse is to try to homogenize everything, to set up elaborate training programmes and teach immigrants to say 'have a nice day' and 'watch your step' in the hope that they will eventually make baseball fans out of them. As if two Vietnamese clerks, a Hong Kong accountant, and six Canadian factory workers could work together, just like that. Consider the so-called guest workers in Germany and France. Even if Turks could speak flawless German, would they be accepted? I think most people want to be generous and egalitarian, but if they believe their family, their job, or their neighbourhood is threatened, their tolerance for tribal co-existence evaporates.

Discrimination will always exist, since it is tied up with tribalism, but there is plenty that can be done to diminish its effects. At Semco, we have built an organization without first- and second-class citizens. Our workers wear collars of many colours, not just blue and white, and we don't condone symbols of power or exclusivity such as executive cafeterias or reserved parking places.

I know the co-existence of tribes is possible. I have witnessed it to a degree I would not have suspected. In 1992, a demonstration for the impeachment of Brazilian President Collor brought tens of thousands of workers to a large square in the centre of São Paulo. I was watching from the sidelines when I was spotted by a director of the radical Worker's Party, who called me to the podium and insisted I speak to the demonstrators, some of whom were waving signs reading 'Down With Business' and worse. After I finished, I got an embrace from the party's president.

There I was, Brazil's Business Leader of the Year, being cheered by the most extreme of workers.

*

In the 1920s, an engineer named DeForest went to see Harry Warner, of Hollywood's famous Warner Brothers. DeForest had managed to synchronize sound and image and could, he said, transform silent movies into talking pictures. Warner listened to him, then replied: 'Are you crazy? Who wants to hear an actor talk?'

Henry Ford would sell his Model T's in any colour, as long as it was black. Legend has it that he adopted this monochromatic philosophy to simplify production and keep prices down. To this day Ford is regarded as a marketing hero. I have a revisionist view. Old Henry's stubborn thinking cost Ford the leadership of America's biggest industry, for William Durant, of the then smaller General Motors, decided to offer cars in a variety of colours, and was soon looking at Ford through his rearview mirror.

And then there was Chester Carlson, who visited IBM, GE and RCA, trying to sell his new invention. They thanked him for his time but regretted that, in their view, his idea had no future. A stubborn man, Carlson persisted. Finally, he met Joseph Wilson, who owned a small firm named the Haloid Company. Wilson saw the potential of Carlson's device. With time, he even renamed his company after it: Xerox.

Corporations have notoriously short life spans. Even in the stable and relatively prosperous United States, a company has a less than 5 per cent chance of being in a better position 50 years from now. These cautionary tales illustrate what I believe is the biggest challenge any business faces: change. Semco has succeeded despite some of the harshest economic conditions imaginable because we have learned to see the need for change and have been smart enough to seek our employees' help in implementing it.

To survive in modern times, a company must have an organizational structure that accepts change as its basic premise, lets tribal customs thrive, and fosters a power that is derived from respect, not rules. In other words, the successful companies will be the ones that put quality of life first. Do this and the rest – quality of product, productivity of workers, profits for all – will follow.

At Semco we did away with strictures that dictate the 'hows' and created fertile soil for differences. We gave people an opportunity to test, question and disagree. We let them determine their own training and their own futures. We let them come and go as they wanted, work at home if they wished, set their own salaries, choose their own bosses. We let them change their minds and ours, prove us wrong when we are wrong, make us humbler. Such a system relishes change, which is the only antidote to the corporate brainwashing that has consigned giant businesses with brilliant pasts into uncertain futures.

People often assume that at Semco we have strict selection procedures to ensure that those who come to work for us are philosophically attuned with our system. In fact, it's the other way around. We look for competence, and ignore all else. Many of our employees regularly question our concepts. There are even pockets at Semco that are autocratic, and people who like to work in that kind of environment have slowly migrated there. But how can we lock out people who don't think the same way we do without becoming people who say things like, 'This is not the way we do things around here.'

Semco is more than novel programmes or procedures. What is important is our open-mindedness, our trust in our employees and distrust of dogma. We are neither socialist nor purely capitalist, but we take the best of these failed systems and others to re-organize work so that collective thinking does not overpower individualistic flights of grandeur; that leadership does not get lost in an endless search for consensus; that people are free to work as they like, when they like; that bosses don't have to be parents and workers don't act like children. At the heart of our bold experiment is a truth so simple it would be silly if it wasn't so rarely recognized: *A company should trust its destiny to its employees.*

No, Semco isn't a model, with programmes to be followed with precision, so many recipes for participation, productivity, and profits. Semco is an invitation. I hope our story will cause other companies to reconsider themselves, and their employees. To forget socialism, capitalism, just-in-time deliveries, salary surveys, and the rest of it, and to concentrate on building organizations that accomplish that most difficult of all challenges: to make people look forward to coming to work in the morning.

APPENDIXES

SEEN FROM BELOW: HOW SEMCO EMPLOYEES EVALUATE THEIR SUPERVISORS

The following questionnaire is anonymously completed by all Semco employees every six months as part of the process of evaluating their supervisors. The questions are weighted according to their importance and the results are posted. A score of 80 out of 100 is average.

1. When an employee makes a small mistake, the subject is:
   a. *Irritated and unwilling to discuss the mistake*
   b. *Irritated but willing to discuss it*
   c. *Realizes the mistake and discusses it in a constructive manner*
   d. *Ignores the mistake and only pays attention to more important matters*

2. The subject reacts to criticism:
   a. *Poorly, ignoring it*
   b. *Poorly, rejecting it*
   c. *Reasonably well*
   d. *Well, accepting it*

3. The subject is:
   a. *Constantly tense*
   b. *Usually tense, but relaxed on occasion*
   c. *Usually relaxed, but tense on occasion*
   d. *Constantly relaxed*

4. The subject is:
    a. Insecure
    b. More often insecure than secure
    c. More often secure than insecure
    d. Secure

5. As far as professional and personal relationships are concerned, the subject is:
    a. Incapable of separating them
    b. Frequently incapable of separating them
    c. Usually capable of separating them
    d. Capable of separating them

6. When the subject's department achieves a high level of productivity, he usually:
    a. Takes credit for others' success
    b. Gives credit to those who did the work
    c. Gives credit to the team as a whole

7. The subject is seen as:
    a. Always unfair
    b. More often unfair than fair
    c. More often fair than unfair
    d. Always fair

8. The subject conveys to his team feelings of:
    a. Fear and insecurity
    b. Indifference
    c. Security and tranquillity

9. The subject transmits to his team a sense of:
    a. Coldness and unwillingness to talk
    b. Distance, but willingness to talk
    c. Friendliness, but indifference to others' problems
    d. Friendliness and concern with others' problems

10. When dealing with people in inferior positions (custodians, messengers, drivers, etc.), the subject usually:

    a. Has an attitude of superiority
    b. Ignores them
    c. Treats them politely, but with an air of superiority
    d. Respects them

11. The subject treats his subordinates:
    a. Much worse than he treats his superiors
    b. A little worse than he treats his superiors
    c. Treats both the same

12. The subject:
    a. Constantly reminds everyone he is the boss
    b. Occasionally reminds everyone he is the boss
    c. Rarely makes a point of being the boss

13. The subject is:
    a. A weak leader, unable to motivate his team
    b. A weak leader, but able to motivate his team
    c. A strong leader, but unable to motivate his team
    d. A strong leader, and able to motivate his team

14. When his team has a specific goal, the subject:
    a. Demands results, but doesn't participate in the effort to achieve them
    b. Demands results, and participates superficially
    c. Participates in the effort when necessary to meet the goal

15. The subject:
    a. Is openly held in disrespect by his team
    b. Is held in disrespect by his team, but not publicly
    c. Generates neither respect nor disrespect
    d. Is respected by his team

16. The subject:
    a. Gives obvious preferential treatment to some people because of their colour, religion, or origin
    b. Denies being biased, but doesn't give equal opportunity to everyone
    c. Isn't biased and gives equal opportunity to everyone

17. The subject:
   a. *Gives obvious preference to people of a certain gender*
   b. *Denies being biased, but doesn't give equal opportunity to everyone*
   c. *Isn't biased and gives equal opportunity to everyone*

18. When promotions and prizes are concerned, the subject:
   a. *Gives them to those he likes*
   b. *Sometimes gives them to those who deserve them and sometimes gives them to 'followers'*
   c. *Almost always is just and impartial*

19. During a crisis, the subject:
   a. *Disrupts the group's unity*
   b. *Doesn't affect the group's unity*
   c. *Helps the group stick together*

20. Which is more important to the subject:
   a. *Work to be performed perfectly*
   b. *Work to be performed quickly*
   c. *Either speed or perfection, depending on the situation*

21. The subject is:
   a. *Excessively involved in all situations*
   b. *Not involved enough in all situations*
   c. *Adequately involved in all situations*

22. The subject's knowledge of his area is:
   a. *Insufficient*
   b. *Sufficient*
   c. *Profound*

23. If the subject were to replace you temporarily, his performance would be:
   a. *Unsatisfactory*
   b. *Regular*
   c. *Good*
   d. *Better than yours*

24. In choosing between the urgent and the important, the subject:
    a. *Doesn't know the difference between them*
    b. *Usually tends towards the urgent*
    c. *Distinguishes well between the two*

25. The subject:
    a. *Wastes too much time on urgent problems*
    b. *Gives equal time to urgent and important matters*
    c. *Gives more time to important matters*

26. The subject is:
    a. *Not very creative and resists new ideas*
    b. *Too creative and change-oriented, disturbing the atmosphere*
    c. *Is adequately creative and change-oriented*

27. As far as creating an environment where people feel free to be creative or suggest changes, the subject:
    a. *Blocks innovative and creative ideas*
    b. *Doesn't block them, but also doesn't create them*
    c. *Promotes creative or innovative ideas*

28. As far as the team is concerned, the subject:
    a. *Usually chooses the wrong people*
    b. *Sometimes chooses well and sometimes chooses poorly*
    c. *Usually chooses the right people*

29. The people who work around the subject:
    a. *Rarely feel motivated to work*
    b. *Sometimes feel motivated to work*
    c. *Usually feel motivated to work*

30. The subject's use of financial resources given to him is:
    a. *Poor*
    b. *Average*
    c. *Good*
    d. *Excellent*

31. The subject's use of his own time is:
    a. *Bad*
    b. *Average*
    c. *Good*
    d. *Excellent*

32. The value the subject gives to training and related matters is:
    a. *Too small*
    b. *Sufficient*
    c. *Great*

33. The subject performs tasks:
    a. *Almost always poorly*
    b. *Sometimes poorly and sometimes well*
    c. *Almost always well*

34. Regarding opinions that differ from his, the subject:
    a. *Never accepts them*
    b. *Usually doesn't accept them*
    c. *Sometimes accepts them*
    d. *Almost always accepts them*

35. People find the subject:
    a. *Untrustworthy*
    b. *Occasionally trustworthy*
    c. *Very trustworthy*

36. The subject represents the company:
    a. *Poorly, raising concern about it*
    b. *Neither poorly nor well*
    c. *Well, leading people to trust it*

appendix B

TIME MANAGEMENT

I promised in Chapter Nine to reveal my cure for time sickness. (All eyes on the top hat, please. Here comes the rabbit.)

1. Begin at the end. Set a certain hour at which to leave the office and obey it blindly. I chose 7 p.m., but before I had often worked until midnight. If you normally work until 7 p.m., move your leaving time to 5.30 or 6.00. If you take work home at weekends, establish a 60-day programme to halt this insidious practice.

2. Sift through that stack of papers on your desk and decide which are most important. (Deciding that everything is equally important is cheating. Start again.) Spend several hours, or even a whole day, if that's what it takes, discovering what's in that pile. Begin with the most difficult, complex, or time-consuming documents. In other words, go through the pile in order of importance, not appearance. You won't get a false sense of accomplishment that way. As you go through it, divide the papers into three categories:

- Priority items, which require your personal attention and represent matters of indisputable importance. Don't put more than five documents in this category.
- Items that can be handled only by you, but can wait. At first this category seems the most enjoyable, because so much appears to fit in it. Think hard about whether you are really the only one who can deal with an item. Whether your subordinates or colleagues are overworked should not weigh in your decision; the control of time is nothing if not an exercise in selfishness. Load them up with everything that fails

'The Test of the Seventies'. (No, this isn't a quiz to see if you remember Watergate.) Ask yourself: 'Is it possible that someone else could do this task at least 70 per cent as well as I could?' If the answer is yes, let him.

• Items you think would be good to look at, but never quite get around to. These include newspapers and magazines, lengthy reports, copies of memos – you get the idea. We've all grown accustomed to receiving vast quantities of information. As a defence, we tend to read a little of everything. This is among the most serious causes of time illness.

The key to time management is self-esteem. You must maintain it even though you may not be as well informed about some essentially meaningless report or arcane issue as your associates. You must be prepared to go to a meeting and endure comments such as, 'You mean you didn't read "Short-Cuts to a Better Casting Project" in the latest *Foundry Lovers' News?*' Better to suffer the humiliation of saying you didn't and ask someone to please be kind enough to summarize it than to have had to read all the articles that cross your desk. Legions of executives believe they will be regarded as ill-informed dunces if they let their subscriptions lapse to *The Wall Street Journal*, *The Financial Times*, *Newsweek*, *Time*, and *L'Express*, not to mention assorted local papers, financial newsletters, *Fortune*, *Forbes*, *Business Week*, and so on. Publications work hard to convey their indispensability. Don't let too many succeed.

Due to (what else?) lack of time, I used to leave magazines and newspapers on a table in my office to read later. When more periodicals would arrive, I would carefully add them to the pile. I felt depressed just looking at it, fearful of all the information I had not absorbed. Then one evening the pile collapsed. That was my cue, and I finally gave the magazines the dignified burial they deserved, without opening them.

I estimate that the ratio of useless to relevant reading material is about 20 to 1. With that in mind, my advice is to reduce the literary inflow to a maximum of two newspapers a day, two weekly magazines, and two publications in a specialized field. Start being proud of not being aware of everything. Get off distribution lists. The reward will be an opportunity to engage in that under-appreciated occupation, contemplation. Aristotle, who didn't subscribe to *The Wall Street Journal*, once said 'Thinking requires leisure time.' If you are not in possession of leisure time, you can't be thinking all that much.

3. If you think you can manage your time without making any investment in fixed assets, you are wrong. There is one essential acquisition: another rubbish bin.

I know. You already have a perfectly good one. But most people have enough on their desk to fill two. At first, using this second bin will take courage. You will have to toss into it impressive reports and unread magazines. But remember the question Alfred Sloan, the legendary head of General Motors, used to ask: 'What is the worst thing that can happen if I throw this out?' If you don't tremble, sweat, or grow short of breath, go ahead and pitch it. Eventually, your second rubbish bin will become a baby-sitter for your in-tray. Leave it in place a few more months, a magnificent symbol of freedom.

4. Think hard before accepting that invitation to lunch or to visit a supplier or to make a speech to a trade group. The first response is usually to reach for the Filofax and, if the appropriate space is blank, scrawl in the new commitment. Adopt a new party line: 'Thanks, but I just can't fit it in.' Or, you might ask, 'Have you tried X?' Or: 'I can't make it, but do let me know what happened.' Or, as a last resort: 'I'm really sorry, but I'll be on my honeymoon.' Say what you have to, but take part only in events that are absolutely, positively essential. That lunch to get to know supplier Z better or to impress customer Y, like those 'it's-probably-a-good-idea-to-be-there' meetings, play upon insecurities. I've never met a supplier who lowered his price because he found me great company at lunch or a customer who gave me an order because the Beaujolais I served at dinner made him giddy. Participate only in what you're sure will generate a return for your investment of precious time.

If you have to meet someone, do it at the office. The surroundings discourage people from drifting from the subject. But don't provide visitors with a cup of coffee: it's an invitation to an easygoing, unproductive conversation. By leaving an intruder uncaffeinated, you are contributing to his health, and he may not be so quick to return, either.

5. Rationalizing time without talking about meetings is like a soccer match without a riot. Is there anyone who works in an office who doesn't go to too many meetings?

For starters, remember that man is a social animal. We feel more comfortable in the presence of others. Meetings give rise to the sense of being part of a group, of solidarity even with the ever-present rifts and jealousies of business. And, of course, corporate communications systems are usually slow and often inadequate, so meetings let us catch up.

To eliminate meetings is to go against human nature and diminish corporate efficiency. But making meetings more effective is not all that difficult. Through trial and error, we at Semco have come up with some recommendations.

- Begin on time. (Five or ten minutes late is still on time, unless you're Swedish.) Just start with whoever is there. Do this a few times and those who are usually late will get the message.
- Don't start a meeting without first setting a time to stop. And don't go beyond it by more than a few minutes. When you are in your own office, get up from your chair and say, 'OK then,' when you want to end a session. Sometimes I sit on the edge of my desk from the start. It may not be polite, but it works.
- Go over the agenda in front of everyone. List subjects in order of importance. Don't give in to the temptation of clearing up old items, or getting rid of uncomplicated new items, first.
- Delegate to one or more people any item that might take more time than is allotted for it, or that provokes a discussion that drags on without hope of resolution.

- Don't have meetings that last longer than two hours. After that, attention drops by the minute.
- Avoid 'dog and pony shows'. Keep reports short and discourage the use of charts and tables. Avoid overhead transparencies, too, and don't *ever* turn out the lights.
- Be a bear about interruptions. The only excuse for breaking into a meeting is a customer with a problem.
- Transform as many meetings as possible into telephone calls or quick conversations in the hall. People tend to call meetings for problems that can be resolved in 10 or 15 minutes over the phone, or even in a fax.

6. About the telephone: anyone who takes a message at Semco asks the caller to detail the subject – that's detail, not state. Ask your secretary or assistant to say automatically that you cannot take a call – before the caller is asked who he is, of course. Take the list of callers from a given day (or several days) and return only those from people you truly need to talk to, such as customers. As for the others, they will either:

—Call again and again, until they give up, at which point you know the subject was not important.

—Call one of your associates.

In any case, prepare to hear how talking to you is harder than talking to the Pope. Take it as a compliment.

7. Make time to think. Try blocking out a half-day a week on your agenda. I find that Monday and Friday mornings are good, because I can clear away post- and pre-weekend distractions. During this half-day, avoid your office. Camp out in an unused conference room or, even better, stay at home.

Thinking is difficult. It requires concentration and discipline. Give it the time it deserves. Aristotle would approve.

A SEMCO LEXICON

Bosses: Semco doesn't have as many as it used to, and those who remain aren't very bossy. As workers began to exercise more control over their jobs, the need for supervisors diminished. We also have reduced our corporate staff, which provides legal, accounting and marketing expertise to our manufacturing units, by more than 75 per cent, eliminating the date processing, training, and quality control departments, among others.

Circular Organization: We slashed Semco's bureaucracy from twelve layers of management to three and devised a new organization structure based on fluid concentric circles instead of a rigidly hierarchical pyramid. All employees have one of only four titles: Counsellors, who are like vice presidents and higher in conventional companies and co-ordinate our general policies and strategies; Partners, who run our business units; Co-ordinators, who comprise that first, crucial level of management, such as marketing, sales, and production supervisors or engineering and assembly-area foremen; and Associates, which is what we call everyone else. (*See Chapter 24.*)

Clean-Outs: Twice a year Semco shuts down for an afternoon and everyone cleans out his work place. Office workers pitch useless files, factory workers get rid of scrap and old machinery. This programme started in our offices, but now no one is exempt and nothing safe. (*See Chapter 17.*)

Corruption: More than a few government inspectors who set out to extort Semco have ended up in jail. This has caused us plenty of trouble with the government inspectors all over Brazil, but it's worth it rather than send a signal to our employees and customers that we tolerate dishonesty. (*See Chapter 28.*)

Democracy: A cornerstone of the Semco system. We have representative democracy through our factory committees; on important decisions, such as plant relocations, all our employees get a direct vote. Subordinates essentially vote on their bosses. And to make the point absolutely clear, we don't have executive dining rooms or reserved parking spaces.

Factory Committees: At each Semco business unit groups of workers – machinists, office personnel, maintenance workers, stockroom personnel, draftsmen, and other types of employees except management – elect representatives to serve on committees. (The union is also represented.) These committees meet regularly with the top managers at each unit to discuss any and all work place issues or policies. They are empowered to declare strikes, audit the books, and question all aspects of management. (*See Chapter 10.*)

Family Silverware: When a job opening occurs or a new position is created, a Semco employee who meets 70 per cent of the requirements is given preferential consideration over an outsider. (*See Chapter 22.*)

Flexitime: Many companies let office workers set their own hours. We are the only company I know of to extend this freedom to factory workers. This is potentially disruptive, since each shop floor worker so heavily depends on his teammates, but our people have always subordinated individual preferences to group schedules. (*See Chapter 30.*)

Headline Memo: All memos at Semco are limited to a single page, topped with a newspaper-like headline that gets right to the point. There are no exceptions, not even for marketing reports. (*See Chapter 18.*)

Hepatitis Leave: Our version of sabbaticals. Professionals can take a few weeks or even a few months every year or two away from their usual duties to learn new skills, redesign their job, or simply recharge. This programme began when several harried managers told us they didn't have time to think. We responded by asking them to consider what would happen if they suddenly contracted hepatitis and were forced to spend two months recuperating. Then we let them. (*See Chapter 20.*)

Job Rotation: We encourage our managers to exchange jobs with one another and in a given year up to 25 per cent do. A minimum of two years and a maximum of five years in the same job are ample, but as with other programmes at Semco it's up to the employees to take the initiative. Job rotation can be unsettling, but offers some considerable advantages, including: 1) obliging people to learn new skills; 2) discouraging empire-building; 3) providing employees with a broader view of a company, which lets them appreciate colleagues' problems; 4) forcing management to prepare more than one person for a job; 5) creating additional opportunities for those who might otherwise be trapped. (*See Chapter 20.*)

Job Security: There was a time not too long ago when IBM and Bridgestone Tires, 3M, and Kyocera, among others, boasted credos that read, 'lifetime employment guaranteed here'. The American executives of these companies would nod to their Japanese counterparts, and vice versa, through interviews in *Fortune*, *The Financial Times* and *The Asahi Shimbun* in which they would extol the high-minded strategy of 'believing in people'. Now all this is legend and Japanese and American multinationals alike have laid off thousands of experienced workers. At Semco, we never promised anyone job security, so we never had to break this promise.

Lost in Space: Each good year we choose several young people from our entry-level applicants and turn them loose. With no job description, no boss, no set responsibilities, they are free to roam, so long as they work in at least 12 departments in their first 12 months. Then they can negotiate a more permanent arrangement with any of those departments. (*See Chapter 29.*)

Management by Wandering Around: Semco is designed to allow people to mingle. Our offices typically don't have walls; people are instead separated only by plants. Sometimes we intentionally mix departments. In fact, we don't like barriers of any kind separating our employees.

Manufacturing Cells: Instead of assembly lines, we cluster production machines so that teams of workers can assemble a complete scale, dishwasher, mixer or other product, not just an isolated component. That gives workers more autonomy and responsibility, which makes them happier and our products better. Nearly all factory workers have mastered several production jobs and some even drive forklifts to keep teammates supplied with raw materials and spare parts, which workers have been known to purchase themselves from suppliers. Often factory workers set production quotas and develop improvements for our products. (*See Chapter 16.*)

Natural Business: A guiding principal. At Semco we have stripped away the unnecessary perks and privileges, such as executive dining rooms and fancy office furniture, that feed the ego but hurt the balance sheet and distract everyone from the crucial corporate tasks of making, selling, billing and collecting.

Nucleus of Technological Innovation: A small group of employees, mostly engineers, who are free of any day-to-day production or managerial responsibilities and have all their time to invent new products, refine old ones, devise market strategies, unearth cost reductions and efficiencies, even dream up new lines of business. Their compensation depends in part on the success of their entrepreneurial efforts. (*See Chapter 29.*)

Paternalism: A dirty word at Semco. We don't want to be a big, happy family. We want to be a successful business. We're only concerned with our employees' performance on the job, not their personal lives. You won't find a running track, swimming pool, or gym at Semco. If our people want to join a health club, that's their business. We do offer health insurance and other benefits, but we ask employees to help manage them. Occasionally, Semco will lend employees money, but only for unpredictable emergencies. Instead of treating employees as children who need looking after, we treat them as adults who are capable of making decisions on the job. (*See Chapter 21.*)

Profit-Sharing: Unlike typical plans, in which management unilaterally decides how much will be distributed and to whom, Semco negotiated with our workers over the basic percentage to be distributed – about a quarter of corporate profits – and then they decide how to split it. (*See Chapter 17.*)

Reverse Evaluation: Before anyone is hired or promoted to a leadership position, he must be interviewed, evaluated, and approved by all the people who will work for him. Also, every six months Semco managers are evaluated by the people they supervise, who anonymously complete a multiple choice questionnaire we developed for this purpose. The grades are posted for all to see. There are no hard and fast rules, but those who consistently get poor marks (80 out of 100 is average) usually leave Semco sooner or later. (*See Chapter 22.*)

Risk Salary: About a third of all Semco employees have the option of taking a pay cut of up to 25 per cent and then receiving a supplement raising their compensation to 125 per cent of normal if the company has a good year. If Semco does poorly, on the other hand, they're stuck with 75 per cent of their salary. This programme rewards those willing to take a risk, and lets some of our labour costs fluctuate with profits or losses. (*See Chapter 25.*)

Rules: We have as few as possible. There are no dress codes, for example, or regulations on travel. And we no longer have an internal auditing department to check up on our people. All we say is: use your common sense. (*See Chapter 10.*)

Salary Surveys: Many companies rely on off-the-shelf wage surveys to re-evaluate salary scales. Semco is the only.company I know of that has asked its factory and office workers to help in this process. They visit other manufacturing companies that are comparable to Semco, interview their counterparts, and tally the findings. As a result, no one distrusts our surveys. Eventually, though, we hope all Semco employees will set their own salaries.

Satellite Programme: An effort to contract out basic manufacturing, with a twist: instead of doing business with outsiders, we help our own workers set up their own companies, transforming them from employees to partners. To ease the transition, we lease them our production machines at favourable rates and offer them advice on such matters as pricing, quality, and taxes. They are free to sell to our competitors, too. (*See Chapter 32.*)

Self-Set Pay: Paying people whatever they want seems a sure route to bankruptcy, but we've been doing this for years and we've never done better. A 10 per cent rise turns out to be an exception. Nearly 25 per cent of our employees now set their own salaries, including most of our Co-ordinators, and I don't see any reason why factory workers shouldn't one day determine their own pay. (*See Chapter 25.*)

Size: Large, centralized organizations foster alienation as stagnant ponds breed algae. We believe people reach their potential only when they know almost everyone around them, which is generally when there are no more than 150 co-workers. When our business units grow bigger than that, we split them. (*See Chapters 14 and 15.*)

Strikes: Regrettably, we haven't eliminated them. But when there's a walkout we: 1) treat everyone as adults; 2) tell the strikers that no one will be punished when they return; 3) don't keep records of who came to work and who led the walkout; 4) never call the police or try to break up a picket line; 5) maintain all benefits; 6) don't keep workers or union leaders out of the factory; 7) insist that everyone respects the right of those who want to work; 8) don't fire anyone during or after the strike. (*See Chapter 13.*)

Support staff: We have completely eliminated secretaries, receptionists, personal assistants, and other ungratifying, dead-end jobs from our payroll. In keeping with our philosophy of natural business, everyone at Semco fetches their own guests, copies their own papers, and sends their own faxes. (*See Chapter 18.*)

Training: Rather than have formal training programmes, we respond in various ways when employees ask for a chance to develop new skills. We ask people to think about what they would like to be doing in five years and then prod them to request training that takes them there. The expenses are then approved at the weekly meetings of our business units.

Transparency: We make public virtually all corporate information, from salaries to strategies and productivity statistics to profit margins. We also give courses to teach workers to read financial documents such as balance sheets and income statements. Employees are free to question managers on any aspect of our business, and to talk to media without fear of repercussion. (*See Chapter 18.*)

Working at Home: I do it at least three mornings a week, and encourage everyone else who can work at home to do so. It enhances concentration and productivity and gives people more flexibility.

appendix D

THE SURVIVAL MANUAL

What follows are excerpts from the small booklet we give to each new Semco employee. It constitutes our only written set of rules.

Organization Chart

© Miguel Paiva

Semco doesn't use a formal organization chart. Only the respect of the led creates a leader. When it is absolutely necessary to sketch the structure of some part of the company, we always do it in pencil, and dispense with it as soon as possible.

Hiring

Before people are hired or promoted, the others in that unit have the opportunity to interview and evaluate the candidates.

Working Hours

Semco has flexible working hours, and the responsibility for setting and keeping track of them rests with each employee. People work at different speeds and differ in their performance depending on the time of day. Semco does its best to adapt to each person's desires and needs.

Working Environment

We all want our people to feel free to change and adapt their working area as they please. Painting walls or machines, adding plants or decorating the space around you is up to you. The company has no rules about this, and doesn't want to have any. Change the area around you, according to your tastes and desires and those of the people who work with you.

Clothing and Appearance

Neither has any importance at Semco. A person's appearance is not a factor in hiring or promotion. Everyone knows what he or she likes or needs to wear. Feel at ease – wear just your common sense.

Authority

Many positions at Semco carry with them hierarchical authority. But efforts to pressure subordinates or cause them to work out of fear or insecurity, or behaviour that shows any type of disrespect, are considered an unacceptable use of authority and will not be tolerated.

Unions

Unions are an important form of worker protection. At Semco, workers are free to unionize and the persecution of those connected with unions is absolutely forbidden. Unions and the company don't always agree or even get along, but we insist on mutual respect and dialogue.

Strikes

Strikes are considered normal. They are part and parcel of democracy. No one is persecuted for participating in strikes, as long as they represent what the people of the company think and feel. The workers' assemblies are sovereign in this respect.

Absence from work because of a strike is considered as normal absenteeism, without further consequences or punishment.

Change

Semco is a place where there are big changes from time to time. Don't worry about them. We consider them healthy and positive. Watch the changes without fear. They are characteristic of our company.

Participation

Our philosophy is built on participation and involvement. Don't settle down. Give opinions, seek opportunities and advancement, always say what you think. Don't be just one more person in the company.

Your opinion is always interesting, even if no one asked you for it. Get in touch with the factory committees, and participate in elections. Make your voice count.

Factory Committees

Employees at Semco are guaranteed representation through the factory committee of each business unit. Read the charter, participate, make sure your committee effectively defends your interests – which many times will not coincide with Semco's interests. We see this conflict as healthy and necessary.

Evaluation by Subordinates

Twice a year you will receive a questionnaire to fill in that enables you to say what you think of your boss. Be very frank and honest, not just on the form but also in the discussion that follows.

Job Security and Age

Anyone who has been with us for three years, or has reached the age of 50, has special protection and can only be dismissed after a long series of approvals. This doesn't mean Semco has a no-layoff policy, but it helps to increase the security of our people.

Suggestions

Semco doesn't believe in giving prizes for suggestions. We want everyone to speak out, and all opinions are welcome, but we don't think it is healthy to reward them with prizes or money.

Private Life

Everyone owns his or her life, and a person's private affairs are considered sacred by the company. Semco never interferes with what people do when they are away from work, as long as it doesn't interfere with work. Of course, our human resources department is at your service for any help or support you may need.

Semco Woman

Women in Brazil have fewer employment, promotion, and financial opportunities than men. At Semco, women have various programmes, run by women, that seek to reduce this discrimination. They are known as The Semco Woman programmes.

If you are a woman, participate.

If you aren't, don't feel threatened and don't fight against this effort. Try to understand and respect it.

Vacations

Semco is not one of those companies that believes anyone is irreplaceable. You should all take your 30 days of vacation every year. It's vital for your health and the company's welfare. No excuse is good enough for accumulating vacation days for later.

Readers with questions or comments may write to me at:

Ricardo Semler
Rua Dom Aguirre 438
Jardim Marajoara
São Paulo – SP 04671
Brazil

The new bestseller from Ricardo Semler

THE SEVEN-DAY WEEKEND

Feeding Ducks and Making Millions

The new book from the author of **Maverick!** which sold 1.1 million copies worldwide.

Everyone knows how to work long hours and take work home on weekends – but few of us know how to go to the movies on Monday afternoon. Ricardo Semler knows. He doesn't always have time, of course – sometimes he has to feed ducks with his young son instead.

In **The Seven-Day Weekend**, Semler explains how he transformed a small family business into a highly profitable manufacturing, services and high-tech powerhouse – 40 times larger – while watching his favorite movies or relaxing with his son in the middle of the business day.

He did it because he found the elusive 'balance' between work and personal life, for himself and his 3,000 employees. He jettisoned the 'boarding school' habits and replaced them with a new architecture. Now Semco employees create their own jobs and generate new ideas and business, all while protecting their personal lives.

Any organization can emulate Semco. Any employee can enjoy his job just as Semler and his people do. Semler proves this with stories drawn from day-to-day operations at Semco. After 20 years spent testing his radical ideas, this book makes it clear that it's not only easy to find balance between work and leisure – it's the natural result of creating the seven-day weekend.

The Seven-Day Weekend is publishing on 3 April 2003.

The Seven-Day Weekend

The Wisdom Revolution:
Feeding Ducks and Making
Millions

Ricardo SEMLER

Author of the bestselling *Maverick!*

So even though Semco is in large part a sociological or anthropological experiment, we also make an excellent business case. We fit neatly into any MBA examination of success, because the right approach to employees always creates profit.

It's very simple – the repetition, boredom and aggravation that too many people accept as an inherent part of working can be replaced with joy, inspiration and freedom.

That's what I wish for everyone who reads this book.

Ricardo Semler
(Lying in a hammock with a laptop and my little boy, having fed the ducks at a nearby pond)
On a Monday in May, 2002